◆ A LITERARY COMPANION TO TRAVEL IN GREECE ◆

·A LITERARY·
COMPANION
TO TRAVEL IN
GREECE

Edited by

RICHARD STONEMAN

The J. Paul Getty Museum

Malibu, California

© 1994 J. Paul Getty Trust
1200 Getty Center Drive Suite 500
Los Angeles, CA 90049-1682

Fourth printing

Christopher Hudson, Publisher
Mark Greenberg, Editor in Chief

Library of Congress Cataloging-in-
Publication Data
A Literary companion to travel in
Greece / edited by Richard Stoneman.
        p. cm.
    Includes bibliographical references
    and index.

    ISBN 13: 978-0-89236-298-1 (pbk)
    ISBN 10: 0-89236-298-7 (pbk)

1. Greece—Description and travel.
2. Greece in literature. 3. Literary land-
marks—Greece. 4. Travelers' writings—
History and criticism. 5. Travelers—
Greece—History. I. Stoneman, Richard.
DF720.5.L58   1994
914.9504—dc20   94-9813
                              CIP

Project Staff
Manuscript Editor: Anita Keys
Designer: Leslie Thomas Fitch
Production Coordinator: Martha Drury
Cartographer: Patricia Isaacs
Typesetter: Andresen Typographics,
    Tucson, Arizona
Printer: Malloy Lithographing
Cover Printer: Phoenix Color Corporation

Previous edition published 1984
by Penguin Books Ltd, Harmondsworth,
Middlesex, England

For Althea

Contents

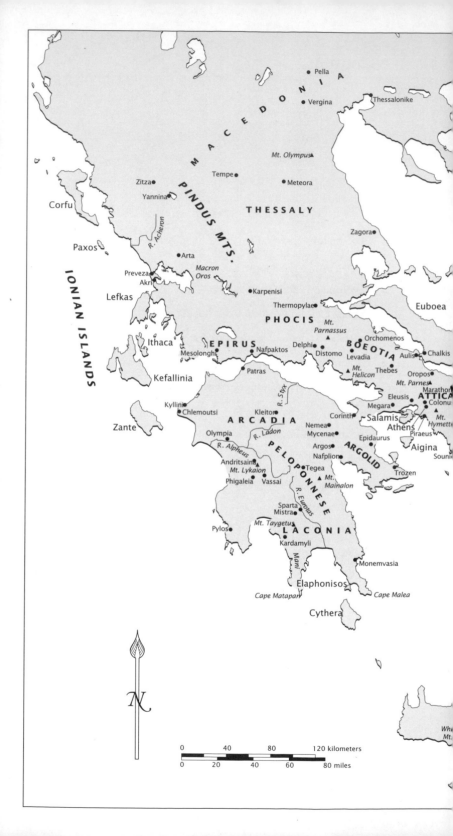

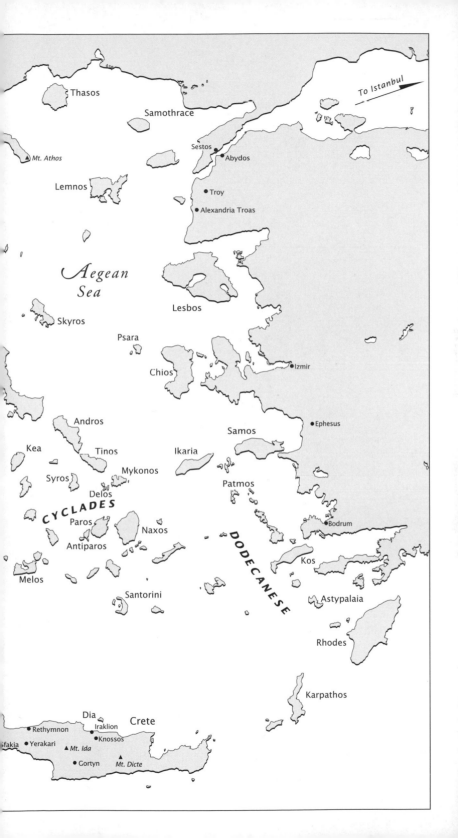

Preface

This book is a personal one. It is the kind of book I would have liked to have had with me when I first visited Greece, a record of sensibility at large in Greek places rather than an account of historical data, which are available in many publications. I hope that the selections I have made convey sufficient of the wealth and variety of the written records of Greek history and lore, landscape and poetry, and of the reactions of travelers from overseas, to make the reader seek for more of these and other authors; but I have not read everything I might have, and I think a lifetime would not be long enough to do so.

I should have read far less but for the invaluable services generously provided by several libraries: the British Library, the Bodleian Library in Oxford, the Bibliothèque Nationale in Paris, and, above all, the London Library. I am grateful to the Royal Society for the opportunity to consult the manuscript of Francis Vernon's journal in their library. Olga Palagia, in Athens, provided valuable bibliographical information and other assistance. Fenella Gentleman gave material assistance in many ways.

I have taken the opportunity offered by this new edition to add a few additional passages from recent writers and to update the bibliography.

Time has gone into the making of this book that should rightly have been devoted to my wife; the least I can do is to dedicate the finished product to her, with love.

RS, London

Philippos Margaritis, *The Temple of
Athena Nike*. The J. Paul Getty Museum,
Malibu, California.

Introduction:
Travelers in an Antique Land

Of all books, the most difficult, in my opinion, is a translation. Now, to travel is to translate; it is to translate to the eye,
thought and soul of the reader, the places, colours, impressions
and sentiments which nature or human monuments give to the
traveller. He must be able, at the same time, to look, to feel,
and to express; and how to express?—not with lines and
colours like the painter—a simple and easy matter; not with
sounds like the musician; but with words, with ideas, which
contain neither sounds, nor lines, nor colours. Such were the
reflections which I made, seated on the steps of the Parthenon,
having before my view Athens and the olive wood of the
Piraeus, and the blue sea of Aegea, and over my head the
majestic shadows of the frieze of the temple of temples. I
wished to carry away for myself a living memorandum, a written memorandum of this moment of my life. I felt that this
chaos of marble, so sublime, so picturesque to my sight, would
vanish from my memory, and I wished to be able to find it
again amid the commonplace of my future life. Let us write,
then: it will not be the Parthenon, but it will be at least a shade
of that great shade that hovers this day above me.

> Alphonse de Lamartine, *Travels in the East*

There must have been many travelers who have felt as Lamartine
did in the face of the overwhelming experience of an unfamiliar and
ancient country. Lamartine was sufficiently aware that his account
could be no more than personal; but the test of the interest of a
travel book is the interestingness of the traveler who writes it. As
Norman Douglas once wrote:

It seems to me that the reader of a good travel book is
entitled not only to an exterior voyage, to descriptions of
scenery and so forth, but to an interior, a sentimental or tem-
peramental voyage, which takes place side by side with that
outer one; and that the ideal book of this kind offers us,
indeed, a triple opportunity of exploration—abroad, into
the author's brain, and into our own. The writer should

therefore possess a brain worth exploring; some philosophy of life—not necessarily, though by preference, of his own forging—and the courage to proclaim it and put it to the test, he must be naif and profound, both child and sage.

This has by no means been the aim of all travelers who have described their experiences. Many, before knowledge was already well catalogued, aimed chiefly to gather and convey information back to their countrymen, even when, like the ponderous Henry Blount, they recognized that autopsy is the truest source of knowledge.

> Intellectual complections have no desire so strong, as that of knowledge; nor is any knowledge unto man so certain and pertinent, as that of human affairs: this experience advances best, in observing of people whose institutions much differ from ours; for customs conformable to our own, or to such wherewith we are already acquainted, do but repeat our old observations, with little acquist of new . . . I was of opinion, that he who would behold these times in their greatest glory, could not find a better scene than Turky. These considerations sent me thither . . .
>
> *A Voyage into the Levant* (London, 1636)

Though his own improvement was Blount's explicit aim, the publication of his travels (which became very popular) implied a desire to inform others, too. And his friend, the poet Henry King, acknowledged his success in this.

> Sir I must ever own myself to be
> Possest with human curiosity
> Of seeing all that might the sense invite
> By those two baits of profit and delight.
> And since I had the wit to understand
> The terms of native or of foreign land;
> I have had strong and oft desires to tread
> Some of those voyages which I have read.
> Yet still so fruitless have my wishes proved
> That from my country's smoke I never moved:
> Nor ever had the fortune (though designed)
> To satisfy the wanderings of my mind.
>
> ·᷄
>
>   By your eyes
> I here have made my full discoveries;

And all your countries so exactly seen,
As in the voyage I had sharer been.
By this you make me so: and the whole land
Your debtor.

Information is but ephemeral when it is gathered from travelers'
tales (like Blount's own account of Samos—see page 246), unless
it is part of a voyage of self-discovery or, like William Lithgow's, an
odyssey of experience, both pleasant and unpleasant, not of learning. Then even misinformation takes its place in the varied gallery
of the mind displayed. The writers who retain their value are
the egotists—Tom Coryate, William Lithgow, Chateaubriand,
Lamartine, Byron, Schliemann, even the archetypal bad-tempered
Englishmen, to whom everything foreign is disagreeable, like
Tobias Smollett and William Thackeray. The topographers and
antiquaries, botanists and archaeologists, have their value, and it is
a real value in the learned authors like George Wheeler, whose
writings became the guidebook of an era, or George Sandys; but
it is in their anecdotes or in their scientific achievements that they
live, and not in the works of their pens. Some respond to this inter-
mittency of liveliness by encapsulating their best moments in
poems—Richard Monckton Milnes, Professor J. D. Carlyle,
Aubrey de Vere—and the habit seems to become commoner as
the centuries advance.

But if there are few travel books on Greece of which one
would still wish to read the whole, the variety of reasons that led
men and women to travel in Greek lands is well worth contemplation. Leaving aside the writers of antiquity, for whom Greek travel
was not an "experience" in this sense, we can find the widest and
most intriguing variety of motivation in the gallery of independent spirits who set off for the Levant in the hundred years or so
succeeding the accession of Queen Elizabeth I.

Many had the simple thirst for knowledge of Henry Blount,
Grand Tourists before their time. Such was Francis Vernon, the
botanist whose travels culminated in his murder in Isfahan during
a quarrel over a penknife, and whose crabbed manuscript journal
is now in the Royal Society library in London; he avowed an "insatiable desire for knowledge," which impelled him in his perpetual
travels. Travelers such as Wheeler or Sandys equaled him in his
eagerness for knowledge, of which they brought as much from
books to their journeying as they reimported from their travels to
their books. Their successors have included many who traveled
out of a fascination with the lore of contemporary Greece: Pierre
Augustin Guys, author of the *Voyage Littéraire de la Grèce* (1771),

one of the first travelers to record Greek folk songs; his fellow-countryman Claude Etienne Savary (though his thirst for knowledge was attenuated by a penchant for picturesque writing); Robert Pashley, the Cambridge don whose *Travels in Crete* (1837) remains a valuable and delightful source; and, in our own century, J. C. Lawson, Rennell Rodd, and Patrick Leigh Fermor.

The phylum of naturalists, into which Vernon falls, is well represented: The book of the early traveler Pierre Belon (1553) contains much information on the plants and fauna of Greece, expressed in elegant French and with reference to the best authorities. (He had been in Greece between 1544 and 1547; he was later assassinated in the Bois de Boulogne, probably for reasons of religious politics, in 1565.) The botanist Joseph Pitton de Tournefort, whose book was published in 1717, devotes more of it to the customs of, and frequent tribulations imposed by, the natives than to information on plants. At the end of the eighteenth century, John Sibthorp pursued similar researches, culminating in the monumental posthumous *Flora Graeca;* he endowed a chair of rural economy at Oxford, and, like Tournefort, has given his name to several Greek plant species.

Others again traveled on mercantile or diplomatic business, like the Seigneur de la Borderie in 1542, or simply, like Sir Kenelm Digby, for fair adventure to win the King's favor. Even in the seventeenth century the route for the traveler still followed the course of the Crusaders of previous centuries, and of pilgrims like Sir Richard Guylforde, who published his account in 1511, and Matthew Paris. One of the most informative histories of a Greek island is the account of Santorini by Père Richard, one of a colony of Jesuits dispatched there in 1613 by the Pope to convert the inhabitants.

But the biggest draw for the West was antiquity. Cyriac of Ancona has the unchallenged distinction of being the father of archaeology in Greek lands, and his scattered and fragmentary works are still valuable documents for archaeologists, though written five and a half centuries ago. Though ignorance of antiquity was fairly prevalent among travelers (Guylforde thought Delphi was on Cythera; Bernard Randolph apparently did not know the legend of the Cretan Minotaur), an interest in ancient remains provided the impetus for travelers like Cristoforo Buondelmonti (in Crete in 1414), for George Sandys (who also wrote a translation of Ovid's *Metamorphoses* which became a contemporary classic), and later the Abbé Fourmont and Chateaubriand. Most lettered travelers, from Thomas Dallam, Tom Coryate, and William Lithgow onward, visited what they supposed to be Troy, scene of the most famous work of Western literature; they had not the archaeological sense of period to know that what they saw were the ruins of Alexandria Troas, a thousand years younger in date than Homer's Troy. (Even Schliemann identified as Priam's city a stratum of the Hill of Hisarlik too young by many centuries.) More often than not archaeological enthusiasm was expressed by theft. From the time of Charles I, when the Earl of Arundel sent his agents to collect statuary for him, despoliation was rife. Even earlier, Thomas Dallam breezily described his use of the hammer to remove desirable chunks of "Troy"; Bernard Randolph remarks of Delos, "The ruins are carried away by all ships who come to anchor there, so as part are in England, France, Holland, but most at Venice." Later, in 1795, J. B. S. Morritt traveled through Greece with the express purpose of collecting some distinguished decorations for Rokeby. From Athens he writes:

> I am wanted by the Centaurs and Lapithae. Goodbye for a moment. Scruples of conscience had arisen in the mind of the old scoundrel at the citadel; that is to say, he did not think we had offered him enough. We have, however, rather smoothed over his difficulties, and are to have the marble the first opportunity we can find to send it off from Athens. I, only being sensible for the extreme awkwardness of Grecian workmen, tremble lest it should be entirely broken to pieces on taking it out; if any accident happens to it I shall be quite crazy, as now there is nothing damaged but the faces and one of the hands. If I get it safe I shall be quite happy, and long to show it you at Rokeby.

The connoisseur as vandal of course reached his apogee in the Earl of Elgin.

Then, some traveled simply for the hell of it. The irrepressible Tom Coryate is the best example of this in the seventeenth century, as his account of Troy shows (page 316). He continued his career by traveling via Isfahan to Kandahar, Lahore, and Agra, where he distinguished himself by making a speech to the Mogul in the native tongue. The frontispiece of his travels shows him perched, characteristically, on an elephant.

William Lithgow's frontispiece shows him in full Turkish regalia, standing on a map of the Troad, containing the tombs of Achilles and Patroclus, with the following inscription:

> Loe here's mine Effigie, and Turkish suite;
> My staffe, my Shasse, as I did Asia foote:
> Plac'd in old Ilium; Priams Scepter thralles:

The Grecian Campe design'd; lost Dardan falles
Gird'd with small Simois: Idaes tops, a Gate;
Two fatall Tombes, an Eagle, sackt Troyes State.

The pride of the dour Scot at reaching beyond Europe's confines shines out of this emblem. If the life of the traveler got him down at times, he at least extracted full value from his enforced flight from Lanark.

The style of these two is not unlike that which later characterized Trelawny and Byron, who reckoned the Troad as good a hunting-ground for snipe as for antiquities and clearly preferred to concentrate on the former while his companion, the painstaking John Hobhouse, sketched and measured. One can imagine the rather vapid Richard Monckton Milnes, traveling with the dogged scholarly Christopher Wordsworth, taking a similarly light, if less sportsmanlike, view.

These figures have brought us to the age of the Grand Tour (Extended) which the Napoleonic Wars imposed on those whose predecessors had been accustomed to confine their peregrinations to France, Switzerland, and Italy. The number of those who made picturesque tours of Greece in the last years of the eighteenth century and the first of the nineteenth is considerable. Several of the more interesting personalities have been sketched by Hugh Tregaskis in *Beyond the Grand Tour* (1980): Among the liveliest of the writers are Edward Dodwell, the painter, Edward Daniel Clarke, the Cambridge mineralogist, Thomas S. Hughes, and Henry W. Williams, one of the foremost painters of Grecian scenes; Byron, Charles Cockerell, and Elgin have earned their own fame. It is amusing to consider the list of necessities for travel in Greece which Williams provides:

> Nothing can be more inconvenient in travelling than a superfluity of luggage; but the following articles will be found indispensable: A small camp-bed, with a bear-skin, sheet, and blanket; a small canteen; a tea-kettle, tin tea-pot and canisters; a silver cup; a pocket knife and fork. The French or English dress is most respected. Two or three pairs of shoes will be absolutely necessary. Few clothes will be sufficient, but they ought to be strong and good. It is unnecessary to take a great quantity of shirts, neckcloths, and stockings, as these may be had anywhere. A cap lined with an additional piece of leather will be found extremely useful, to protect the head from the heat of the sun. English saddles may be dispensed with, as the mules and horses are apt to be restive under them; our bed-

ding, as a substitute, we found convenient and comfortable. As vessels not unfrequently sail from London for Corfu, it may be advisable to forward the luggage to that island, consigned to a merchant of respectability.

Without a servant who can speak the Italian and Romaic (Greek) languages, the traveller will be exposed to much inconvenience and trouble. Such servants may be procured in Rome, in the islands of Corfu or Zante, and are occasionally to be met with in London; their usual charge is a dollar a-day. The English consul generally recommends a janizary.

The traveler compelled to keep his requirements to those permitted on a charter airplane may perhaps rejoice in his freedom as much as he envies the greater leisure of the Grand Tourist.

It is in the pens and the brushes of these men that we find sketched that portrait of "Fair Greece! sad relic of departed worth" which is a leitmotif of the age, and which provides the title for T. J. B. Spencer's masterly survey of Romantic Hellenism in England. Many of the paintings of these travelers, from Williams to Edward Lear, are reproduced in Fani-Maria Tsigakou's *The Rediscovery of Greece* (1981). Where the poets lamented departed glories, the painters depicted the picturesque present, and to Tennyson it seemed that Lear's painterly verbal account abolished the intervening centuries.

> Illyrian woodlands, echoing falls
> > Of water, sheets of summer glass,
> > The long divine Peneian pass,
> The vast Akrokeraunian walls,
>
> Tomohrit, Athos, all things fair,
> > With such a pencil, such a pen,
> > You shadow forth to distant men,
> I read and felt that I was there:
>
> And trust me while I turn'd the page,
> > And track'd you still on classic ground,
> > I grew in gladness till I found
> My spirits in the golden age.
>
> For me the torrent ever pour'd
> > And glisten'd—here and there alone
> > The broad-limb'd Gods at random thrown
> By fountain-urns;—and Naiads oar'd

A glimmering shoulder under gloom
    Of cavern pillars; on the swell
    The silver lily heaved and fell;
And many a slope was rich in bloom

From him that on the mountain lea
    By dancing rivulets fed his flocks
    To him who sat upon the rocks,
And fluted to the morning sea.

Alongside the laments of the poets for fallen glory, plentifully represented later in this book, there ran another strand of phil-hellenic sentiment, which had taken its impulse from the Crusades of Christendom against the Turks. The Greeks became the cen-terpiece of a vision of a regenerated Christian Byzantine Empire, such as had been the dream of Gemistus Plethon in Mistra before the Turkish Conquest, and which remained firmly alive among expatriates and interested parties many centuries later. In the sev-enteenth century, it seemed that anyone who dared lead an army against the Turkish Sultan could have the leadership of that Empire. The battle of Lepanto became a symbol of the possible defeat of the Turks, and James I of England wrote a long and turgid poem about it which expresses Christians' joy at the defeat of the infidel:

Iehova als hath ballances,
    Wherewith hee weighs aright
The greatest and the heaviest sinnes
    With smaller faults and light,
These grace did move him for to take,
    And so he weighed in heaven,
The Christian faults with faithlesse Turkes
    The ballance stood not eaven,
But sweid upon the faithlesse side:
    And then with awfull face,
Frownd God of Hosts, the whirling Heavens
    For feare did tremble apace,
The staiest mountains shuddred all,
    The grounds of earth did shake,
The Seas did bray, and Plutoes Realme
    For horrour cold did quake.

Not many years later Edmund Waller wrote a birthday poem for James's grandson, James II, in which he was envisaged as the leader of a new Crusade:

The British monarch shall the glory have,
That famous Greece remains no longer slave;
That source of art and cultivated thought!
Which they to Rome, and Romans hither brought.

The banished Muses shall no longer mourn,
But may with liberty to Greece return;
Though slaves, (like birds that sing not in a cage)
They lost their genius, and poetic rage;
Homers again, and Pindars, may be found,
And his great actions with their numbers crowned.

The Turk's vast empire does united stand;
Christians divided under the command
Of jarring princes, would be soon undone,
Did not this hero make their interest one;
Peace to embrace, ruin the common foe,
Exalt the Cross, and lay the Crescent low.

Thus may the Gospel to the rising sun
Be spread, and flourish where it first begun;
And this great day (so justly honoured here!)
Known to the East, and celebrated there

"A Presage of the Ruin of the Turkish Empire.
Presented to his Majesty on his birthday"

Not many years before this, in 1642, Leone Allacci, an intellectual from Chios living in Rome, addressed to the Dauphin of France a lengthy poem in classical iambics, urging him to liberate Greece from the Turkish yoke:

The solemn dignity and the achievements of Greece are falling to nothing. The god-established hearth of Athens is sinking, whose foundations Zeus established, and which Ares walled around; Poseidon of the Isthmus erected its tall towers, Pallas Athena straightened its roads, Hephaestus built its dwellings and Hermes its colonnades; Phoebus designed and Artemis raised up the Parthenon, Aphrodite laboured to establish its baths, Bacchus its dancing places, Themis its courthouse; and Justice is the guardian of its laws. Should not such a city have received honour from all cities, work of the gods that it was? Yet it has perished, it has been torn in fragments by rabid dogs, falling, wretched in its fate, to the doom of the gods.

Hellas, 514–28

The privateer, Thomas Sherley, whose brothers Robert and Anthony became distinguished figures at the court of Persia, took advantage of his long stay at Constantinople in the early years of the century to engage in discussions with prominent Greeks about the possibility of a rising against their Turkish overlords. Here lay the seeds of the "Great Idea" that dominated intellectual Greek thinking for centuries.

In the circumstances it is perhaps surprising that it was so long before sufficient support was mobilized to carry out the plan, by which time the Greeks had taken affairs into their own hands in the Revolution of 1821. At this point many Westerners of all nations flocked to assist the Greek cause, some with their persons and enthusiasm, others with money as well. The spirit of revolution flowed into countless poems by now forgotten French writers (their troops are catalogued by Eugène Asse in *Les Petits Romantiques* (1900)) and into those of a slightly better remembered German poet, Wilhelm Müller. It provided the impetus for collections of folk songs like that of Charles Brinsley Sheridan and the important compilation of Charles Fauriel (both 1825). The death of Byron crystallized the enthusiasm of the Greeks and the philhellenes, and Byron was himself celebrated in Greek songs, and in many poems by foreigners, including an ode by Casimir Delavigne and a long heroic poem by A. E. Gaulmier (*Oeuvres Poétiques*, 1850), who pinpointed Byron's achievement succinctly in an address to Delavigne:

> Qu'ils surent l'inspirer de sublimes accords,
> Ces Grecs régénérés, ces illustres rebelles,
> Osant, trahis de tous, se demeurer fidèles,
> Et toujours abattus, se relevant toujours,
> Lutter sans espérance, et vaincre sans secours!
> Ils avaient Marathon, Salamine et Platée,
> En chantant leurs exploits tu leur rendis Tyrtée.[1]
> Hélas! un favori des Muses et des cieux
> Admira, comme toi, leurs faits audacieux.
> La Grèce l'enflammait, et sa lyre sans cesse
> Modulait dans ses chants le doux nom de la Grèce.
> Enfin à ces héros, qu'ont délaissés les rois,
> Il voue et sa fortune, et sa vie, et sa voix,
> Et court sur une terre, en merveille féconde,
> Partager avec eux l'étonnement du monde.
> Mais de la Grèce à peine il a touché les bords,

1. A poet of sixth-century Sparta, whose poems reflect patriotic and martial ardor.

Le trépas a glacé ses généreux transports.
Il tombe; le destin enviait à sa gloire
L'honneur de succomber sur un champ de victoire.
Sans doute sur son front c'était trop d'allier
La palme du poète et celle du guerrier;
Les dieux n'ont pas voulu qu'un mortel téméraire
Fût à la fois d'un peuple et l'Achille et l'Homère.
Mais en vain leurs décrets, trahissant sa valeur,
L'ont surpris dans sa course et frappé dans sa fleur:
Les larmes des héros ont coulé sur sa cendre;
Au tombeau fraternel ton luth' s'est fait entendre,
Et son nom cher aux Grecs, cher à l'humanité,
A reçu de tes mains son immortalité.

They knew how to inspire him [Byron] with sublime agreement, these regenerated Greeks, these illustrious rebels; who dared, betrayed by all, to remain loyal to themselves; beaten down by all, to raise themselves continually, to struggle without hope, and to conquer without assistance. They had their Marathon, Salamis and Plataca, and in singing of their exploits you gave them back a Tyrtaeus. Alas! a favourite of the Muses and of the heavens wondered, like yourself, at their bold deeds. Greece inflamed him, and his lyre unceasingly chimed in his songs with the sweet name of Greece. At last, to these heroes whom kings had abandoned, he vowed his fortune, his life and his voice, and hastened to a land, fruitful to a wonder, to share with them the astonishment of the world. But scarcely had he touched the coast of Greece, when death froze his generous ecstasy. He fell; destiny begrudged his fame the honour of falling on a field of victory. Doubtless it was too much to ally on his brow the palm of the poet and that of the warrior; the gods did not wish that a presumptuous mortal should be both the Achilles and the Homer of a single people. But it was in vain that their decrees, betraying his valour, took him by surprise and felled him in his flower: the tears of the heroes fell on his ashes; at his tomb your lute has made heard its fraternal tones, and his name dear to the Greeks, dear to humanity, has received its immortality at your hands.

Translated by RS

The revolution inspired enthusiasm in many American breasts too, and, in its aftermath, brought travelers like Julia Ward Howe (1819–1910), the abolitionist, suffragist, and reformer, with strong views on how the place could be improved. An extreme example is Lydia H. Sigourney, whose poems on Greece included one entitled "Female Education for Greece" (1837).

The anarchy that ensued on the War of Independence formed the backdrop to the visits of Lamartine, Chateaubriand, and Samuel S. Cox, before calmer days welcomed Mark Twain, Herman Melville, W. M. Thackeray, Gustave Flaubert, Robert Pashley, and more recent travelers.

It is time we said a word of the people whose country Greece was and is, and of what they have written of it. It used to be common-place that the ancient Greeks had no feeling for landscape, and no interest in conveying its beauties in words. The first assumption cannot long survive a visit to one of the spectacular sites like Del-phi, Vassai, or Sounion: How could a people indifferent to nature have chosen spots so magnificent, have fitted their own little edifices so perfectly into the whole? As for the second charge, it is true that Greek writers do not, like a Wordsworth, prey on their landscape to fuel and to convey their own deepest perceptions. When Homer describes Ithaca, it is the scene of an action, a set-ting fit for history; when Pindar celebrates his hero's victory "under the shady mountains of Phleious," that brief and precise phrase sets human achievement directly in its place in the enduring order of nature: Men's talents blossom and fade, take turn and turn about, like the leaves or fallow fields; when Sophocles celebrates Colonus his focus is all on the place and its qualities: The grave of Oedipus is holy ground and not amenable to the interpretation of mere men.

There is scarcely any classical Greek travel-writing as such. The *Periplus* of Dionysius and the *Geography* of Strabo are scientific geography according to the standards of the time; even Pausanias' *Description* is not *belles-lettres* but a practical guide and compendium of history. The lively Heracleides himself aimed mainly at an account of the customs of men, not of the terrain. The harshness of Greek landscape leaves little leisure for mere admiration to those who wrest a living from it; but, like the gods, the land is inescapable and essential, a stage as well as a backdrop. There is more truth than one might expect in the following account, by Wordsworth, of the ancient pagan's response to his natural surroundings, even if we do not share the implied corollary that a Wordsworthian feeling for nature is automatically better than one which peoples the landscape with its own spirits. Of course he overstates the case in this descrip-tion of false Arcadias: Shocked though he might be to recognize it, it is out of Tiepolo, not Homer or Pausanias:

Once more to distant ages of the world
Let us revert, and place before our thoughts
The face which rural solitude might wear
To the unenlightened swains of pagan Greece.
—In that fair clime, the lonely herdsman, stretched
On the soft grass through half a summer's day,
With music lulled his indolent repose:
And, in some fit of weariness, if he,
When his own breath was silent, chanced to hear
A distant strain, far sweeter than the sounds
Which his poor skill could make, his fancy fetched,
Even from the blazing chariot of the sun,
A beardless Youth, who touched a golden lute,
And filled the illumined groves with ravishment.
The nightly hunter, lifting a bright eye
Up towards the crescent moon, with grateful heart
Called on the lovely wanderer who bestowed
That timely light, to share his joyous sport:
And hence, a beaming Goddess with her Nymphs,
Across the lawn and through the darksome grove,
Not unaccompanied with tuneful notes
By echo multiplied from rock or cave,
Swept in the storm of chase; as moon and stars
Glance rapidly along the clouded heaven,
When winds are blowing strong. The traveller slaked
His thirst from rill or gushing fount, and thanked
The Naiad. Sunbeams, upon distant hills
Gliding apace, with shadows in their train,
Might, with small help from fancy, be transformed
Into fleet Oreads sporting visibly.
The Zephyrs fanning, as they passed, their wings,
Lacked not, for love, fair objects whom they wooed
With gentle whisper. Withered boughs grotesque,
Stripped of their leaves and twigs by hoary age,
From depth of shaggy covert peeping forth
In the low vale, or on steep mountain-side;
And, sometimes, intermixed with stirring horns
Of the live deer, or goat's depending beard,—
These were the lurking Satyrs, a wild brood
Of gamesome Deities; or Pan himself,
The simple shepherd's awe-inspiring God!

The Excursion, IV, 847–88

Collectors of Greek folklore have revealed a world which is still, even in the twentieth century, populated with the spirits of the countryside: the Nereids, the Kallikantzari, vampires, and *revenants.*

The long and continuous tradition of Greek literature—though what lies between the death of Callimachus and the birth of Cavafy is only beginning to be studied and appreciated—has always been in intimate relation to the history of the places and the times that produced it. Kazantzakis has said of the Greek landscape that it "is a palimpsest bearing twelve successive inscriptions: contemporary; the period of 1821; the Turkish yoke; the Frankish sway; the Byzantine; the Roman; the Hellenistic epoch; the Classic; the Dorian middle ages; the Mycenaean; the Aegean; and the Stone Age" (*Travels in Greece*). All of these, except the two most ancient, before writing was known or memory prized, have left their imprint in the literature. The face of Greece figures only in anthropomorphic form, as in the *Quarrel of Olympos and Kissavos*, or as background to human events; the works of man, even those of the *Bridge of Arta* (page 196), are the center of attention. The lush (and not altogether truthful) description of Mount Ida in the *Erotokritos* is exceptional, clearly influenced by Italian poetry. Most of the major historical events are celebrated in the heroic folk poetry which, although oral, has survived until very recently in many parts of Greece, so that collectors like J. A. Notopoulos have been able to record songs closely related in theme, attitude, and verbal arrangement to those first published by Fauriel, Legrand, and Pashley a hundred years earlier. The songs of the klephts, the bands of brigands who effectively ruled large tracts of Roumeli and the Morea, the *paraloges*, or narrative poems, and the *rizitika* and *mantinades* of Crete are but a few of the traditional forms in which it is still possible to come across songs celebrating the events of the War of Independence. A Cretan song on the conquest of Rhodes has been adapted with minimal alteration to treat of the Turkish sway in Cyprus.

Few before Fauriel troubled to record such material. The Jesuit, F. Richard, and the French traveler, Pierre Augustin Guys, were exceptions. On the whole travelers noticed only the Turks and the distinctive features of the Turkish civilization. The serf-like condition of the Greeks clearly put them beneath notice. It is the more remarkable that the native tradition remained so vigorous.

The sense of the tremendous accumulated weight of tradition, of being buried under layer after geological layer of example to be lived up to, determining the shape of life and making a man unfree, compelling him to an Aeschylean inexorability of destiny, is well expressed in Seferis's poem:

I woke with this marble head in my hands;
it exhausts my elbows and I don't know where to put
      it down . . .
so our life became one and it will be very difficult for it to
      separate again.

Since the liberation, the Greek intelligentsia have struggled with that weight of tradition, overvaluing it—as did Adamantios Korais (1748–1833), who lived in Paris from 1788, and remodeled the Greek language on the template of New Testament Greek to create a tongue worthy of a literate and advanced people, even though no one actually spoke it, so that the rivalry of "pure" and demotic speech has been a political football ever since—or strenuously ignoring it to concentrate on *Realien*, as in the poetry of Yannis Ritsos. Those Greek writers who have achieved the widest reputation are those who have to some extent reconciled these conflicting forces, so that myth, literature, and the present form a true whole. This is achieved, perhaps, by Andreas Kalvos in his celebration of the blessings of Zante or by Angelos Sikelianos with his fervently mystical appreciation of the Greek landscape, and more surely by the intellectual George Seferis or the often surrealist Odysseus Elytis. Elytis's *Axion Esti* is a litany of the scenes of Greece which illuminates them with meaning. These poets celebrate their country through particulars.

Particulars, as William Blake was wont to aver, are the way to knowledge. "To generalize is to be an idiot." The poems, anecdotes, and discoveries, the ecstasies and cruelties recorded in this book are all, I hope, particular and truthful. If they bring the reader to love Greece more, and to reap more from visiting it, they will have served their purpose.

2

Romantic Overture

Hail, nature's utmost boast! unrivalled Greece!
My fairest reign! where every power benign
Conspired to blow the flower of human kind,
And lavished all that genius can inspire.
Clear sunny climates, by the breezy main,
Ionian or Aegean, tempered kind:
Light, airy soils: a country rich and gay,
Broke into hills with balmy odours crowned,
And, bright with purple harvest, joyous vales:
Mountains and streams where verse spontaneous flowed,
Whence deemed by wondering men the seat of gods,
And still the mountains and the streams of song:
All that boon nature could luxuriant pour
Of high materials, and my restless arts
Frame into finished life. How many states,
And clustering towns, and monuments of fame,
And scenes of glorious deeds in little bounds!
From the rough tract of bending mountains, beat
By Adria's here, there by Aegean waves,
To where the deep-adorning Cyclad Isles
In shining prospect rise, and on the shores
Of farthest Crete resounds the Libyan main!

.ے

'These were the wonders that illumined Greece,
From end to end'—Here interrupting warm,
'Where are they now? (I cried) say, goddess, where?
And what the land, thy darling thus of old?'
'Sunk! (she resumed), deep in the kindred gloom
Of superstition and of slavery sunk!
No glory now can touch their hearts, benumbed
By loose dejected sloth and servile fear;
No science pierce the darkness of their minds;
No nobler art the quick ambitious soul
Of imitation in their breast awake.
Even to supply the needful arts of life

Mechanic toil denies the hopeless hand.
Scarce any trace remaining, vestige grey,
Or nodding column on the desert shore
To point where Corinth or where Athens stood.'
                    James Thomson, *Liberty*, ii, 84–107, 391–406

Fair Greece! sad relic of departed worth!
Immortal, though no more; though fallen, great!
Who now shall lead thy scatter'd children forth,
And long accustom'd bondage uncreate?
Not such thy sons who whilome did await,
The hopeless warriors of a willing doom,
In bleak Thermopylae's sepulchral strait—
Oh! who that gallant spirit shall resume,
Leap from Eurotas' banks, and call thee from the tomb?

Spirit of Freedom! when on Phyle's brow
Thou sat'st with Thrasybulus and his train,
Couldst thou forebode the dismal hour which now
Dims the green beauties of thine Attic plain?
Not thirty tyrants now enforce the chain,
But every carle can lord it o'er thy land;
Nor rise thy sons, but idly rail in vain,
Trembling beneath the scourge of Turkish hand;
From birth till death enslaved; in word, in deed, unmann'd.

In all save form alone, how changed! and who
That marks the fire still sparkling in each eye,
Who but would deem their bosoms burn'd anew
With thy unquenched beam, lost Liberty!
And many dream withal the hour is nigh
That gives them back their father's heritage:
For foreign arms and aid they fondly sigh,
Nor solely dare encounter hostile rage,
Or tear their name defiled from Slavery's mournful page.

Hereditary bondsmen! know ye not
Who would be free themselves must strike the blow?
By their right arms the conquest must be wrought?
Will Gaul or Muscovite redress ye? no!
True, they may lay your proud despoilers low,
But not for you will Freedom's altars flame,
Shades of the Helots! triumph o'er your foe!
Greece! change thy lords, thy state is still the same;
Thy glorious day is o'er, but not thine years of shame.

·᷒

And yet how lovely in thine age of woe,
Land of lost gods and godlike men, art thou!
Thy vales of evergreen, thy hills of snow,
Proclaim thee Nature's varied favourite now:
Thy fanes, thy temples to thy surface bow,
Commingling slowly with heroic earth,
Broke by the share of every rustic plough:
So perish monuments of mortal birth,
So perish all in turn, save well-recorded Worth;

Save where some solitary column mourns
Above its prostrate brethren of the cave;
Save where Tritonia's airy shrine adorns
Colonna's cliff, and gleams along the wave;
Save o'er some warrior's half-forgotten grave,
Where the gray stones and unmolested grass
Ages, but not oblivion, feebly brave;
While strangers only not regardless pass,
Lingering like me, perchance, to gaze, and sigh 'Alas!'

Yet are thy skies as blue, thy crags as wild;
Sweet are thy groves, and verdant are thy fields,
Thine olive ripe as when Minerva smiled,
And still his honied wealth Hymettus yields;
There the blithe bee his fragrant fortress builds,
The freeborn wanderer of thy mountain air;
Apollo still thy long, long summer gilds,
Still in his beam Mendeli's marbles glare;
Art, Glory, Freedom fail, but Nature still is fair.

Where'er we tread 'tis haunted, holy ground;
No earth of thine is lost in vulgar mould,
But one vast realm of wonder spreads around,
And all the Muse's tales seem truly told,
Till the sense aches with gazing to behold
The scenes our earliest dreams have dwelt upon;
Each hill and dale, each deepening glen and wold
Defies the power which crush'd thy temples gone:
Age shakes Athena's tower, but spares gray Marathon.

> Lord Byron, *Childe Harold's Pilgrimage*, ii, 73–76, 85–88

ODE ON A GRECIAN URN

Thou still unravish'd bride of quietness,
    Thou foster-child of silence and slow time,
Sylvan historian, who canst thus express

A flowery tale more sweetly than our rhyme:
What leaf-fring'd legend haunts about thy shape
   Of deities or mortals, or of both,
      In Tempe or the dales of Arcady?
What men or gods are these? What maidens loth?
   What mad pursuit? What struggle to escape?
      What pipes and timbrels? What wild ecstasy?

Heard melodies are sweet, but those unheard
   Are sweeter; therefore, ye soft pipes, play on;
Not to the sensual ear, but, more endear'd,
   Pipe to the spirit ditties of no tone:
Fair youth, beneath the trees, thou canst not leave
   Thy song, nor ever can those trees be bare;
      Bold Lover, never, never canst thou kiss,
Though winning near the goal—yet, do not grieve;
   She cannot fade, though thou hast not thy bliss,
      For ever wilt thou love, and she be fair!

Ah, happy, happy boughs! that cannot shed
   Your leaves, nor ever bid the Spring adieu;
And, happy melodist, unwearied,
   For ever piping songs for ever new;
More happy love! more happy, happy love!
   For ever warm and still to be enjoy'd,
      For ever panting, and for ever young;
All breathing human passion far above,
   That leaves a heart high-sorrowful and cloy'd,
      A burning forehead, and a parching tongue.

Who are these coming to the sacrifice?
   To what green altar, O mysterious priest,
Lead'st thou that heifer lowing at the skies,
   And all her silken flanks with garlands drest?
What little town by river or sea-shore,
   Or mountain-built with peaceful citadel,
      Is emptied of this folk, this pious morn?
And, little town, thy streets for evermore
   Will silent be; and not a soul to tell
      Why thou art desolate, can e'er return.

O Attic Shape! Fair attitude! With brede
   Of marble men and maidens overwrought,
With forest branches and the trodden weed;

Thou, silent form, dost tease us out of thought
As doth eternity: Cold Pastoral!
When old age shall this generation waste,
        Thou shalt remain, in midst of other woe
Than ours, a friend to man, to whom thou say'st,
        'Beauty is truth, truth beauty,—that is all
                Ye know on earth, and all ye need to know.'

John Keats

3

The Ionian Islands

For centuries, most travelers making their way to or through Greek lands followed the sea route from the Italian coast, making their first landfall on one of the Ionian Islands. This book follows their example, even though the modern traveler is more likely to arrive at Athens by airplane or at Piraeus by ship. To proceed from west to east at least offers a more or less continuous and comprehensive itinerary.

It also brings the traveler directly to Ithaca, which lies almost at the center of the group, in the embrace of Cephalonia. Ithaca is the home of the best known of Greek heroes, Odysseus.

> I am Ulysses Laertiades,
> The fear of all the world for policies,
> For which my facts as high as heav'n resound.
> I dwell in Ithaca, earth's most renown'd,
> All over-shadow'd with the shake-leaf ill,
> Tree-fam'd Neritus; whose near confines fill
> Islands a number, well-inhabited,
> That under my observance taste their bread;
> Dulichius, Samos, and the full-of-food
> Zacynthus, likewise grac'd with store of wood.
> But Ithaca, though in the seas it lie,
> Yet lies she so aloft she casts her eye
> Quite over all the neighbour continent;
> Far northward situate, and, being lent
> But little favour of the morn and sun,
> With barren rocks and cliffs is over-run;
> And yet of hardy youths a nurse of name;
> Nor could I see a soil, where'er I came,
> More sweet and wishful.
>
> Homer, *Odyssey*, IX, 21–28;
> translated by George Chapman

Corfu

The more northerly Corfu has been a strong contender for the identification with the Kingdom of Phaeacia, that lush idyll where

King Alcinous ruled and his charming daughter, Nausicaa, res-
cued Odysseus from his many days at sea. Both Ernle Bradford
and Lawrence Durrell identify features of Corfu with Homer's
Phaeacia. It is hard to believe that Odysseus could have lived so
close to such a fairyland and not have known of it until he was
washed up there: But Homer's poetry no doubt needed the inspiration of locality. The description of Alcinous's garden could reflect
the rich vegetation of Corfu:

> There grew luxuriant many a lofty tree,
> Pomegranate, pear, the apple blushing bright,
> The honied fig, and unctuous olive smooth.
> Those fruits, nor winter's cold nor summer's heat
> Fear ever, fail not, wither not, but hang
> Perennial, whose unceasing zephyr breathes
> Gently on all, enlarging these, and those
> Maturing genial; in an endless course
> Pears after pears to full dimensions swell,
> Figs follow figs, grapes clust'ring grow again
> Where clusters grew, and (ev'ry apple stript)
> The boughs soon tempt the gath'rer as before.
> There too, well-rooted, and of fruit profuse,
> His vineyard grows; part, wide-extended, basks,
> In the sun's beams; the arid level glows;
> In part they gather, and in part they tread
> The wine-press, while, before the eye, the grapes
> Here put their blossom forth, there, gather fast
> Their blackness. On the garden's verge extreme
> Flow'rs of all hues smile all the year, arranged
> With neatest art judicious, and amid
> The lovely scene two fountains welling forth,
> One visits, into ev'ry part diffus'd,
> The garden-ground, the other soft beneath
> The threshold steals into the palace-court,
> Whence ev'ry citizen his vase supplies.

Homer, *Odyssey*, VII, 112–31;
translated by William Cowper

Waller Rodwell Wright, who had been Consul-General for the
Seven Islands from 1800 to 1804, accepts the identification of
Corfu with Phaeacia, and takes the opportunity for a description
of the scene:

> Here gushing founts and springs that never fail
> Pour health and plenty through the smiling vale;

Edward Lear, *Corfu from the Island of Vido*. The Fine Art Society, London (detail).

Fair smiles the vale, with myrtle hedges crown'd,
And aromatic fragrance breathes around;
The rising hill wide-spreading olives shade,
Skirt the deep ravine, and embow'r the glade
With sober tints of never-fading green;
While distant mountains close the varied scene,
Beyond the cultivated landscape rise,
And sternly frown amid the cloudless skies.
    Such is the spot where flows Crissida's stream;
The peasant's solace, and the poet's theme:
From the cold rock her limpid fount distils;
A rocky bed receives the falling rills.
'Twas here, sequester'd 'midst embow'ring shades,
The bright Nausicaa sported with her maids,
What time Laertes' god-like son address'd
His tale of sorrow to her pitying breast . . .
        Wright, *Horae Ionicae* (London, 1809)

Byron admired Wright's poetry, and hailed him in *English Bards and Scotch Reviewers* (written before Byron's first journey to Greece):

Wright! 'twas thy happy lot at once to view
Those shores of glory, and to sing them too;

And sure no common Muse inspired thy pen
To hail the land of Gods and Godlike men.

Lawrence Durrell discusses the relative claims of Cassopi, Pale-
opolis, and Paleocastritsa for the capital and court of Alcinous. One
may preserve a degree of scepticism about the details of such
identification.

However, Homer certainly described the Cave of the Nymphs
on Ithaca from observed detail:

> There is a port,
> That th'aged sea-god Phorcys makes his fort,
> Whose earth the Ithacensian people own,
> In which two rocks inaccessible are grown
> Far forth into the sea, whose each strength binds
> The boist'rous waves in from the high-flown winds
> On both the out-parts so, that all within
> The well-built ships, that once their harbour win
> In his calm bosom, without anchor rest,
> Save, and unstirr'd. From forth the haven's high crest
> Branch the well-brawn'd arms of an olive-tree;
> Beneath which runs a cave from all sun free,
> Cool, and delightsome, sacred to th'access
> Of Nymphs whose surnames are the Naiades;
> In which flew humming bees, in which lay thrown
> Stone cups, stone vessels, shittles all of stone,
> With which the Nymphs their purple mantles wove,
> In whose contexture art and wonder strove;
> In which pure springs perpetually ran;
> To which two entries were; the one for man,
> On which the North breath'd; th'other for the Gods,
> On which the South; and that bore no abodes
> For earthy men, but only deathless feet
> Had there free way.

> Homer, *Odyssey*, XIII, 96–112;
> translated by George Chapman

Recent research has established the site of the cave not far from
Vathy town, and we are less bound than ever to accept the elab-
orate interpretations, so characteristic of an age that sought
inappropriate wisdom in classical texts, of the Neo-Platonist
scholar Porphyry:

> What does Homer obscurely signify by the cave in
> Ithaca?

That the poet, indeed, does not narrate these particulars from historical information, is evident from this, that those who have given us a description of the island, have, as Cronius says, made no mention of such a cave being found in it. This likewise, says he, is manifest, that it would be absurd for Homer to expect, that in describing a cave fabricated merely by poetic licence and thus artificially opening a path to Gods and men in the region of Ithaca, he should gain the belief of mankind. And it is equally absurd to suppose, that nature herself should point out, in this place, one path for the descent of all mankind, and again another path for all the Gods. For, indeed, the whole world is full of Gods and men; but it is impossible to be persuaded, that in the Ithacensian cave men descend, and Gods ascend. Cronius therefore, having premised this much, says, that it is evident, not only to the wise but also to the vulgar, that the poet, under the veil of allegory, conceals some mysterious signification; thus compelling others to explore what the gate of men is, and also what is the gate of the Gods; what he means by asserting that this cave of the Nymphs has two gates; and why it is both pleasant and obscure, since darkness is by no means delightful, but is rather productive of aversion and horror. Likewise, what is the reason why it is not simply said to be the cave of the Nymphs, but it is accurately added, of the Nymphs that are called Naiades? Why also, is the cave represented as containing bowls and amphorae, when no mention is made of their receiving any liquor, but bees are said to deposit their honey in these vessels as in hives? Then, again, why are oblong beams adapted to weaving placed here for the Nymphs? . . . Hence, since this narration is full of such obscurities, it can neither be a fiction casually devised for the purpose of procuring delight, nor an exposition of a topical history; but something allegorical must be indicated in it by the poet, who likewise mystically places an olive near the cave . . . For, neither did the ancients establish temples without fabulous symbols, nor does Homer rashly narrate the particulars pertaining to things of this kind. But how much the more anyone endeavours to show that this description of the cave is not an Homeric fiction, but prior to Homer was consecrated to the Gods, by so much the more will this consecrated cave be found to be full of ancient wisdom.

Porphyry, *Cave of the Nymphs*;
translated by Thomas Taylor (London, 1789)

Paxos

In the Ionian Islands, too, off Paxos, took place, according to legend, one of the most melancholy events of the dying pagan world.

> Epitherses told me that, designing a voyage to Italy, he
> embarked himself on a vessel well laden both with goods and
> passengers. About the evening the vessel was becalmed about
> the Isles Echinades, whereupon their ship drove with the tide
> till it was carried near the Isles of Paxi; when immediately a
> voice was heard by most of the passengers (who were then
> awake, and taking a cup after supper) calling unto one
> Thamus, and that with so loud a voice as made all the com-
> pany amazed; which Thamus was a mariner of Egypt, whose
> name was scarcely known in the ship. He returned no answer
> to the first calls; but at the third he replied, Here! here! I am
> the man. Then the voice said aloud to him, When you are
> arrived at Palodes, take care to make it known that the great
> God Pan is dead. Epitherses told us, this voice did much
> astonish all that heard it, and caused much arguing whether
> this voice was to be obeyed or slighted. Thamus, for his part,
> was resolved, if the wind permitted, to sail by the place with-
> out saying a word; but if the wind ceased and there ensued a
> calm, to speak and cry out as loud as he was able what he was
> enjoined. Being come to Palodes, there was no wind stirring,
> and the sea was as smooth as glass. Whereupon Thamus
> standing on the deck, with his face towards the land, uttered
> with a loud voice his message, saying, The great Pan is dead.
> He had no sooner said this, but they heard a dreadful noise,
> not only of one, but of several, who, to their thinking, groaned
> and lamented with a kind of astonishment. And there being
> many persons in the ship, an account of this was soon spread
> over Rome, which made Tiberius the Emperor send for
> Thamus; and he seemed to give such heed to what he told
> him, that he earnestly enquired who this Pan was; and the
> learned men about him gave in their judgments, that it was the
> son of Mercury by Penelope.

> Plutarch, *Why the Oracles Cease to Give Answers*, 419;
> translated by R. Midgley (London, 1870)

Zante

The travelers of the seventeenth century felt themselves leaving
civilization as they coasted the Ionian shore. What terrors lay ahead

they might only guess, like Thomas Dallam, an organ-maker of Lancashire who was delegated by Queen Elizabeth I to deliver to the Sultan an organ of which she wished to make him a present. He left England in February 1599; here is his first landing in "Turkey":

Whyleste we laye, thus for sixe dayes upon the seae before the towne, I touke great notis of a little mountayne, the which, as I thought, did ly close to the seae, and semed to be a verrie pleasante place to take a vew of the whole iland and the seae before it. It showed to be verrie greene and playen ground on the tope of it, and a whyte thinge lyke a rocke in the mydle tharof. I touke suche pleasur in behouldinge this hill that I made a kinde of vow or promise to my selfe that assowne as I sett foute on shore I would nether eate nor drinke untill I had bene on the tope tharof; and in the meane time did labur with tow of my companyons, and perswaded them to beare me company. One of there names was Myghell Watson, my joyner; the other's name Edward Hale, a cotchman. The day beinge come that we should go a shore, I chalinged my associates with there promise, and gott there good wils to go with me before we wente into the towne. This hill is called by the Greekes Scopo (i.e., outlook). It is from the town more than a myle, but I gave our sayleres somthinge to carrie us in the coke boote, as we thoughte to the foute of the hill; but when we weare sett a shore we found it to be almoste tow myles unto it. When we cam to the foute of it, by great fortune we hapened on the ryghte waye, the which was verrie narrow and crouked. It was arlye in the morninge, and we weare toulde, 2 or 3 days before, that no man muste carrie any weapern with him when he wente a shore, and tharfore we wente only with cudgels in our handes. So, assendinge the hill aboute halfe a myle, and loukinge up, we sawe upon a storie of the hill above us a man goinge with a greate staffe on his shoulder, havinge a clubed end, and on his heade a cape which seemed to hus to have five horns standinge outryghte, and a greate heard of gootes and shepe folloed him.

My frende Myghell Watson, when he saw this, he seemed to be verrie fearfull, and would have perswaded us to go no farther, tellinge us that surly those that did inhabite thare weare savidge men, and myghte easalye wronge us, we hauinge no sordes or dageres, nether any more Company; but I tould him that yf thei weare divers, I would, with Godes help, be as good as my worde. So, with muche adow, we gott him to go to that storie wheare we sawe the man with his club; and than we saw that man was a heardman. Yeate, for all this, Myghell Watson swore that he would goo no farther, com of it what would. Edward Hale sayd somethinge fayntly that he would not leave me, but se the end. So we tow traveled forwarde, and when we cam somthinge neare the topp, we saw tow horsis grasinge, with packe sadls on ther backes, and one man cominge downe the hill towardes us, having nothinge in his handes. Cothe I to my fellow: Nede, we shall see by this man what people they be that inhabit heare. When this man came unto us he lay his hand upon his breste, and boued his head and bodye with smylinge countinance, makinge us a sine to go up still. Yeat than Ned Hall began to diswade me from goinge any further; but I tould him it would not stand with my othe to go backe until I had bene as farr as I could go. Cominge to the top thare was a prittie fair grene, and on one sid of it a whyte house bulte of lyme, and some square, the whyche had bene the house of an ancoriste, who, as I harde after wardes, died but a litle before our cominge thether, and that she had lived five hundrethe years. Ryghte before us, on the farther side of the greene, I saw a house of som 20 pacis longe, and waled aboute one yarde hie, and than opene to the eaves; which was aboute a yarde more. And I se a man on the inside reatche oute a coper kettell to one that stood with oute the wale. Than saide I to Ned Hale: I will go to yender house and gitt som drinke, for I have greate neede. The wether was verrie hote, and I was fastinge. But Ned Hale tould me that I had no reason to drinke at there handes, nether to go any nearer them. Yeate I wente bouldly to the sid of the house, whear I saw another man drinke, and made a sine to him within that I woulde drinke. Than he touke up the same ketle which had water in it, and offer it me to drinke. And when I did put out my hande to take it, he would not give it me, but sett it further of, and than cam near the wale againe, and lifte up a carpit which lay on the ground, and thar was six bottels full of verrie good wyne, and a faire silver cupe, and he filed that silver boule full of a redeishe wyne, which they do cale Rebola, and he gave it me to drinke; and when I had it in my hande I caled to my frende Nede Hale, who stood a far of, for he was a fraide to com neare. Hear, Nede, cothe I, a carrouse to all our frendes in Inglande. I pray you, cothe he, take heede what you dow. Will you take what drinke they give you? Yeae, truly, cothe I; for it is better than I have as yeat disarved of. When I had give God thankes for it, I drank it of, and it was the beste that ever I dranke. Then he filled me the same boule with whyte Rebola, the which was more pleasante than the other. When I had muche comended the wyne, and tould Ned Hale that he was a foule to refuse suche a cup of wyne, than he come neare the house, and desiered to have som water; so he had the kettle to drinke in. When this was all done, I was so well pleasede with this entertaynmente, that I knew not how to thanke this man.

Thomas Dallam, Diary, 1599–1600*

Henry Teonge (1621–90) of Warwickshire took holy orders and held three livings in England before becoming a chaplain in the navy. In 1675 he joined the *Assistance* on her voyage to the Mediterranean. In 1678 he joined the *Bristol,* and was then moved to the *Royal Oak* on which he returned to England and his living at Spernall. His first voyage brought him to Zante, and he recorded his sojourn there in these lively verses:

A Relation of some Passages happening when we were at Zante; where we tried which wine was the best; viz. of that which we had at Malta or that which we found then at Zante. Composed September 28.

Two great commanders at this place fell out,
A Malta gallant and a Grecian stout;
True Trojans both, equal for birth and valour,
Small difference in habit or in colour;
> Ambitious only which should have the honour
> To fight the Turks under the English banner.

Brave Syracusa, Malta's warlike knight,
Displays his bloody flag much like a wight
Of peerless courage (drawing forth his forces,
Whose colours all were red, both foot and horses).
> Thus Hector once, that noble son of Priam,
> Dared out the Grecian lads, only to try 'um.

Rubola, bold as ere was Alexander,
At this place was the merry Greeks' commander;
Like a stout champion and a man of might
Set up his standard, which was red and white.
> Thus Ajax with Ulysses had a fray
> Which should Achilles' armour bear away.

Whilst these two combatants with large pretences
Do praise, and boast, and brag their excellences,

---

*NOTE: Authors and titles indicated thus * in the text have a full reference in the bibliography.

Our English squadron, being much in wrath
Vowed by St George to be revenged on both.
    Thus Jove enraged, with thunder-bolts controlled
    The daring giants, 'cause they were so bold.

Th' *Assistance, Dragon, Dartmouth*, all consent
As firm as by an Act of Parliament;
And quickly too, because they were no starters,
Surprised Syracusa in his quarters:
    Whilst suddenly our gentry on the shore
    Spared not to turn Rubola o'er and o'er.

But two to one is odds, and so we found,
For many of our men were run aground:
Some would have stole away, but could not stand;
Some were aboard, and could not get to land;
    Some lost their feeling, and ('twas strange to see't)
    They went as well upon their heads as feet.

Some would have fought, but, lifting up their hands
Scarce to their heads, fell backwards on the sands:
One lost his hearing; another could not see
Which was his friend or which his enemy:
    And, having lost those senses which they had,
    They whooped and holloa'd as they had been mad.

Some by their friends were carried to their hammocks,
And bed-rid lay, with pains in sides and stomachs;
With fiery faces, and with aching brain,
Their hands all dirt, their pulses beat amain;
    Which when the doctor did but touch would spue
    Good Syracusa and Rubola too.

Some talk, and swear like men in frantic fits,
Whose vain discourse did much outrun their wits;
Some were stroke dumb, not able to afford
Their minds or meanings by a sign or word;
    Some, loth to speak, made signs, whose silent
        speeches
    Shewed the disease was sunk into their breeches.

Some so outrageous that the corporal
Was forced to cloister them in bilboes-hall;[1]
Some, seized to th' mainmast, do their backs expose

1. Leg-irons or stocks.

To th' nine-tailed cat or cherriliccum's[2] blows;
  Some ready to be ducked, some left ashore,
  And many mischiefs I could tell you more.

The strangeness of their weapons, and their number,
Caused us to lose the day, the field, the plunder:
The English used to fight with swords and guns,
But here they met with barrels, butts, and tuns.
  Boast now no more: you see what odds will do;
  Hector himself would never fight with two.

An Adventure off Lefkas

Some dangers were real enough. William Lithgow of Lanark, known to his friends as Cut-lugged Willie on account of a mutilation meted out by the relatives of a certain lady—an escapade which caused him to leave Lanark under a cloud and follow the pilgrimage route to the Middle East, about 1610—describes an adventure off Lefkas:

From th' Ithac rocks we fled Laerte's shore,
And curs'd the land that dire Ulysses bore,
For Ilion's sake, with Dardan blood attir'd,
Whose wooden horse the Trojan temples fir'd.

On our left hand toward the main, we saw an island called St Maure, formerly Leucas, or Leucada; which is only inhabited by Jews, to whom Bajazet II gave it in possession, after their expulsion from Spain: the chief city is St Maure, which not long ago was subject to Venice. This isle St Maure was anciently joined with the continent, but now rent asunder, and environed with the sea. During the course of our passage, the captain of the vessel espied a sail coming from sea; he presently being moved therewith, sent a mariner to the top, who certified him she was a Turkish galley of Biserta, prosecuting a straight course to invade our back: which sudden affrighting news overwhelmed us almost in despair. The affrighted master having demanded of every man what was most proper to be done, some replied one way, and some another; insomuch, that the most part of the passengers gave counsel, rather to surrender than fight; being confident their friends would pay their ransom, and so relieve them. But I, the wandering pilgrim,

2. The bo'sun's cane.

pondering in my pensive breast my solitary estate, the distance of my country and my friends, could conceive no hope of deliverance. Upon the which troublesome and fearful appearance of slavery, I absolutely arose, and spoke to the master, saying, 'The half of the carmoesalo is your own, and the most part also of the loading, (all which he had told me before); wherefore my counsel is, that you prepare yourself to fight, and go encourage your passengers, promise to your mariners double wages, make ready your two pieces of ordnance, your muskets, powder, lead, and half-pikes; for who knoweth but the Lord may deliver us from the thraldom of these infidels.' My exhortation ended, he was greatly animated therewith, and gave me thanks; whereupon, assembling the passengers and mariners, he gave good comfort, and large promises, to them all: so that their affrighted hopes were converted to a courageous resolution; seeming rather to give the first assault, than to receive the second wrong.

To perform the method of our defence every man was busy in the work; some below in the gun-room, others cleansing the muskets, some preparing the powder and balls, some their swords, and short weapons, some dressing the half-pikes, and others making fast the doors above; for so the master resolved to make combat below, both to save us from small shot, and besides for boarding us on a sudden. The dexterous courage of all men was so forward to defend their lives and liberty, that truly, in my opinion, we seemed thrice as many as we were. All things below and above being cunningly perfected, and everyone ranked in order with his harquebuss and pike, to stand in readiness for his own defence, we recommended ourselves into the hands of the Almighty; and in the mean while attend their fiery salutations.

In a furious spleen, the first hola of their courtesy was the progress of a martial conflict, thundering forth a terrible noise of galley-roaring pieces; and we, in a sad reply, sent out a back-sounding echo of fiery flying shots, which made an equivox to the clouds, rebounding backward in our perturbed breasts the ambiguous sounds of fear and hope. After a long and doubtful fight, both with great and small shot, (night parting us) the Turks retired till morning, and then were mindful to give us the new rencounter of a second alarm. But as it pleased him, who never faileth his, to send down an irresistible tempest, about the break of day we escaped their furious designs; and were enforced to seeke into the bay of Largostolo in Cephalonia; both because of the violent weather, and also for that a great hole was sprung in our ship. In this fight there were of us killed, three Italians, two Greeks, and two Jews, with eleven others deadly wounded, and I also hurt in the right arm with a small shot. But what harm was done by us amongst the infidels, we were not assured thereof, save only this, we shot away their midde mast, and the hinder part of the poop; for the Greeks are not expert gunners, neither could our har-quebusadoes much annoy them, in respect they never boarded. But howsoever it was, being all disbarked on shore, we gave thanks to the Lord for our unexpected safety, and buried the dead Christians in a Greekish churchyard, and the Jews were interred by the sea-side.

William Lithgow, *Totall Discourse of the Rare Adventures and Painefull Peregrinations* (London, 1632)

Ithaca

In the eighteenth century, many ruinous buildings on Ithaca had been optimistically identified with sites named in Homer or otherwise connected with antique legends; some of these are detailed in this poem from a volume published in 1824 by the philhellenic poet Donald MacPherson:

A VIEW FROM MOUNT NERITOS,
IN THE ISLAND OF ITHACA

Hail, rugged Isle! whose mountains wild are seen
Heaving abrupt their heads of hoary gray,
With here and there a lively spot of green,
Like Winter mingling with the bloom of May;
Yet, to fair plains, to courts luxurious, gay,
Did thy sage chief prefer these barren hills—
Full twenty years a wanderer did he stray,
Of life, for thee, despising all the ills—
Much can the man endure whose breast the patriot fills.

See yonder pile,[3] torn by the teeth of Time,
In moss-grown fragments scattered all around!
Oft did those walls to many a theme sublime,
In matchless eloquence of verse resound—
'Twas thence the sage philosopher, profound
In moral maxims, all his maxims drew.
Thence keen eyed Science looked fair Nature round,

3. Homer's School.

In all her ways, with microscopic view;
There warriors learnt to fight and be victorious too.

Yon other ruin[4] crumbling into dust,
Where spotless Chastity once found a home,
The pride of architecture rose, august;
The arch, the column, and the gorgeous dome;
There pensive Penelope plied the loom,
All day, and sad, the tedious task unwove,
When sable Night envelop'd all in gloom;
A blest example of unaltered love!
Not all the youth of Greece her steady faith could move.

Deep in the bosom of that woody glen,
Where Echo whispers to the passing breeze
Of rosy Spring, or, from his hollow den,
Roars to the blast that bends the groaning trees;
Where once the bath, for elegance and ease,
Surrounded with fair seats of swardy green,
Stately arose, the wandering stranger sees
The lonely Arethusa, Naiad queen!
Who, murmuring, seems to mourn the changes she has seen.

These heroes erst, when toil their nerves unstrung,
Imbibed fresh vigour from her cooling streams,
There lovely Beauties, sprightly, fair, and young,
Would oft repair to lave their snowy limbs—
Ah! how degrading the mutation seems!
Now there fond Indolence, in female shape,
In squalid tatters, basks in noon-day beams;
And Sloth and Apathy their bodies scrape,
In form of men, with many a gaunt and gape.

Say, ye deep learned in the book of Fate!
Of Change and Chance ye who can trace the laws!
Say, whence this change? Did Luxury create
Of this effect, this dire effect, the cause?
Did she bid Avarice, with harpy claws,
With hollow-hearted Fraud and Power and combine,
To immolate fair Freedom, maid divine!
Midst peals of sensual mirth, at Epicurus' shrine?

Did she bid cruelty, infuriate, burn
In the dark guileful breast of Tyranny?

4. Castle of Ulysses, Mt. Aito.

Did she make man so base as not to scorn
Before a fellow man to bow the knee?
Did she bid men, by nature born free,
Become the slaves of superstition wild;
And, led by Falsehood and Hypocrisy,
In labyrinths of error stray beguiled,
And be by Ignorance and Vice debas'd, defil'd?

Or does th' unalterable voice of Fate
Thus speak the doom of Empires as they rise;
'Rejoice awhile, for by a certain date,
Your greatness withers, and your glory dies?'
Ah! is it so? and must the curious eyes
Of strangers yet behold Augusta[5] low?
Must she, whose fame o'er earth and ocean flies,
To some new Goth or some new Vandal bow?
And must her sons be doom'd to slavery and woe?

Celestial spirit! whatsoe'er thou art,
That warm'st the breast with patriotic fire,
Thy influence shed on every Briton's heart!
With love of Britain, Britons still inspire!
Be thou around her still a wall of fire!
Guard her from foreign and domestic wrong!
Of foaming Faction, furious, false, and dire,
Foil the devices, and strike mute the tongue!
And British Freedom 'till the wreck of Time prolong!

Donald McPherson, *Melodies from the Gaelic . . .*

(London, 1824)

Travelers like Lord Byron, however, had little time for such things; the present (1823) was exciting enough.

> Our party made an excursion to the neighbouring island of Ithaca; contrasted with the arid wastes and barren red hills of Cephalonia, the verdant valleys, sparkling streams, and high land, clothed in evergreen shrubs, were strikingly beautiful. After landing, it was proposed to Byron to visit some of the localities that antiquaries have dubbed with the titles of Homer's school,—Ulysses' stronghold, etc.: he turned peevishly away, saying to me, 'Do I look like one of those emasculated fogies? Let's have a swim. I detest antiquarian twaddle. Do people think I have no lucid intervals, that I came to

5. London.

Greece to scribble more nonsense? I will show them I can do something better: I wish I had never written a line, to have it cast in my teeth at every turn.' Brown and Gamba went to look for some place where he might pass the night, as we could not get mules to go on until the next day.

After a long swim, Byron clambered up the rocks, and, exhausted by his day's work, fell asleep under the shade of a wild fig-tree at the mouth of a cavern. Gamba, having nothing to do, hunted him out, and awakened him from a pleasant dream, for which the Poet cursed him. We fed off figs and olives, and passed our night at a goatherd's cottage.

E. J. Trelawny, *Records of Shelley,*
Byron and the Author (London, 1878)

Ithaca had been a favorite of Byron's since his previous visit in 1810; a letter to Hobhouse of 4 October 1810 contains the remark: "I have some idea of purchasing the Island of Ithaca. I suppose you will add me to the Levant lunatics."

For Heinrich Schliemann, later to achieve fame as the excavator of Troy and Mycenae, it was the rediscovery of the past alive in the present that gave Homer's Ithaca its allure.

The next day, July 12, [1868] I got up as usual at 5 a.m., with my guide, to examine the old road the traces of which I had discovered the previous day, and to visit the north of the island . . . As I could not reach the place on horseback, and had discovered that the old road past the village Agiou Ioannou (St John) leads to the seashore via the vineyards which tradition calls Agros Laertou (Field of Laertes), I sent my guide there with the horse, and had myself conducted by another man over the old way to the estate of Odysseus' father . . .

I soon came to the Field of Laertes, where I sat down to rest, and to read the 24th book of the Odyssey. The arrival of a stranger is an event even in the main town of Ithaca: how much more so in the countryside! I had scarcely sat down, when the villagers crowded round me and bombarded me with questions. I thought the best plan would be, to read aloud lines 205 to 412 of the twentyfourth book of the Odyssey, and to translate it word for word into their dialect. Their excitement was boundless as they listened to the account, in the musical language of Homer, in the language of their glorious forbears of three thousand years ago, of the terrible sufferings which King Laertes had endured on that very spot where we were gathered, and to the description of his great joy when he found again, after twenty years' separation, his beloved son Odysseus whom he had held for dead. The eyes of all were swimming with tears, and when I had concluded my reading, men women and children all came up to me and embraced me with the words: 'You have given us great joy, we thank you a thousand times.' I was carried in triumph to the city, where they all competed to give of their hospitality in abundance, without the least sense of being incommoded. I was not allowed to leave until I had promised to visit them a second time in the village.

Heinrich Schliemann, *Ithaka, der Peloponnes und Troja:*
(Leipzig, 1869); translated by RS

The modern German poet, Peter Huchel, was less sanguine than Schliemann about the possibility of finding direct access to the ghosts of the legendary past.

THE GRAVE OF ODYSSEUS

No one will find
the grave of Odysseus,
no stab of a spade
the encrusted helmet
in the haze of petrified bones.

Do not look for the cave
where down below the earth
a wafting soot, a mere shadow,
damaged by pitch from torches,
went to its dead companions,
raising weaponless hands,
splattered with blood of slaughtered sheep.

All is mine, said the dust,
the sun's grave behind the desert,
the reefs full of the sea's roar,
unending noon that still warns
the pirate's boy from Ithaca,
the rudder jagged with salt,
the maritime charts and lists
of ancient Homer.

Peter Huchel, *The Garden of Theophrastus*
(Manchester, 1983);
translated by Michael Hamburger

Zante Revisited

Zante's chief export, currants, was the occasion of some scornful mirth in Lithgow, and more genial wit from Edward Lear, who toured the islands to paint them in 1862.

> The islanders are Greeks, a kind of subtle people and great dissemblers; but the signiory thereof belongeth to Venice. And if it were not for that great provision of corn which is daily transported from the firm land of Peloponnesus to them, the inhabitants in a short time would famish.
>
> I was credibly informed here by the better sort, that this little isle maketh yearly (besides oil and wine) only of currants, one hundred and sixty thousand zechins, paying yearly over and above for custom, twenty-two thousand piasters, every zechin of gold being nine shillings English, and every piaster, being white money, six shillings: A rent or sum of money which these silly Islanders could never afford, (they being not above sixty years ago, but a base beggarly people, and an obscure place), if it were not for some liquorish lips here in England of late, who forsooth can hardly digest bread, pasties, broth, and (*verbi gratia*) bag-puddings, without these currants. And as these rascal Greeks becoming proud of late with this lavish expence, contemn justly this sensual prodigality, I have heard them often demand the English, in filthy derision, what they did with such liquorish stuff, and if they carried them home to feed their swine and hogs withal. A question indeed worthy of such a female traffick; the inference of which I suspend: there is no other nation, but this, thus addicted to that miserable isle.

William Lithgow, *Totall Discourse of the Rare Adventures and Painefull Peregrinations* (London, 1632)

VIEW FROM THE VILLAGE OF GALARO, ZANTE

This view, taken from a village on the slope of the western hills of Zante, shows the Plain of Currant-vines before mentioned, which is only varied by scattered olive-trees and sparkling white villas.

The old nursery rhyme—

> If all the world were apple-pie,
> And all the trees were bread and cheese—

supposes a sort of Food-landscape hardly more remarkable than that presented by this vast green plain, which may be, in truth, called one unbroken continuance of future currant-dumplings and plum-puddings.

Edward Lear, Views in the Seven Ionian Islands
(London, 1863)

The Ionian Islands have been unusually prolific of poets and writers, particularly during the period when talent was fostered by the academy recently founded in 1824 by Frederick North, fifth earl of Guildford. Lefkas gave birth to Valaoritis and to Angelos Sikelianos, as well as to Lafcadio Hearn who became an authority on Japan; from Zante came the Italian poet Foscolo and the Greek ones Kalvos and Solomos. Edgar Allan Poe translated Foscolo's "To Zante"; and Oscar Wilde, too, was moved by his first sight of Greece in this place.

To Zante

Fair isle, that from the fairest of all flowers,
Thy gentlest of all gentle names dost take!
How many memories of what radiant hours
At sight of thee and thine at once awake!
How many scenes of what departed bliss!
How many thoughts of what entombed hopes!
How many visions of a maiden that is
No more,—no more upon thy verdant slopes!
No more! alas, that magical, sad sound
Transforming all! Thy charms shall please no more,
Thy memory no more! Accursed ground
Henceforth I hold thy flower-enamelled shore,
O hyacinthine isle! O purple Zante!
'Isola d'oro! Fior di Levante!'

U. Foscolo;
translated by Edgar Allan Poe

Zante

O beloved homeland,
loveliest of islands,
Zante, you have given me
breath, and given Apollo's
golden gifts.

Now receive my praises:
immortals all detest

mean spirits, and hurl down
their thunder on the heads
of the ungrateful.

I never have forgotten
you, never, though chance has flung me
far from you; twenty years
saw me exiled among
alien nations.

The thickets of Zante
and her shadowy hills
once heard the sharp whistle
of Artemis' silver arrows.

Today shepherds revere
the trees, honour the dewy
springs, that still draw home
from their wanderings
the Nereids.

Ionian waves first kissed
the newly foam-born body,
Ionian winds first caressed
the bosom of Cytherea.

The same wave kisses,
the same winds caress
the bodies and the breasts
of Zante's bright daughters,
girlhood's flower.

Your air, beloved homeland,
is fragrant; it enriches the sea
with the scent of golden lemons.

The king of the immortals
has graced you with full vines
and feathery transparent
pure clouds.

The eternal sun
pours light on all your fruits
by day, and the night's tears
become your lilies.

Snow when it falls upon you
Remains not; the fierce dog star
has never dulled your emeralds.

You are blest. I call you more
Blest, who never knew
the harsh whip of the foe,
the tyrant.

Fate, give me no foreign grave.
Death is only sweet
When we sleep in our
own homeland.

Andreas Kalvos;
translated by RS

IMPRESSION DU VOYAGE

The sea was sapphire coloured, and the sky
    Burned like a heated opal through the air,
    We hoisted sail; the wind was blowing fair
For the blue lands that to the eastward lie.
From the steep prow I marked with quickening eye
    Zakynthos, every olive grove and creek,
    Ithaca's cliff, Lycaon's snowy peak,
And all the flower-strewn hills of Arcady.
The flapping of the sail against the mast,
    The ripple of the water on the side,
    The ripple of girls' laughter at the stern,
The only sounds:—when 'gan the West to burn,
    And a red sun upon the seas to ride,
    I stood upon the soil of Greece at last!

Oscar Wilde

But our conclusion must bring us back to Ithaca, to Cavafy's great poem on indomitable persistence and sensual opportunism—the journey not the arrival matters.

Return to Ithaca

ITHAKA

Setting out on the voyage to Ithaka
You must pray that the way be long,
Full of adventures and experiences.

The Laistrygonians, and the Kyklopes,
Angry Poseidon,—don't be afraid of them;
You will never find such things on your way,
If only your thoughts be high, and a select
Emotion touch your spirit and your body.
The Laistrygonians, the Kyklopes,
Poseidon raging—you will never meet them,
Unless you carry them with you in your soul,
If your soul does not raise them up before you.

You must pray that the way be long;
Many be the summer mornings
When with what pleasure, with what delight
You enter harbours never seen before;
At Phœnician trading stations you must stop,
And must acquire good merchandise,
Mother of pearl and coral, amber and ebony,
And sensuous perfumes of every kind;
As much as you can get of sensuous perfumes;
You must go to many cities of Egypt,
To learn and still to learn from those who know.

You must always have Ithaka in your mind,
Arrival there is your predestination.
But do not hurry the journey at all.
Better that it should last many years;
Be quite old when you anchor at the island,
Rich with all you have gained on the way,
Not expecting Ithaka to give you riches.
Ithaka has given you your lovely journey.
Without Ithaka you would not have set out.
Ithaka has no more to give you now.

Poor though you find it, Ithaka has not cheated you.
Wise as you have become, with all your experience,
You will have understood the meaning of an Ithaka.
                C. P. Cavafy; translated by John Mavrogordato

4

Arcadia
and the Western Peloponnese

Arcadia was discovered in the year 42 or 41 B.C. Not, of course, the Arcadia of which the encyclopaedia says: 'The central Alpine region of the Peloponnesus, limited off on all sides from the other areas of the peninsula by mountains, some of them very high. In the interior, numerous ridges divide the section into a number of small cantons.' This humdrum Arcadia had always been known, in fact it was regarded as the home of Pelasgus, the earliest man. But the Arcadia which the name suggests to the minds of most of us today is a very different one; it is the land of shepherds and shepherdesses, the land of poetry and love, and its discoverer is Virgil.

Bruno Snell, *The Discovery of the Mind*
(New York, 1960), 281

Arcadia is perhaps a unique example of the transformation of a real country into a "spiritual landscape." Paradises have been sited on earth by hindsight, but here Virgil took a hint from Polybius and made the transformation from real to ideal. Polybius writes:

> All men know, that Arcadia is almost the only country, in which the children, even from their most tender age, are taught to sing in measure the songs and hymns that are composed in honour of their gods and heroes; and that afterwards, when they have learned the music of Timotheus and Philoxenus, they assemble once in every year in the public theatres, at the feast of Bacchus, and there dance with emulation to the sound of flutes; and celebrate, according to their proper age, the children those that are called the puerile, and the young men the manly games. And even in their private feasts and meetings, they are never known to employ any hired bands of music for their entertainment; but each man is himself obliged to sing in turn.

Polybius, *Histories*, 4, 20;
translated by J. Hampton (London, 1823)

So Virgil's bucolic singing contests are set in Arcadia (while The-ocritus's, his predecessor's, had been set in Sicily or Cos), and the lasting consolatory power of the pastoral vision is given full expression in his lament for Gallus:

What lawns detain'd you, Naiads, or what grove,
When he was perishing of slighted love?
From him indeed, no steeps of Pindus grey,
Or cleft Parnassus, very long might stay
Your ready feet, nor Aganippe's well:
'Twas thereabouts he loved to dream and dwell;
And him their laurels, him their myrtles mourn:
Him, stretch'd beside a desert rock forlorn,
Maenalian pines and cold Lycaeus wept.

The shepherd came and the slow herdsmen, last
Menalcas, wet with gathering winter mast:
Their homely help was ready, if they knew
Alas! where balm for such a sorrow grew.
Apollo came: he said, 'Why rav'st thou thus
For false Lycoris? She, libidinous,
Hies her to a new paramour, and goes
Through bristling camps and ventures Alpine snows.'
Thither, as wont, with forest honours crown'd,
His way the tutelary Silvan found,
All weather-swarth'd, and with his flowering rod
And full-blown lilies shaking as he trod.
Pan came, Arcadian tetrarch ever good;
I myself saw him, glowing as he stood,
With wall-wort berries, crimson'd like the West.
'Is there no mean?' he said, 'and for the rest
Love cares not: cruel Love no tears can sate,
Nor rivulets the lust of meads abate,
Wild-thyme of bees, of goats the sapling-sprays.'
    At last the lover spoke: we saw him raise,
As waking from a dream, his languish'd head.
'Yet, henceforth in your mountains, you,' he said,
'Arcadians, will in verse her name prolong
With mine; you, ever excellent in song;
And O! how softly then these bones will rest,
Our story by your plaintive reeds express'd.'

Virgil, *Eclogue* 10;
translated by Samuel Palmer

The scenery and population were fixed by tradition; Virgil spread an aura of enchantment over a land already haunted by Pan. This country of shepherds required its own distinctive god. Homer celebrated him already in the eighth century B.C.

> Sing, Muse, this chief of Hermes' love-got joys,
> Goat-footed, two-horn'd, amorous of noise,
> That through the fair greens, all adorn'd with trees,
> Together goes with Nymphs, whose nimble knees
> Can every dance foot, that affect to scale
> The most inaccessible tops of all
> Uprightest rocks, and ever use to call
> On Pan, the bright-hair'd God of pastoral;
> Who yet is lean and loveless, and doth owe
> By lot all loftiest mountains crown'd with snow;
> All tops of hills, and cliffy highnesses,
> All sylvan copses, and the fortresses
> Of thorniest queaches, here and there doth rove,
> And sometimes, by allurement of his love,
> Will wade the wat'ry softnesses. Sometimes
> (In quite oppos'd *capriccios*) he climbs
> The hardest rocks, and highest, every way
> Running their ridges.

> (When Hesperus calls to fold the flocks of men)
> From the green closets of his loftiest reeds
> He rushes forth, and joy with song he feeds.
> When, under shadow of their motions set,
> He plays a verse forth so profoundly sweet,
> As not the bird that in the flow'ry spring,
> Amidst the leaves set, makes the thickets ring
> Of her sour sorrows, sweetened with her song,
> Runs her divisions varied so and strong.
> And then the sweet-voic'd Nymphs that crown his mountains
> (Flock'd round about the deep-black-water'd fountains)
> Fall in with their contention of song.
> To which the echoes all the hills along
> Their repercussions add.

Homeric Hymn to Pan;
translated by George Chapman

The madness of Panic terror is still feared, but its progenitors are now called the Nereids; for great Pan is dead. Arcadia was throughout antiquity filled with strange legends, like that of the temple of Zeus on Mt. Lycaion, where a man might lose his shadow; of the powers of the waters of the Styx; of the statue of Demeter at Phigaleia; or of the spring at Kleitor.

The water which trickles from the precipice near Nonacris, falls first of all upon a lofty rock: and from thence, passing through the rock, it falls into the river Crathis. It is said, that this water is destructive both to men and animals of every kind. In after-times, indeed, it was found that goats perished through drinking of this water.

The following also is a wonderful circumstance respecting this water. Crystal and porphyry vessels, and indeed all vessels made of stone or earth, are broken by the water of Styx. Vessels, too, of horn and bone; likewise brass, lead, pewter, silver, and amber, are dissolved by this water. Even gold is not able to resist its dissolving quality; though the Lesbian poetess asserts, and gold itself evinces, that it is incapable of being defiled by rust. Divinity, however, confers on more abject substances a power superior to what those possess which are the most esteemed by men. Thus pearls are dissolved by vinegar: and the blood of a goat liquefies a diamond, which is the hardest of all stones. In like manner the water of Styx is not able to vanquish the hoof of a horse; for when thrown into this water it remains undivided. Whether or not Alexander the son of Philip died through this poison, I am not perfectly certain.

Pausanias, VIII, 18; translated by Thomas Taylor

The Phigalenses dedicated to Ceres a wooden statue, which was made in the following manner: The figure of a woman in every other part except the head, was represented sitting on a rock; but she had the head and mane of a horse, and the images of dragons and other wild beasts were represented as naturally belonging to her head. A garment with which she was clothed, reached to the extremities of her feet; and in one of her hands she held a dolphin, and in the other a dove. Why the statue was made after this manner, will be obvious to a man who is not destitute of sagacity, and who is endued with a good memory. But they say that she was called *black*, because she clothed herself in a black garment. They cannot however tell either the name of the person by whom the statue was made, or in what manner it was destroyed by fire.

But the Phigalenses, having lost this ancient statue, did not dedicate another statue to the goddess, and neglected a great part of the ceremonies pertaining to her festivals and sacrifices, in consequence of which the land became barren; and on their supplicating the Pythian deity, he answered them as follows: 'Azanian Arcadians, who inhabit Phigalea, the concealed cavern of horse-delivered Ceres, you are come hither inquiring a remedy for distressful famine, you who alone are twice Nomades, who alone are fed with rustic food. Ceres has deprived you of your food, and she will again compel you to feed on the sweet beech-tree and acorns, taking from you the gifts of your ancestors, and your ancient honours; and still more, she will compel you to devour each other, and your own children, unless you appease her anger by public libations, and adorn with divine honours the profundities of her cavern.' The Phigalenses, having received this answer, venerated Ceres in a more august manner than before.

Pausanias, VIII, 42; translated by Thomas Taylor

Herdsman, if midday thirst assails your lips
as you approach the outskirts of high Kleitor,
Stop and draw water from this well; let all
your herd enjoy the water-nymph's largesse.
But do not bathe in it, for if you do
the scent of wine thereafter makes you sick.
Flee the wine-hating fountain, where Melampus,
when he had cured the Proetides of madness,
Hid his medicaments (they came from Argos
to the rough mountains of Arcadia).

Anonymous Greek epigram,
in A. S. F. Gow and D. L. Page,
Further Greek Epigrams (1981), no. 452;
translated by RS

It is not in the relics of ancient worship only that traces of the Dryads are to be found. The traveller in Greece will commonly hear that such and such a tree is haunted by a Nereid. Particularly famous in north Arcadia is a magnificent pine tree on the path from the monastery of Megaspelaeon to the village of Solos. My muleteer enthusiastically compared it to the gigantic tree which is believed to uphold the world; and piously crossed himself, as we passed it, for fear of the nymph who made it her home.

J. C. Lawson, *Modern Greek Folklore and Ancient Greek Religion* (London, 1910), 155

The belief is exactly that of the ancients, as described in the Homeric *Hymn to Aphrodite:*

> And with the lives of these doth life invade
> Or odorous fir-trees, or high-foreheaded oaks,
> Together taking their begetting strokes,
> And have their lives and deaths of equal dates,
> Trees bearing lovely and delightsome states,
> Whom Earth first feeds, that men initiates.
> On her high hills she doth their states sustain,
> And they their own heights raise as high again.
> Their growths together made, Nymphs call their groves
> Vow'd to th'Immortals' services and loves;
> Which men's steels therefore touch not, but let grow.
> But when wise Fates times for their fadings know,
> The fair trees still before the fair Nymphs die,
> The bark about them grown corrupt and dry,
> And all their boughs fall'n yield to Earth her right;
> And then the Nymphs' lives leave the lovely night.

Homeric Hymn to Aphrodite;
translated by George Chapman

For Sir Philip Sidney, Arcadia typified archetypal pleasance, all fear and melancholy dispelled. Here is his imaginary description of the river Ladon, that grand but arid-banked river:

> . . . their sober dinner being come and gone, to recreate themselves something they determined to go, while the heat of the day lasted, to bathe themselves (such being the manner of Arcadian nymphs often to do) in the river of Ladon, and take with them a lute, meaning to delight them under some shadow . . . they came to the river's side, which of all the rivers of Greece had the prize for excellent pureness and sweetness, insomuch as the very bathing in it was accounted exceeding healthful. It ran upon so fine and delicate a ground as one could not easily judge whether the river did more wash the ground or the gravel did purify the river; the river not running forth right but almost continually winding, as if the lower streams would return to their spring, or that the river had a delight to play with itself. The banks of either side seeming arms of the loving earth that fain would embrace it, and the river a wanton nymph which still would slip from it; either side of the bank being fringed with most beautiful trees, which resisted the sun's darts with overmuch piercing the natural coldness of the river.

Sir Philip Sidney, *Arcadia*, II, XI, 3, 4

The pleasance retained its dark shadow in the painting of Poussin, which shows shepherds picking out on a tomb the words ET IN ARCADIA EGO (i.e., death). Goethe remorselessly distorted the words to ET EGO IN ARCADIA, "I too have been in Arcadia." The Romantic dream was dispersed by a Romantic poet, Byron, who glossed Virgil's "Arcades ambo" with "that is: blackguards both."

Trelawny, who, like Byron, fought in the Greek War of Independence, gives a vivid picture of the Arcadian scene at this period:

> We stopped two or three days at Tripolitza, and then passed on to Argos and Napoli di Romania; every step of our way was marked by the ravages of the war. On our way to Corinth, we passed through the defiles of Dervenakia; our road was a mere mule-path for about two leagues, winding along in the bed of a brook, flanked by rugged precipices. In this gorge, and a more rugged path above it, a large Ottoman force, principally cavalry, had been stopped, in the previous autumn, by barricades of rocks and trees, and slaughtered like droves of cattle by the wild and exasperated Greeks. It was a perfect picture of the war, and told its own story; the sagacity of the nimble-footed Greeks, and the hopeless stupidity of the Turkish commanders, were palpable: detached from the heaps of dead, we saw the skeletons of some bold riders who had attempted to scale the acclivities, still astride the skeletons of their horses, and in the rear, as if in the attempt to back out of the fray, the bleached bones of the negroes' hands still holding the hair ropes attached to the skulls of their camels—death, like sleep, is a strange posture-master. There were grouped in a narrow space five thousand or more skeletons of men, horses, camels, and mules; vultures had eaten their flesh, and the sun had bleached their bones. In this picture the Turks looked like a herd of bisons trapped and butchered in the gorges of the rocky mountains. The rest of their battles, amidst scenery generally of the same rugged character, only differed in their magnitude. The Asiatic Turks are lazy, brave, and stupid. The Greeks, too crafty to fight if they could run, were only formidable in their fastnesses. It is a marvel that Greece and Greeks should be again resuscitated after so many ages of death-like slavery. No people, if they retain their name and language, need despair; 'There is nothing constant but mutability!'
>
> E. J. Trelawny, *Records of Shelley, Byron and the Author*
> (London, 1878)

Vassai (Bassae)

Travelers and explorers in the nineteenth century were overawed by the grandeur of the lonely temple of Apollo Epicourios at Vassai, in the mountains above Andritsaina. The temple is the work of Ictinus, the architect of the Parthenon.

> Far from the haunts of men, amidst these scenes
> Sequester'd, which have never heard a sound
> Ruder than shepherd's plaintive reed, or bleat
> Of flocks returning to their ev'ning fold
> A ruin'd temple stands. Devotion rais'd
> The hallow'd shrine, and Fancy still surveys
> The long procession of her hoary priests,
> Her altars wreath'd with chaplets, and the smoke
> Of incense rising from those ancient woods.
> The eye of Taste that forms from Nature's stores
> Ideal scenes of beauteous and sublime,
> Views here a perfect picture. Broken shafts
> And mossy stones, half hid by flower and shrub,
> Break the rough fore-ground where the peasant leans
> His lazy length against a knotted oak,
> Listening with vacant gaze to the wild tale
> Of simple goatherd. In the middle space,
> Mould'ring and gray, the Doric columns nod
> O'er scattered heaps of massy pediment
> And sculptur'd frize, round which the myrtle waves
> Its wither'd branches; from the temple's base
> The rocky knoll precipitous and bare
> Sweeps down to yonder vale, whose clust'ring woods
> Sleep in the lustre of the setting sun.
> Distant, and fading in the clouds of eve,
> The blue hills bend their vast circumference,
> A stately amphitheatre, and close
> Within their arms the peaceful solitude
>
> William Haygarth, *Greece: A Poem* (London, 1814)

SUGGESTED BY THE RUINS OF A MOUNTAIN TEMPLE IN ARCADIA, ONE BUILT BY THE ARCHITECT OF THE PARTHENON

> Like stranded ice when freshets die
> These shattered marbles tumbled lie:
> They trouble me.

William Haygarth, *Bassae*. From William Haygarth, *Greece, A Poem* (1814).

What solace?—Old in inexhaustion,
Interred alive from storms of fortune,
   The quarries be!

Herman Melville

Olympia

Olympia, where in 776 B.C. the first Panhellenic Games were held, is only a short journey out of Arcadia. As Nikos Kazantzakis comments: "In all Greece there is no landscape more inspiring, none that so gently and perseveringly invites peace and reconciliation. The ancients chose it with unerring eye, so that every four years all the clans of Greece might gather here, to sport and to fraternize" (Nikos Kazantzakis, *Travels in Greece*; translated by F. A. Reed, London, 1965).

According to legend, the Games had been founded by Heracles. Pindar describes the first celebration of the Games:

> The strong son of Zeus drove the whole of his host
> And all his booty to Pisa,
> And measured a holy place
> For his mighty Father.
> He fenced the Altis and marked it off

In a clean space, and the ground encircling it
He set for rest at supper,
In honour of the Ford of Alpheos

And the twelve Kings of the Gods.
To Kronos' Hill he gave a name; for before
It was nameless when Oinomaos ruled,
And drenched with many a snowstorm.
In this first birthday-rite
The Fates stood near at hand,
And he who alone proves the very truth,

Time. In his forward march
He has revealed all clearly:
How Herakles portioned the booty, war's gift,
Made sacrifice and founded
The fourth year's feast
With the first Olympiad
And the winning of victories.

⁙

The evening was lit
By the lovely light of the fair-faced moon.

All the holy place was loud with song
In the glad feasting like the music of banquets.

Pindar, *Olympian*, 8, 43–58, 74–77;
translated by C. M. Bowra

Many legends attached themselves to the hero-like feats of ath-
letes at Olympia, several of which are recorded by Pausanias. The
following is typical:

> In the seventy-first Olympiad, it is said, that Cleomedes
> the Astypalaean slew in boxing the Epidaurian Iccus; for which
> action being deprived by the judges of the crown of victory,
> he became insane through grief. Afterwards, however, he
> returned to Astypalaea, and entering into the gymnasium, in
> which sixty boys were instructed, he tore down the pillar which
> supported the roof of the building. In consequence, therefore,
> of the roof falling on the boys, the citizens pursued him with
> stones, and he fled for refuge to the temple of Minerva. Here
> he shut himself up in a chest which was in the temple; and the
> Astypalaeans having for a long time endeavoured to raise the
> lid, but without success, at length broke the chest. In this,
> however, they neither found Cleomedes alive nor dead; and

having sent to Delphos to inquire into the meaning of this affair, the Pythian deity answered them as follows: 'Cleomedes the Astypalaean was the last of the heroes. Him honour with sacrifices, as he is no longer a mortal.' In consequence of this, the Astypalaeans afterwards honoured Cleomedes as a hero.

Pausanias, VI, 9; translated by Thomas Taylor

The river Alpheus was the subject of a legend, attached also to a number of other rivers in Greece and elsewhere in antiquity, that its waters disappeared under the sea and reemerged elsewhere; in this case, Alpheus was thought to pursue the nymph Arethusa and to reemerge at the spring Arethusa in Sicily. An epigram of Moschus and Shelley's lush "Arethusa" both celebrate this legend:

From Pisa, where the sea his flood receives,
Alpheus, olive-crown'd, the gift of leaves,
And flowers, and sacred dust is known to bring,
With secret course, to Arethusa's spring;
For, plunging deep beneath the briny tide,
Unmix'd, and unperceiv'd his waters glide.
Thus wonder-working Love, with mischief fraught,
The art of diving to the river taught.

Moschus, *Idyll 8*; translated by Francis Fawkes (1760)

Arethusa arose
From her couch of snows
In the Acroceraunian mountains,—
From cloud and from crag,
With many a jag,
Shepherding her bright fountains.
She leapt down the rocks,
With her rainbow locks
Streaming among the streams;—
Her steps paved with green
The downward ravine
Which slopes to the western gleams;
And gliding and springing
She went, ever singing,
In murmurs as soft as sleep;
The Earth seemed to love her,
And Heaven smiled above her,
As she lingered towards the deep.

Then Alpheus bold,
On his glacier cold,

With his trident the mountains strook;
    And opened a chasm
    In the rocks—with the spasm
All Erymanthus shook.
    And the black south wind
    It unsealed behind
The urns of the silent snow,
    And earthquake and thunder
    Did rend in sunder
The bars of the springs below.
    And the beard and the hair
    Of the River-god were
Seen through the torrent's sweep,
    As he followed the light
    Of the fleet nymph's flight
To the brink of the Dorian deep.

P. B. Shelley

As the ancient world declined, the site of Olympia, where the
Games were last celebrated in A.D. 261, was buried and lost, until in
1765 Richard Chandler made some observations of the temple,
and, a few years later, the French consul Fauvel, friend to so many
Western travelers to Athens. . .

> arrived upon the banks of the Cladeus . . . It runs in a bed, or
> rather in a deep ravine, to join the Alpheus, after having
> watered a plain to the north, in which are some fine ruins. Per-
> ceiving on this river the relics of an ancient bridge, I examined
> the nature of its banks both to the right and to the left, and I
> remarked every where, at the depth of about six feet from the
> surface of the ground above, relics of pottery, of bricks and of
> antique tiles; I also perceived some fragments of marble. These
> discoveries, joined to that of the bridge, convinced me that I
> was among the ruins of some town noted in antiquity . . . Some
> men, sent by the aga of a neighbouring village to seek materi-
> als for building, were at this moment turning up the ground.
> What was my surprise, when on inquiry I found that they called
> their village Andilalo, or *the Village of the Echo!* I could not then
> forbear calling to mind, that the Greeks who assisted at the
> Olympic Games were accustomed, as Pausanias relates, to listen
> to a remarkable echo, which repeated sounds seven times over.
> This discovery impressed me still more strongly with the idea
> that I was upon the very ground where once stood Olympia.
>
> Quoted in F. Pouqueville, *Travels in the Morea . . .* (London, 1813)

The Italian poet, Salvatore Quasimodo, wrote a number of poems about Greece; one centers on Olympia:

FOLLOWING THE ALPHEUS

The harmonies of the earth,
the sound of the clay,
the mildewed reeds, low green
leaves along the bank of Alpheus
towards Olympia, Zeus' and Hera's place.
But above concord, the signs inside
an obstinate ruin, the absurdity
of obscure contrasts: wreckage, in fact,
of negations protracted like life.
The harmony of the waters is unimportant,
Alpheus, you are kindly, silent here
in Elis; on the stones shivers
a chrysalis sun which,
it seems, will set only by deception,
so long is its flight. I look only
for dissonances, Alpheus,
something more than perfection.
You could bypass Olympia now,
bypass the tangle of pines, forms still
repulsed by death, and bypass
the closed arch I know. A gate
to storm, Olympia wise place
of holidaymakers, a robber's leap is enough
on a horse from a pediment,
the fieriest. I do not seek
a place for infancy, nor to follow the river underseas,
already at its hearth in Arethusa,
and to tie up the cord
broken by arrival.
The continuation quiet and indistinct,
Olympia, like Zeus like Hera.
I look at your head detached on the green earth,
lit with a straw moon.

Salvatore Quasimodo; translated by RS

Kyllini (Glarentza)

Kyllini's chief claim to fame is delightfully expounded by Robert Byron over a bottle of wine in Patras:

We ordered a bottle of syrupy brown wine, named Malvasia, first manufactured at Monemvasia in Sparta. This wine, which we had also tasted at Ferrara, was the original Malmsey, exported to our notoriously drunken island, in which the Duke of Clarence, whose bones now hang in a glass case on the walls of the crypt of Tewkesbury Abbey, met his unfortunate end. It is a strange coincidence that not only did the wine of Malmsey have its birthplace in Greece, but also the Dukedom of Clarence. One of the oldest titles of the English monarchy takes its name from a small town on the west coast of the Peloponnese.

Glarentza, as it is properly called, first assumed its position as a ducal appendage, in the peerage of the principality of Achaia, under the rule of Geoffroy de Villehardouin, the second of the Frankish princes of that province. Later it became the chief port of the Morea and the seat of the Achaian royal mint. By the marriage of Count Florence of Hainault with Isabella de Villehardouin, the title eventually descended to the Counts of Hainault; and was arbitrarily revived by Edward III and his Queen, Philippa of that family, in favour of their second son, Lionel. The town itself was destroyed in 1436 by order of the then exarch of Mistra, Constantine Dragatses, future and last emperor of the East.

As our dinner progressed, enough Malmsey to have drowned a hundred Dukes of Clarence seemed to disappear . . .

Robert Byron, *Europe in the Looking Glass* (London, 1926)

The town of Kyllini seems never to have recovered from that savage destruction. But its medieval splendor is vividly evoked by Nikos Kazantzakis:

Here, six or seven centuries ago at the now decrepit harbour of Glarentza, what activity, what delights and profits! Ships set sail hence for Venice, Ancona, Durazzo, Alexandria, laden with silks, raisins, acorns, figs, honey, oil, wax . . . Here, in the now invisible palace, the Grand Court of Achaia gathered to decide on war or peace, or princely marriages. Here in Glarentza the Court of the Bourgeoisie, of the townsmen, convened to arbitrate the quarrels of the natives, or those between Franks and natives. And in this toppled Gothic church Franciscan monks from Assisi intoned their vespers, and gazed through the slitlike windows at the cool and enduring sea. When the first of the Villehardouins died, he who had so loved Glarentza, on this very shore the dirge which the chronicle relates would have broken out:

> Great mourning spread throughout the Morea,
> for he was held in high esteem, and much beloved
> for his benign dominion, and the wisdom that
> he showed.

Nikos Kazantzakis, *Travels in Greece*;
translated by F. A. Reed (London, 1965)

It was Geoffroy II de Villehardouin who built, in 1220–23, the castle of Chlemoutsi, or Clermont (also known as Castel Tornese), which stands high on an eminence above modern Kyllini, commanding the straits between the mainland and Zakynthos, and the whole plain of Elis. It is the best-preserved Frankish castle in Greece, though a modern plaque at the entrance records only that the Emperor Constantine Dragatses made it his dwelling from 1428 to 1432, a late outpost in the wars that ended with his death in the last battle for Byzantium in 1453. Kazantzakis describes its first days:

> Villehardouin worked on it for three years. He seized the rich incomes of the insatiable Latin clergy and transformed them into walls, gates and battlements. The Frankish priests anathematized him, but he chuckled and raised his fortress high. It had become so impregnable that even if the Franks had been expelled from everywhere else, as the chronicles relate, possession of Clermont would have enabled them to reconquer the Peloponnesos. A few years later the Franks began to mint their own coinage here, the *tournesia*, with squared crosses, fortresses and royal lilies embossed upon them.

> As I passed through the narrow, open fortress gate, crossed the devastated Gothic chambers and grass-choked courtyards, and, scaling a wild fig-tree, reached the upper level and stood atop a rock, I felt like uttering a piercing cry, like a hawk. Sudden joy seized me. In a flash the Franks returned to the Peloponnese, ravished it, filled it with blond-headed children and savage fortresses, and vanished. I was delighted because for an instant, sluggish time assumed the rhythm craved by every impatient soul.

Nikos Kazantzakis, *Travels in Greece*

Pylos

The ancient bay of Pylos is first mentioned by Homer, and the discovery of a Mycenaean palace there confirmed that this is the site of ancient Pylos, the home of aged Nestor.

> The sun now left the great and goodly lake,
> And to the firm heav'n bright ascent did make,
> The shine as well upon the mortal birth,
> Inhabiting the plow'd life-giving earth,
> As on the ever-treaders upon death.
> And now to Pylos, that so garnisheth
> Herself with buildings, old Neleus' town,
> The prince and Goddess come had strange sights shown,
> For, on the marine shore, the people there
> To Neptune, that the azure locks doth wear,
> Beeves that were wholly black gave holy flame.
>
> Homer, *Odyssey*, 3, 1ff.;
> translated by George Chapman

In the Ottoman period, the city was called Navarino, and was the scene of a decisive battle against the Turks, celebrated by Victor Hugo in his long poem "Navarin":

> Now—Navarino, the town of painted houses
> And golden domes, white Navarino,
> Set on its hill among the terebinths,
> Lends its calm bay to the fiery embrace
> Of two fleets, bruising each other's brazen prows.
>
> Behold them there: the sea is full of them,
> Ready to swamp their fire, ready to drink their blood.
> Each side drawn up in the ranks of his god,
> One stretched out like a cross over the waves,
> One spreading its thick arms to form a crescent.
>
> On this side Europe fights for liberty,
> Its great three-masters swaying like tall towers;
> There, Turkish Egypt, Africa's own Asia,
> Spirited pirates, scarcely conquered by Duquesne
> Who stamped upon the vulture's nest in vain.
>
> Victor Hugo, "Navarin"; translated by RS

The resounding victory of the Western powers produced a crop of Greek ballads, too, such as this Cretan one by Anagnostis Chaziris of Lakka:

Who wishes to learn it, let him know
How the Turkish armada was lost.
A galley makes in strength
To Niokastro, and moors in the harbour.
Ibrahim Pasha played a trick
To destroy Nydhra which was burnt.
They came loaded up to the masts,
They came and put out boats
The watchmen began to cry
'They have put out a boat, kapetanii!
They have put out a great boat,
They are not like any Turkish armada;
Forward, forward three frigates are plying,
And there is a Frankish armada.
And behind them are the criers
And they are playing music and singing—
They stand on the lookout and watch
—The three powers are coming at top speed.'
'Are the three powers coming at top speed
To help the Greeks against the Turks?'
'They have tied up and are beginning the bombardment,
The aghas are fleeing in confusion,
From all the thunder and turmoil
A black cloud has covered the harbour.
It was on a Wednesday, and on a Thursday,
Their rain fell upon the armada.'
'Has Ibrahim Pasha brought out his army
To take it away, to go into exile?'
'He has collected together his troops of attack and defence,
His picked and chosen weaponry.'

Jeannaraki*; translated by RS

In 1865 the philologist Friedrich Gottlob Welcker published an account of an extended journey through Greece. He was one of the first German scholars to link the studies of philology and archaeology and allow the findings of each to illuminate the other; reading his texts with the attention of an archaeologist, he surveys the Greek scene with the eye of one familiar with its legends and literary past. The effects of the combination are nicely illustrated in his comments on Pylos:

> The journey across the bay took fifty minutes, under sail and oars, by the steep cliffs of Sphacteria. The appearance of the surroundings, bare, grey, charmless, only the occasional

village or group of houses visible—how disadvantageous the comparison with Lake Geneva! One walks a quarter of an hour under the rocks of Pylos, then over the dam or spit of land between the two breasts. The rocks peter out eventually in sand-dunes, and it is through sand, thick as the ash of Vesuvius, that one climbs strenuously up the side of the acropolis. Sand surrounds the little old harbour, and covers the hill above it and that which leads to the acropolis. Homer's 'sandy Pylos' is completely accurate for this side. A little way above the sand is the entrance to the famous grotto, almost like that of the Treasury (of Atreus), with another aperture after the first step. The cave goes more or less straight inwards for sixty paces, so that it displays a general similarity to a Gothic cathedral, and thereafter turns only unobtrusively towards our left. It has been quarried at various times, and is thus full of potholes and heaps of stones. Several small, and a few larger, holes and niches in the walls, especially near the entrance, point to votive offerings. One can imagine the hanging ox-skins, without being able to indicate the forms either of the dry, long-suspended, shrivelled hides, or of the extended ones, or even of the heads and bones. I would guess that the cave was dedicated to Hermes, because of the wealth of the royal house of Neleus, long before the legend of Hermes' stealing the cattle was connected with it and their remains recognized in the stalagmite formations. As I emerged, the sun did me the favour of setting, and thereat to position itself directly opposite the hill in which the cave lies; it could also have illuminated the cave sideways, if it had not been somewhat obscured by cloud. So the cave was—especially at this season—a place for the evening sun, as in Athens Lycabettus is for sunrise—and the physical illumination of that myth gains considerably from the phenomenon. The setting of the great ball of fire in the middle of the sea, which I had never observed before, was also astonishing.

F. G. Welcker,
Tagebuch einer griechischen Reise (Berlin, 1865);
translated by RS

5

Sparta and Laconia;
Mani; Cythera

Thucydides observed that future ages would be amazed that Athens
and Sparta had been equal rivals for the leadership of Greece, for,
while Athens would leave glorious monuments in marble, Sparta,
whose buildings were all of wood, would vanish completely. The
buildings of Sparta of the fifth century B.C. have indeed vanished,
but the legend of the city proved surprisingly persistent, and its
supposedly Stoic virtues were perhaps a more pervasive model in
the Renaissance than those of Athenian democracy. The Enlight-
enment took, perhaps, a more equivocal view, and James Thomson dispensed praise to each equally.

> O'er all two rival cities reared the brow,
> And balanced all. Spread on Eurotas' bank,
> Amid a circle of soft-rising hills,
> The patient Sparta one: the sober, hard,
> And man-subduing city, which no shape
> Of pain could conquer, nor of pleasure charm.
> Lycurgus there built, on the solid base
> Of equal life, so well a tempered state,
> Where mixed each government in such just poise,
> Each power so checking and supporting each,
> That firm for ages and unmoved it stood,
> The fort of Greece! without one giddy hour,
> One shock of faction or of party rage.
> For, drained the springs of wealth, corruption there
> Lay withered at the root. Thrice happy land!
> Had not neglected art, with weedy vice
> Confounded, sunk. But, if Athenian arts
> Loved not the soil, yet there the calm abode
> Of wisdom, virtue, philosophic ease,
> Of manly sense and wit, in frugal phrase
> Confined, and pressed into Laconic force.
> There too, by rooting thence still treacherous self,
> The public and the private grew the same.
> The children and the nursing public all,
> And at its table fed—for that they toiled,

For that they lived entire, and even for that
The tender mother urged her son to die.
James Thomson, Liberty, ii, 108–35

Whatever the austerity of the perception of Sparta by later ages the archaic city of Alcman and Terpander was no foe to the Muses. One of the loveliest, if most mysterious, of archaic poems is Alcman's fragmentary *Partheneion*, or Maiden-song:

> Is not Hagesichora, she of the lovely ankles, here beside us? Is she not close to Agido, praising our festival? Receive their prayers, ye gods: for the gods' is the power and the fulfilment. Choir-leader, I would speak out, though I am but a girl who, like an owl from a rafter, chatters emptily; I too wish most of all to please the goddess of the dawn. She is our healer; but by Hagesichora's grace the maidens have set their feet upon lovely peace.

Some of the atmosphere of these girl-choruses is captured, too, by Aristophanes at the end of the *Lysistrata*:

CHORUS OF SPARTAN WOMEN:

Leave the lovely Taygetus, and come back again, O Spartan Muse, thou that celebratest the god of Amyclae, adored by us, and Athene of the Brazen House, and the bold Tyndaridae, who sport beside the Eurotas. Oh come, bounding lightly! so that we may extol Sparta that loves the choruses of the gods and the rhythmic trampling of feet; the nimble-footed damsels bound like fillies along the banks of the Eurotas, and toss the tresses of their hair like Bacchanals sporting with the thyrsus, and comely is their chorus-leader, the chaste daughter of Leda. But come, bind a fillet round your hair with your hands, and with your feet leap, leap like a stag: gladden also the chorus with your happy din and hymn again the peerless warrior-goddess of the Brazen House.

Aristophanes, Lysistrata, 1296ff.;
translated by Aubrey Beardsley

In the Middle Ages, the city of Mistra, on the slopes of Mt. Taygetus above Sparta, was the scene of the last flowering of Greek philosophy under the Platonist Gemistus Plethon, scholar and politician. In his tract, *On the Affairs of the Peloponnese*, he dreams of the revival of the Hellenic spirit in contradistinction to the Christian culture of Byzantium, and as a foe to the Ottoman Empire.

Gemistus died in 1452; in his heyday he had been visited there by the Italian antiquary, Cyriac of Ancona. Cyriac is the father of archaeology, the first Renaissance man to devote himself to the recovery and recording of the inscriptions of Greece, of which he collected a prodigious number. A manuscript journal of Cyriac survives, which vividly portrays the mingled excitement and melancholy of the lover of antiquity in classic lands:

From the citadel of Leonardi, accompanied by servants of the Despot, Thomas Palaeologus, we came to the foothills of Mt Taygetus. Here about 30 stades distant we saw the ancient and once noble city of Sparta, an impregnable town on the cliffs which is now called Spartovouni Misistratidi [i.e. Mistra on the Spartan mountain]. Here we found one Constantine Palaeologus, the Despot of the Morea, reigning. At his court was that illustrious man, famous and powerful among Platonic philosophers, for the sake of whose conversation we had come thither. I also came upon a young man in that royal court, named Nicolaus Chalcocondyles, an Athenian, the son of our great friend, that learned man George . . .

And when I had visited Mistra for the sake of the dear Platonist Gemistus, I decided to make a detour to visit the ruins of the once noble city of Sparta. For I felt that a duty of mourning was owed to those great and noble cities now collapsed or destroyed. I felt that more bitterness was due to that calamity of the human race than to those distinguished cities of the world. We saw wonderful temples and beautiful statues, and other noble ornaments of human power and art crumbled from their former splendour. What a decline did that pristine human virtue and famous probity of soul seem to have suffered . . .

Then, when we came to the citadel of Sparta, the plains of the River Eurotas and the hallowed spot where the honoured city of the Lacedaemon had been, I saw from afar an immense spread of ruins. At that pont Calliope descended from heaven, and I heard her utter the following verses in my own Italian tongue:

Sparta, kind queen of broad Laconia,
Glory of Greece, example to the world,
Temple and training ground of war and honour,
Mirror of every virtue, and its spring,

When I survey your policy and laws,
Your customs, and your every excellence,

I stand by the Eurotas, and exclaim
In wonder to Diana, your kind queen:

Where is your good Lycurgus, where are Castor
And Pollux, the divine twin sons of Zeus?
Where Anaxandridas, Orthriadas and Gylippus?

Eurystheus, and Leonidas, and Agis;
Where are Pausanias, and the great Lysander?
Agesilaus, Aristus and Xanthippus?

Not Rome, not Philip,
But now, in Mystra here, a lowlier age
Has brought you to Byzantine vassalage.

> Cyriac of Ancona,* in Sabbadini;
>
> translated by RS

After the death of Plethon and the taking of Mystra by the Franks
under Villehardouin, there only remained, in the words of Kevin
Andrews, "the distant echoes of horns and Burgundian hounds
along the ravines of Achaia." At least the hounds of Sparta itself,
famous in antiquity, are not yet forgotten:

Theseus: My hounds are bred out of the Spartan kind,
So flew'd, so sanded; and their heads are hung
With ears that sweep away the morning dew;
Crook-knee'd and dew-lapp'd like Thessalian bulls;
Slow in pursuit, but match'd in mouth like bells,
Each under each. A cry more tuneable
Was never holla'd to, nor cheer'd with horn,
In Crete, in Sparta, nor in Thessaly:
Judge, when you hear.

> William Shakespeare,
> *A Midsummer Night's Dream*, IV, i

The Frankish culture is vividly imagined by Goethe when he transports Faust to medieval Sparta:

Phorkyas: So many years deserted stood the valley-hills
That in the rear of Sparta northwards rise aloft,
Behind Taygetus; whence, as yet a nimble brook,
Eurotas downward rolls, and then, along our vale,
By reed-beds broadly flowing, nourishes your swans.

Behind there in the mountain-dells a daring breed
Have settled, pressing forth from the Cimmerian Night,

And there have built a fortress inaccessible,
Whence land and people now they harry, as they please. . .

⸙

Faust: With rage restrained, in silence banded,
And certain of the victory feast,
Ye, Northern blossoms, half expanded,
Ye, flowery fervours of the East!

The light upon their armour breaking,
They plundered realm on realm, at will:
They come, and lo! the earth is quacking;
They march away, it thunders still!

In Pylos we forsook the waters;
The ancient Nestor is no more,
And soon our lawless army scatters
The troops of kings on Grecian shore.

Back from these walls, no more delaying,
Drive Menelaus to the sea!
There let him wander, robbing, slaying,
As was his wish and destiny.

I hail you Dukes, as forth you sally
Beneath the rule of Sparta's Queen!
Now lay before her mount and valley,
And you shall share the kingdom green!

Thine, German, be the hand that forges
Defence for Corinth and her bays:
Achaia, with its hundred gorges,
I give thee, Goth, to hold and raise.

Towards Elis, Franks, direct your motion;
Messene be the Saxon's state:
The Norman claim and sweep the ocean,
And Argolis again make great!

Then each shall dwell in homes well-dowered,
And only outer foemen meet;
Yet still by Sparta over-towered,
The Queen's ancestral, ancient seat.

Each one shall she behold, abiding
In lands that lack no liberal right;

And at her feet ye'll seek, confiding,
Your confirmation, law and light!

Goethe, Faust, ii, iii;
translated by Bayard Taylor

Mistra was, in the centuries after its fall, generally supposed to be the site of ancient Sparta. Bernard Randolph describes Mistra as it was in the late seventeenth century, under Turkish domination:

> Mesithra, formerly called Lacedemon is situated at the side of a large Plain on a rising ground, about 25 miles from the sea side, having very high mountains all to the west of the plain. The castle stands to the west on a very high hill, steep on the west and south part, where it is inaccessible, but sloping to the north, have two old walls which cross the hill from the north to the south, dividing the hill almost into three parts. The way into the Castle is very difficult. The walls of the Castle are well built, but very old. It is near half a mile about, having two gates to be pass'd. The town is large, and is esteemed the second for bigness in all the Morea, yet Patras hath more houses. The ruines about it are very great, and towards the South they reach above four miles, having in some places the foundation of a thick wall, which they say was an arch of an aquaeduct. The plain is very pleasant, full of small villages, olive, and mulberry trees. This place and Calamata make more silk than all the other parts of the Morea. The river which runs through the plain is now called Vasili Pottamo. In winter it spreads very large, but in summer towards the city is almost dry. Though the city stands remote from the sea, and free from dangers that ensue from thence; yet the Manjotts are a people apt to prey upon them.

Bernard Randolph, The Present State of the Morea
(London, 1686)

The botanist Francis Vernon (1637?–77) was, as he put it, "possessed of an insatiable desire of seeing." In his early travels, before he took his MA, he was captured and sold by pirates. His last journey was made after his election to the Royal Society in 1672, and ended in his murder in Isfahan during a quarrel over a penknife. Perhaps this prevented him from ever writing up the MS Journal which describes his travels in Greece. Here are his notes on Sparta:

Monday 7th [September 1675]
Up at sun rise and passe plaine to River. Hills of Deibe meete lurkes coine to gaurdes a wall a wood of oakes and ilexes

Pyrastes come out into a hilly plaine, passe woode see *Tayge-tos* . . . passe hills come to river 1 cl. out 3 cl. up hill at the top see the mountaine Taygetos the plaine of *Mistra* come to a spring drinke. downe *Boursia* hill walke come to river Eurotas called Ir. passe it. Plants. Tamariske. Oleander. and ilex a Magpie. Crowes. Vulture. Beccafigi. larkes. pigeons. Conyza augustifolia. sedum spinosum. Lentiscus . . . gramen parnas-sii. Lonilla. come to foot of hill ruine of old house. ruine of aquaeduct. bottome. showe top bricke, come to a spring coole drinke called sua . . . passe a hill passe river againe a mile. grenes infinite. figgs, almonds. mulberries. olive trees, come to another hill passe into a plaine olive trees, see castle towne the walls the Bazar. arrive 7 cl. from Atxuria to *Mistra* 10 legues up into towne enquire for Palaeologo, the fare of St Giovanis, goe to villa without towne. passe two courts of gaurde. Side powder boxes scimitars guns a garden pumpions vines ognions and hall. Lodging bad sup. bread wine.

Francis Vernon, *Journal*

In 1727 two abbés were dispatched by Louis XV of France to seek for manuscripts in the library of the Sultan at Constantinople, and anywhere else such might be found. The Abbé Sevin remained in Constantinople, while the Abbé Fourmont embarked on a tour of the islands and mainland in search not only of manuscripts but of ancient inscriptions, of which he seems to have destroyed as many as he recorded. In the spring of 1729 he reached Sparta.

When the chief men of Mistra knew that M. Fourmont had arrived in their city, they came to see him, and assured him there was no more connection between Mistra and the ancient Sparta than with Athens. They took a day out to visit Sparta; all the elders wished to go there with M. Fourmont, and exam-ine it with him, Pausanias in hand. This author, having passed the bridge over the Eurotas, enters the Platanistas on the right bank of the river, and with this still in sight he ascends to the town, where he finds first the temple of Lycurgus; then many other temples, the palace of the ancient kings, their tombs, the theatre, remarkable in its beauty; finally he goes up to the temple of Minerva, and remarks on the little hills which form a kind of fortress. Following his author, M. Fourmont recog-nized some of the objects of his period, but they were fallen; the Palaeologue princes, who fortified these little hills in recent times, made use of the nearest material, and left nothing of these buildings but their foundations . . .

While M. Fourmont was occupied in reconnoitring Sparta, his nephew, who was running from one side to the other, noticed that some pedestals, half buried near the Palaeologue walls, had inscriptions on them: fifteen men set to work and uncovered more than twenty inscriptions; the number of workmen was increased to sixty, and in thirty-five days which they employed in demolishing all the Palaeologue walls, without sparing even the foundations of the temples of the gods, the shrines of the heroes and the sepulchres of the kings, they unearthed more than three hundred inscriptions. All of these inscriptions were of some consequence . . .

Fourmont*; translated by RS

Fourmont's view of his discoveries was somewhat sanguine, and, as James Stuart remarked in his own record of researches in Greece, he had not only invented inscriptions but had smashed up genuine ones "so that future travellers might not detect his errors and frauds" (cf. F. J. Messmann, *Richard Payne Knight: The Twilight of Virtuosity*, The Hague and Paris, 1974, 57–58).

Sparta seems to have appealed especially to the temperament of the French Romantics. Chateaubriand writes at length about his stay there:

18 August 1806

The view enjoyed, as you walk along the Eurotas, is very different from that commanded by the hill of the citadel. The river pursues a winding course, concealing itself, as I have observed, among reeds and rose-laurels, as large as trees; on the left side, the hills of Mount Menelaion, of a bare and reddish appearance, form a contrast with the freshness and verdure of the channel of the Eurotas. On the right, the Taygetus spreads his magnificent curtain; the whole space comprehended between this curtain and the river, is occupied by small hills, and the ruins of Sparta. These hills and these ruins have not the same desolate aspect as when you are close to them; they seem, on the contrary, to be tinged with purple, violet, and a light gold colour. It is not verdant meads and foliage of a cold and uniform green, but the effects of light, that produce admirable landscapes. On this account the rocks and the heaths of the bay of Naples will ever be superior in beauty to the most fertile vales of France and England.

Thus, after ages of oblivion, this river, whose banks were trodden by the Lacedæmonians whom Plutarch has celebrated, this river, I say, perhaps rejoiced, amid this neglect, at the sound of the footsteps of an obscure stranger upon its shores. It was on the 18th of August, 1806, at nine in the morning, that I took this lonely walk along the Eurotas, which will never be erased from my memory. If I hate the manners of the Spartans, I am not blind to the greatness of a free people, neither was it without emotion that I trampled on their noble dust. One single fact is sufficient to proclaim the glory of this nation. When Nero visited Greece, he durst not enter Lacedæmon. What a magnificent panegyric on that city!

Night drew on apace, when I reluctantly quitted these renowned ruins, the shade of Lycurgus, the recollection of Thermopylæ, and all the fictions of fable and history. The sun sank behind the Taygetus, so that I had beheld him commence and finish his course on the ruins of Lacedæmon. It was three thousand five hundred and forty-three years, since he first rose and set over this infant city. I departed with a mind absorbed by the objects which I had just seen, and indulging in endless reflexions. Such days enable a man to endure many misfortunes with patience, and above all, render him indifferent to many spectacles.

F. de Chateaubriand, *Travels in Greece, Palestine, Egypt and Barbary;* translated by F. Shobel (1811)

The philhellenic poet Pierre Lebrun—who has clearly been studying the paintings of Poussin—devotes a fine passage of his *Voyage de Grèce* (1828) to a vivid tableau by the river Eurotas. As the book is hard to come by, I give the elegant French original with an English version:

Dans la belle vallée où fut Lacedemone,
Non loin de l'Eurotas, et près de ce ruisseau
Qui, formant son canal de débris de colonne,
Va sous des lauriers-rose ensevelir son eau,
Regardez: c'est la Grèce: et toute en un tableau.

Une femme est debout, de beauté ravissante,
Pieds nus; et sous ses doigts un indigent fuseau
File, d'une grenouille empruntée au roseau,
Du coton floconneux la neige éblouissante.
Un pâtre d'Amyclée, auprès d'elle placé,
Du bâton recourbé, de la courte tunique,
Rappelle les bergers d'un bas-relief antique.
Par un instinct charmant, et sans art adossé

Contre un vase de marbre à demi renversé,
Comme aux jours solennels des fêtes d'Hyacinthe,
Des fleurs du platinier sa tête encore est ceinte.
Sous sa couronne à l'ombre, il regarde, surpris,
Trois voyageurs d'Europe, au pied d'un chêne assis.
Le chemin est auprès. Sur un coursier conduite,
La Musulmane y passe, et de l'oeil du mépris
Regarde; et l'Africain marche et porte à sa suite
Dans une cage d'or sa perdrix favorite:
Cependant qu'un aga, dans un riche appareil,
Rapide cavalier au front sombre et sévère,
Sous un galop bruyant fait rouler la poussière.
De ses armes d'argent que frappe le soleil
Parmi les oliviers scintille la lumière.
Il nous lance en passant des regards scrutateurs.
Voilà Sparte: voilà Grèce tout entière:
Un esclave, un tyran, des débris, et des fleurs.

In the fair valley where Lacedaemon stood, not far from the Eurotas—near that river which, forcing its channel around shattered columns, enshrouds its waters in oleander coverts—look, here is Greece, all in a single tableau.

A woman stands, ravishingly beautiful, barefoot; between her fingers she winds a wretched spindle, a distaff borrowed from the reeds, filled with cotton so white as to outshine snow. An Amyclaean herdsman close beside her, with his curved staff and short tunic, reminds one of the shepherds of an antique bas relief. By a charming instinct he leans artlessly against an upturned urn of marble, as on the solemn days of the feast of Hyacinthus, and his head is still twined with plane-flowers. Beneath his shady garland, he looks in surprise at three European travellers, seated at the foot of an oak. The road is close by. Carried on a charger, the Musulman woman passes and looks on with a scornful eye; the Negro, on foot, carries after her her favourite partridge in a golden cage. Meanwhile an aga, in rich apparel, with a sombre and severe countenance, thunders past at a gallop, turning. The twilight, reflected by his silver armour, flashes through the olive trees. He casts a piercing scrutiny on us as he passes.

Behold Sparta; behold Greece itself: a slave, a tyrant, ruins and flowers.

Pierre Lebrun, Le Voyage de Grèce, ii, vi; translated by RS

In 1824 the success of the insurgents in the Greek War of Independence had secured for them the whole of the Morea, and they continued to hold out even after the defeat of the Greeks by Ali Pasha in Western Greece and the fall of Missolonghi. In 1824 the Sultan summoned the aid of a fleet and army from Mehemet Ali of Egypt, which, under the command of Ali's stepson, Ibrahim Pasha, recaptured the Morea. The scale of his atrocities was such that the Great Powers intervened, and the British government sent Captain Hamilton to intercept him. Hamilton was accompanied by the Rev. Charles Swan, who describes the destruction of Mistra on Wednesday 14 September 1824:

> On reaching Bruliah, a point of our descent toward Mistra, the whole range of Taygetus, now called Pendedactylon (Five-fingers) whose summits we had perceived for some time, opened upon us with surprising magnificence . . . From this place we observed Mistra; but we saw with regret that the town was smoking in a variety of places. The way conducted us through many beautiful vallies, ornamented as well as the higher regions with olive-trees . . . As we drew near to Mistra, fire broke from the houses, but not a soul was visible. A few Greeks, attracted by the hope of collecting what had not yet perished, appeared afterwards. We entered the town and beheld the flames all around us; household utensils broken and scattered in every direction. Nothing in short could equal the desolation, or the interest which it excited. In one place a cat remained the only inhabitant; in another, a dog barked at us as we passed, resolved to have the usual gratification of its spleen, though it sounded over the ruined hearth, and the broken shrine of domestic happiness.

> > 'Tis sweet to hear the watch-dog's honest bark
> > Bay deep-mouth'd welcome as we draw near home—

> But what a different feeling must have arisen in the mind of the owner of one of these burnt dwellings, when he returned to witness the wreck of his comforts, and the destruction of his property! The Greeks before mentioned conducted us to a house yet untouched, although surrounded by flames. Here we slept; expecting indeed to have been aroused in the night; but the escape was so easy, that we had no apprehension of the consequence. Ibrahim left Mistra in the state I have described,

only this morning. He has gone forward burning and destroying: we shall follow, and be eyewitnesses of the destructions he has caused.

Charles Swan, *Voyage to the Eastern Mediterranean*
(London, 1826)

The site of two ruined cities and a modest modern village, the valley of the Eurotas and Mount Taygetus now offer only the beauty of desolation and natural majesty. More than one Greek poet has celebrated that awesome and lovely mountain range. Here is Angelos Sikelianos:

> But, Taygetus, when at last my soul
> rested on your wild fragrance,
>
> and my afflicted heart—
> which throughout the night had lamented
> like the Scops owl
> that hangs upside down from the branch
> letting its lament drip,
> still warm, into the earth,
>
> and like the slaughtered lamb
> that they hang head down
> so that the surplus blood can run from its mouth—
>
> when my afflicted heart suddenly felt itself
> as though in an eagle's nest made of dry twigs,
> simple and firm like a trivet,
>
> what new impulses
> nourished my untamable and silent strength,
>
> veil of the tumult on your five peaks
> where the snow was slowly thawing,
>
> aerial cataracts
> of the flowering oleander
> on the escarpments,
>
> dawning of the Doric Apollo
> before my eyes,
> O harsh sculptured form
> on the red unyielding bronze!

Angelos Sikelianos, *Hymn to Artemis Orthia;*
translated by E. Keeley and P. Sherrard

Mani

The central promontory of the Peloponnese is the most impene-
trable and untamed area of Greece, never having submitted to the
rule of any outside invader. Its lore and life are the subject of a mar-
velous book, *Mani* (London, 1958), by Patrick Leigh Fermor. Its
inhabitants have a longstanding and apparently well-deserved reputation for ferocity, and their habits in the seventeenth century
are vividly described by Bernard Randolph:

> If any ship come to anchor on their coast, many arm
> themselves and go to the place, over against where the ship
> doth ride; some of them will be in priests habits, walking by
> the sea side, with their wallets, in which they will have some
> wine and bread. Their companions lye hid behind the bushes
> at some convenient post. When any strangers come ashore,
> who do not understand their language, the feigned priests
> make signes to them, shewing them their bread and wine,
> which they offer to them for money, by which the strangers
> being enticed from the sea side (and it may be to sit down and
> tast their wine) the hidden Manjotts come and make their
> prey. The priests will seem to be sorry, and endeavour to make
> the strangers believe they were altogether ignorant of any
> such design. So a white flagg is put out, and a treaty held with
> the ship for their ransome. The priests endeavour to moderate
> the price, shewing a great deal of respect to their compan-
> ions, who are cloathed in Turkish habits. Many ships have
> been thus served.
>
> Bernard Randolph, *The Present State of the Morea*
> (London, 1689)

By the end of the eighteenth century they were somewhat more
hospitable, and John B. S. Morritt of Rokeby, who made an
extended Grand Tour beginning in 1794, despoiling the odd marble to decorate the family home, is enthusiastic about his reception at Kardamyla:

> To see patriarchal and primitive manners, a traveller
> should visit Maina. Their order of government is this. The
> land is still parcelled out in districts on Lycurgus's own plan;
> on every one of these lives a family, supported by the villagers
> and people of that district, who are as free as their masters,
> with their guns on their shoulders; and thus the head family
> commands about four miles round about, and is indulgent to
> the others, who would otherwise either destroy or desert it.

These rulers often make war on one another, and the plunders then committed bring them into the bad repute their neighbours give them. They acknowledge one man as Bey, who is united by family to many of them, and if attacked by the Turks take their guns, retire to the mountains, and, with a force of six thousand or seven thousand men, carry on a war that is the terror of the Ottoman Empire. They sometimes make peace with the Turks, and pay tribute, if their country does not produce corn enough without importation, but if they can live they never submit to this humiliation. To give you some idea of their confidence in their own strength, and of the complete weakness of their enemies: a party of three hundred wanted to pass into Roumelia across the Morea to join some Pasha then at war. All the Agas opposed their passage, in consequence of which they had their villages plundered and their troops beat. They sent to the Pasha of Tripolizza to give them free passage. He opposed them, and with this small force they marched to Tripolizza and besieged him for seven days in his very capital; then cut their way forward, and joined the Aga in Roumelia, where they wanted to go at first. This you will say, I think, was no way unworthy their ancestors, and it will convince us what their laws must have been, which gave a spirit to the country it has not yet lost, while all the rest of Greece is sunk and degraded. I will go even so far as to say that the very first step in the country is enough to convince you of the freedom of it; the rocks and sides of the Taygetus, which is by nature as barren as ever mountain was, are cut into terraces to support the little earth there is, and covered with corn springing even from the very stones. The agriculture is clean, well kept, and resembling any country more than Turkey; they have so completely made the most of nature that scarce a foot of ground is lost, and it reminded us of Switzerland; and everything shows that the corn and wine spring for themselves, and not for an absent master.

⁓

I left off here to talk with our friends, and resume my letter here, if possible still more pleased with the Mainotes. The lady's castle was really enchantment; her uncle, a hearty, fine old man, dined and supped with us, and we were waited on by beautiful girls, in the true mode of patriarchal times. He lived in one tower with four daughters and his wife. Two of his daughters were children, and visited us—they were beautiful beyond measure; and of his older daughters one was, I think, the handsomest woman I ever saw. To give you some idea of their style of dress: On their heads is a plain small circle, either of shawl worked with gold or, sometimes, a red or green velvet cap embroidered round with gold, forming a coronet. Over this floats a long veil of white embroidered muslin. One end hangs over their right shoulder behind, and the other, hanging loose across their breast, is thrown also over the right shoulder. They wear a tight, high camisole of red silk and gold, buttoned with coloured stones across the breast. A short waistcoat, which is cut quite low, and clasps tight round their waist, is made of muslin and gold, with small globe buttons. A red sash and long flowing robes of white muslin and gold are below. Over these they wear a red, green, or light-blue silk gown, cut straight, and entirely open before, embroidered in the richest manner, the long sleeves sometimes of different colours. On their neck are rows of gold chains in the English mode exactly. They do not wear trousers so low as the women in the other parts of Turkey. This is chiefly the description of the lady of the house; you will suppose the colours are varied for different tastes and different ranks. The contour of the dress is much the same, and as the women are naturally lovely, with complexions you would suppose born in the coldest of climates, you may imagine the enchantment of the place, and will conceive how we regretted leaving our lodging.

J. B. S. Morritt, *Letters* (London, 1794–96)

Patrick Leigh Fermor's unique gift for blending landscape evocation, history, and folklore with dazzling prose is exemplified in his description of the scenery of the Deep Mani:

A tight-meshed network of walls covers this sloping country till the loose ends trail a little distance up the steep flank of the Taygetus and die away among the boulders. They are there for no purpose of delimitation. It is merely a tidy way of disposing of the stones that otherwise cumber the fields in order that, here and there, an inch or two of dusty earth may afford enough purchase for wheat grains to germinate. A little crescent-shaped bastion of flat stones shores up the precious soil round the roots of each olive tree. Winding labyrinths of walled lanes meander among the walls and trees as arbitrarily, it would seem, as the walls themselves. The solid rock of the Mani breaks through the sparse stubble fields in bleached shoulders and whales' backs and tall leaning blades of mineral and all is as white as bone. Sometimes groups of these blades cluster so thick that they give the illusion of whole villages; but when you reach them after clambering a score of walls, there they are in all their bare senselessness: fortuitous dolmens and cromlechs and menhirs. Once in a while, however, the wreck of an almost prehistoric ghost-village does appear: a sudden gathering of walls, the shells of half troglodytic houses with broken slab-roofs and thresholds only to be entered on all fours, the rough-hewn blocks pitched headlong by wild olive and cactus with only a rough cross incised on a lintel or a carved unidentifiable animal to indicate that they date from later than the stone age. The only other buildings are innumerable microscopic chapels, their shallow slab-roofed vaults jutting like the backs of armadilloes; an occasional farmstead, and the abandoned peel-towers of the Nyklians. The pale marble world of rock and gold stubble and thistle and silver-grey olive-leaves shudders in the midday glare, and one feels prone to test the rocks (like spitting on a flat-iron) before daring to lay a hand on them or to lie down in an olive's fragmentary disc of shade. The world holds its breath, and the noonday devil is at hand.

In summer, ghosts are said to roam the Mani in the hottest hour of the day, in winter at the darkest hour of the night. If their mortal predecessors have been killed by an enemy, they wail for revenge. Summer ghosts haunt graveyards, ruined churches and cross roads. A man's blood is supposed to shout out loud the day before he dies and if he perishes by violence his blood remains wet on the spot until a wooden cross is driven into the ground there; then it dries up or drains away. (The Maniots have a death fixation which is almost Mexican; perhaps the blazing light, the naked rock and the cactuses engender the same processes in either place.) The dead are turned into werewolves until forty days after their death and, stealing indoors at night, they eat the dough out of the kneading-troughs—any trough that is empty when it should be full is a werewolf's work. Witches are said to lead people in a trance up the mountainside at dead of night to torture them there. Regular sleepwalkers, of which there seem to be a number, are known as the *stringloparméni*, the witch-taken ones. Then there is a terrible devil called Makrynas, "the faraway one," who invariably appears in deserted places in the haunted hour of noon. I have not been able to learn what he looks like or what harm he does, but he is usually encountered by women who run away shrieking in panic through the rocks and olives. Could he be Pan himself, up to his old game with the latterday descendants of Syrinx and Echo? The nereids, the oreads, the dryads, the hamadryads and the gorgons all survive transposed in the minds of country Greeks. The Faraway One may be the chief woodland god himself.

Patrick Leigh Fermor, *Mani* (London, 1958)

It was on the southernmost promontory of Mani, Cape Tainaron, now Matapan, that one of the entrances to the underworld was situated, that through which Heracles brought up its guardian, the three-headed dog Cerberus. This was the route, too, that Psyche followed when she was sent by Aphrodite to fetch from the Queen of the Underworld a box of her beauty.

> Poore Psyches perceived the end of all fortune, thinking verely that she should never returne, and not without cause, when as she was compelled to go to the gulfe and furies of hell. Wherefore without any further delay, she went up to an high tower to throw her selfe down headlong (thinking it was the next and readiest way to hell) but the tower (as inspired) spake unto her saying O poore miser, why goest thou about to slay thy selfe? Why dost thou rashly yeeld unto thy last perill and danger? know that if thy spirit be once separated from thy body, thou shalt surely go to hell, but never to returne againe, wherefore harken to me; Lacedemon a citie in Greece is not farre hence: go thou thither and enquire for the hill Tenarus, whereas thou shalt find a hold leading to hell, even to the pallace of Pluto, but take heede thou go not with emptie hands to that place of darknesse: but carrie two sops sodden in the flour of barley and honney in thy hands, and two halfepence in thy mouth . . .

Apuleius, *The Golden Asse*, III;
translated by William Adlington (London, 1566)

The hard-headed Cyriac found dire rumors still attaching to the cave on the cape.

> 20 Oct 1447. We set out from the town of Taenarum and came to the tip of the promontory. Near villa Chorasia, outside the port which the sailors call Quaglio, near ancient relics of a Temple of Neptune, we found this first epigram . . . [IG V.1.1236]. Then by some shrine of the archangel Michael, on a very ancient tablet, much damaged by time, an inscription in the most ancient Cadmean letters. [IG V.1.1225]. And at the nearest hill to that same port, in a grove of holm-oaks five stades from the shore, we found that vast cave, from which

they say that the divine Hercules brought back Cerberus from the underworld [Strabo, VIII, 51] although we know that the same is told by others of Heraclea Pontica and the cave of Acheron there, and we had seen that place less than a year before, as we noted in describing our navigation in Pontus.

But here, when we approached the opening, the vast jaws of the abyss, no dragon affrighted us, which the natives, full of rustic terror, assured us was there, but the clatter of three pigeons flying out assailed the trembling hearts of our companions. And then, with the accompaniment of three natives of Porasia and Taenarum, I descended through the rocky mouth to the inner part of the cave.

Going deeper than Magola and John the priest, descending with lighted candles through the gaping entrails of the abyss, we perceived that we were approaching a pit of indeterminate depth. Going out again, when we reached the town of Taenarum, I found these inscriptions on a partly broken stone . . .

Cyriac of Ancona, in Sabbadini*; translated by RS

The Cape is the subject of a poem by Lawrence Durrell:

MATAPAN

Unrevisited perhaps forever
Southward from the capes of smoke
Where past and present to the waters are one
And the peninsula's end points out
Three fingers down the night:
On a corridor of darkness a beam
To where the islands, at last, the islands . . .

Abstract and more lovely
Andros Delos and Santorin,
Transpontine headlands in crisp weather,
Cries amputated by the gulls,
Formless, yet made in marble
Whose calm insoluble statues wear
Stone vines for hair, forever sharing
A sea-penumbra, the darkened arc
Where mythology walks in a wave
And the islands are.

Leaving you, hills, we were unaware
Or only as sleepwalkers are aware
Of a key turned in the heart, a letter

Posted under the door of an empty house;
Now Matapan and her forebodings
Became an identity, a trial of conduct,
Rolled and unrolled by the surges
Like a chart, mapped by a star,
With thistle and trefoil blowing,
An end of everything known
A beginning of water.

> *Here sorrow and beauty shared*
> *Like time and place an eternal relation,*
> *Matapan . . .*
>
> *Here we learned that the lover*
> *Is contained by love, not containing,*
> *Matapan, Matapan:*

Here the lucky in summer
Tied up their boats; a mile from land
The cicada's small machine came like a breath;
Touching bottom saw their feet become
Webbed and monstrous on the sandy floors.
Here wind emptied the snowy caves: the brown
Hands about the tiller unbuckled.
Day lay like a mirror in the sun's eye.
Olives sleeping, rocks hanging, sea shining
And under Arbutus the scriptural music
Of a pipe beside a boy beside a bay
Soliloquised in seven liquid quibbles.

Here the lucky in summer
Made fast like islanders
And saw upon the waters, leaning down
The haunted eyes in faces torn from books:
So painted the two dark-blue Aegean eyes
And θεὸς δίκαιος 'God the Just'
Under them upon the rotting prows.

Inhabitants of reflection going:
We saw the dog-rose abloom in bowls,
Faces of wishing children in the wells
Under the Acropolis the timeless urchin
Carrying the wooden swallow,
Teller of the spring; on the hills of hair
Over Athens saw the night exhaling.

John Linton, *A Greek Couple*. Benaki Museum, Athens.

Later in islands, awaiting passage,
By waters like skin and promontories,
Were blessed by the rotation
Of peach-wind, melon-wind,
Fig-wind and wind of lemons;
Every fruit in the rotation of its breath.
And in the hills encountered
Sagacious and venerable faces
Like horn spoons: forms of address:
Christian names, politeness to strangers.

> *Heard the ant's pastoral reflections:*
> *'Here I go to Arcadia, one two*
> *Saffron, sage, bergamot, rue,*
> *A root, a hair, a bead—all warm.*
> *A human finger swarming*
> *With little currents: a ring:*
> *A married man.'*

In a late winter of mist and pelicans
Saw the thread run out at last; the man
Kiss his wife and child good-bye
Under the olive-press, turning on a heel.

To enter April like swimmer,
And memory opened in him like a vein,
Pushed clear on the tides a pathless keel.

Standing alone on the hills
Saw all Greece, the human
Body of this sky suspending a world
Within a crystal turning,
Guarded by the green wicks of cypresses.

Far out on the blue
Like notes of music on a page
The two heads: the man and his wife.
They are always there.

It is too far to hear the singing.

Lawrence Durrell

Cythera

Opposite Mani lies Cythera, the seventh of the Ionian islands, and
the birthplace of Aphrodite. Sir Richard Guylforde, in 1511 one
of the earliest English pilgrims to describe Greek lands, gives a
somewhat confused account of it:

> Upon tewsdaye ayenst nyght we passed by the yle called
> Cyrigo / whiche yle was somtyme called Citheria where Helena
> the Grekysshe Quene was borne / but she was ravysshed by
> Paris in ye next yle by / called Cicerigo Doynge sacryfyce in the
> Temple / for the whiche Rape folowed the distruccion of
> Troye / as ye famouse Storye therof sheweth / knowen in every
> tonge / and yet is the ymage of the same Quene remaynynge
> in the Citye of Alorys / upon the see of Archipelagus in mem-
> ory of the same Rape wroughte moost sotely and craftly in
> fygne whyte marble / And the sayde yle Cerigo is directly
> ayenst the poynt of Capo maleo in Morea / and in the same
> yle was Venus borne and in the same yle is Delphos / and it is
> all in europa / and so is all the remenaunt of Grece.

In Fénelon's *Télémaque*, the island is endowed with all manner of
pastoral enchantments, which have their visual counterpart in Watteau's paintings and engravings on the theme of Cythera. The reality was a good deal more inhospitable, as Pouqueville observed:

> Cerigo is well known to be the ancient Cythera. Here,
> by a strange caprice of imagination, altars were built to the gay

Antoine Watteau, *Embarcation for Cythera*. Musée du Louvre, Paris
(detail). (Photo: Giraudon/Art Resource, New York).

laughter-loving goddess in the midst of a most wild and desolate country. The view from the rocks, though some cultivated
fields are to be seen from them, is sufficient to disenchant the
ideas of poets and lovers who visit the island to indulge in the
recollections of antiquity. Instead of Celadons they will see
rough peasants; instead of Venus and the Graces, half wild
Greek women; and instead of beautiful lawns enamelled with
flowers, naked and rugged rocks or valleys grown over with
brushwood.

> F. Pouqueville, *Travels in the Morea . . .* (London, 1813)

In 1851 Gérard de Nerval sailed past the enchanted isle, and was
duly disappointed.

> One must admit that Cythera has kept none of its beauties
> except its rocks of porphyry, as gloomy to look at as ordinary
> sandstone rocks. Not a tree on the coast we followed, not a
> rose, alas! not a shell along this shore where the Nereids once
> chose a conch for Aphrodite. I searched for the shepherds and
> shepherdesses of Watteau, their ships adorned with garlands
> made fast to flowery shores; I dreamt of those crazy bands of
> pilgrims of love in cloaks of variegated satin . . . and I saw only
> a gentleman shooting at woodcock and pigeon, and blond and
> dreamy Scottish soldiers, seeking on the horizon, perhaps, the
> fogs of their own country.

As we skirted the coast, before putting in at San-Nicolo, I observed a small monument, vaguely outlined against the azure of the sky, which, atop its rock, seemed to be the statue, yet standing, of some protecting divinity . . . But, as we came closer, we distinguished clearly the object which signalled this coastline to attentive voyagers. It was a gibbet, a gibbet with three branches, one of which alone was adorned. The first real gibbet I had ever seen, and it was given to me to see it on the soil of Cythera, an English possession!

Gérard de Nerval, *Voyage en Orient* (1851); translated by RS

This description caught the imagination of Charles Baudelaire, who based on it his poem *Voyage à Cythère*, first published in 1855:

VOYAGE TO CYTHERA

My heart, a seagull rocketed and spun
about the rigging, dipping joyfully;
our slow prow rocking under cloudless sky
was like an angel drunk with the live sun.

What's that out there? Those leagues of hovering sand?
'It's Cythera famous in the songs,
the gay old dogs' El Dorado, it belongs
to legend. Look closely, it's a poor land.'

Island of secret orgies none profess,
the august shade of Aphrodite plays
like clouds of incense over your blue bays,
and weights the heart with love and weariness.

Island whose myrtle esplanades arouse
our nerves, here heart-sighs and the adoration
of every land and age and generation
ramble like coal-red roses on a house

to the eternal cooing of the dove.
'No, Cythera crumbles, cakes and dries,
a rocky desert troubled by shrill cries . . .
And yet I see one portent stretch above

us. Is it a temple where the pagan powers
hover in naked majesty to bless
the arbours, gold-fish ponds and terraces;
and the young priestess is in love with flowers?

No, nosing through these shoals, and coming near
enough to scare the birds with our white sails,
we saw a man spread-eagled on the nails
of a cross hanging like a cypress there.

Ferocious vultures choking down thick blood
gutted the hanging man, already foul;
each smacked its beak like the flat of a trowel
into the private places of their food.

His eyes were holes and his important paunch
oozed lazy, looping innards down his hips;
those scavengers, licking sweetmeats from their lips,
had hung his pouch and penis on a branch.

Under his foot-soles, shoals of quadrupeds
with lifted muzzles nosed him round and guzzled;
a huge antediluvian reptile muscled
through them like an executioner with his aides.

Native of Cythera, initiate,
how silently you hung and suffered insult
in retribution for your dirty cult
and orgasms only death could expiate.

Ridiculous hanged man, my sins confirm
your desecration; when I saw you seethe,
I felt my nausea mounting to my teeth,
the drying bile-stream of my wasted sperm.

Poor devil with sweet memories, your laws
are mine; before you, I too felt those jaws:
black panther, lancing crow, the Noah's Ark
that loved to chafe my flesh and leave their mark.

I'd lost my vision clinging to those shrouds,
I feared the matching blues of sky and sea;
All things were henceforth black with blood for me,
and plunged my heart in allegoric clouds . . .

Nothing stands upright in your land, oh Lust,
except my double, hanging at full length—
Oh God, give me the courage and the strength
to see my heart and body without disgust.

Baudelaire, Voyage à Cythère;
translated by Robert Lowell

6

Cape Malea to the Argolid;
Corinth

The proverb runs "Double Cape Malea and forget your home" (Strabo, 8, 6, 20). It is one of the most inhospitable parts of the Greek coastline. Alphonse de Lamartine has given us an account of the remarkable sight on the promontory:

> On the steep and inaccessible declivity of the rock that forms the headland of the cape, sharpened by hurricanes, and by the lashing of the spray, accident has suspended three rocks detached from the summit, and arrested half way in their fall. There they remain, like a nest of sea-fowl bending over the foaming abyss of the waters. A quantity of reddish earth, also stopped in its fall by these three unequal rocks, gives root to five or six stunted fig-trees, which themselves hang with their tortuous branches, and their large gray leaves, over the roaring gulf that whirls at their feet. The eye cannot discern any footpath, any practicable declivity, by which this little mound of vegetation could be reached. However, a small low dwelling can be distinguished among the fig-trees—a house of a gray, sombre appearance, like the rock which serves for its base, and with which one confounds it on the first view. Over the flat roof of the house there rises a small open belfry, as over the door of convents in Italy: a bell is suspended from it. To the right are to be seen some ancient ruins of foundations of red bricks, in which there are three open arcades leading to a little terrace that stretches in front of the house. An eagle would have feared to build his eyrie in such a place, without a single bush or trunk of a tree to shelter him from the wind which roars continually, from the eternal noise of the sea breaking, and of the spray licking incessantly the polished rock, under a sky always burning. Well, a man has done what the bird itself would scarcely have dared to do; he has chosen this asylum. He lives there: we perceived him: he is a hermit. We doubled the cape so closely, that we could distinguish his long white beard, his staff, his chaplet, his hood of brown felt, like that of sailors in winter. He went on his knees as we passed, with his face turned towards the sea, as if he were imploring the succour of

Heaven for the unknown strangers on this perilous passage. The wind, which issues furiously from the mountain-gorges of Laconia, as soon as you double the rock of the cape, began to resound in our sails, and make the two vessels roll and stagger, covering the sea with foam as far as the eye could reach. A new sea was opening before us. The hermit, in order to follow us still farther with his eyes, ascended the crest of a rock, and we distinguished him there, on his knees, and motionless, as long as we were in sight of the cape.

What is this man? He must have a soul trebly steeped in wo, to have chosen this frightful abode; he must have a heart and senses eager for strong and eternal emotions, to live in this vulture's nest, alone, with the boundless horizon, the hurricane, and the roar of the sea. His only spectacle is, from time to time, a passing ship, the creaking of the masts, the tearing of the sails, the cannon of distress, the cries of sailors in their agony.

These three fig-trees, that little inaccessible field, this spectacle of the convulsive struggle of the elements, these rough, severe, and meditative impressions of the soul, formed one of the dreams of my childhood and youth. By an instinct which my knowledge of men has since confirmed, I never placed happiness but in solitude—only at that time I placed love there; but now I shall place there love, God, and thought: this desert suspended between the heaven and the sea, shaken by the incessant shock of the winds and waves, would still be one of the charms of my heart. It is the attitude of the bird of the mountains, while yet touching with its foot the sharp summit of the rock; and already flapping its wings to dart still higher into the regions of light. There is no well-organized man who would not become, in such an abode, either a saint or a great poet—perhaps both. But what a violent shock of existence must have been required to inspire me with such thoughts and desires, and to drive thither those other men whom I see there! God knows. Whatever be the case, he cannot be an ordinary man who has felt the pleasure and the necessity of hooking himself like the pendent bindweed to the walls of such an abyss, and to remain hovering there during a whole lifetime, beside the tumult of the elements, the terrible music of the tempest, alone with his own thoughts, in the presence of nature and of God.

A. de Lamartine, *Travels in the East*;
translated by TWR (Edinburgh, 1850)

The itinerary is continued with the Seigneur de la Borderie, who made a description in doggerel verse of most of the main sights of Greece, after traveling to Constantinople in 1542. He accurately describes Monemvasia, though his geography is a little erratic, for he appears to place it where Neapolis now is.

We follow further the Achaean Coast,
Still the Morea, though Laconia's past,
And come upon the island of Cervi[1]
Whose name seems quite unsuitable to me,
Since not one deer has there its habitat,
But only a great quantity of rats:
Our hounds pursued them through the undergrowth,
While the crew took some hours rest, nothing loth,
Illumined by the soft light of the moon,
Until the rising of the lustrous dawn
Announced that Phoebus was about to start,
Admonishing our sailors to depart:
Each one of them commands his underlings,
Each to his place on the oar-benches springs;
They haul the small boats up again on deck,
And spread the sails, and then begin to tack
To Malvaysie, known to the population
As Monemvasia, which is, in translation,
'One Entrance'; so called from the circling cliffs the bay's in.
There was discovered, most authors concede,
The first vine to produce that splendid mead
Called Malmsey from its place of origin,
And brought from there to Candy (which was then
Called Crete), the island of a hundred towns,
Who, subject and enslaved, acknowledged Zeus's crown.
We did not stop to see the ancient castle
Which the Venetians now have made their vassal,
But seized the wind, for fear that it might change,
And hurried on to double Cape St Ang-
elo, formerly known as Malea . . .

> Bertrand de la Borderie,
> *Discours du Voyage de Constantinople* (1542);
> translated by RS

1. Latin Cervi, "deer"; Greek, Elaphonisos.

Asine

Further along the coast is the site of ancient Asine, mentioned once in Homer's catalogue of the ships that sailed to Troy, and nowhere else at all. Seferis has written a memorable poem about this haunting site:

THE KING OF ASINE

We looked all morning round the citadel
starting from the shaded side, there where the sea
green and without luster—breast of a slain peacock—
received us like time without an opening in it.
Veins of rock, dropped down from high above,
twisted vines, naked, many-branched, coming alive
at the water's touch, while the eye following them
struggled to escape the tiresome rocking,
losing strength continually.

On the sunny side a long open beach
and the light striking diamonds on the huge walls.
No living thing, the wild doves gone
and the king of Asine, whom we've been trying to find for
    two years now,

unknown, forgotten by all, even by Homer,
only one word in the *Iliad* and that uncertain,
thrown here like the gold burial mask.
You touched it, remember its sound? Hollow in the light
like a dry jar in dug earth:
the same sound that our oars make in the sea.
The king of Asine a void under the mask
everywhere with us everywhere with us, under a name:
'Ασίνην τε . . . 'Ασίνην τε . . .
        and his children statues
and his desires the fluttering of birds, and the wind
in the gaps between his thoughts, and his ships
anchored in a vanished port:
under the mask a void.

Behind the large eyes the curved lips the curls
carved in relief on the gold cover of our existence
a dark spot that you see travelling like a fish
in the dawn calm of the sea: a void everywhere with us.
And the bird that flew away last winter
with a broken wing—
abode of life,

and the young woman who left to play
with the dogteeth of summer
and the soul that sought the lower world squeaking
and the country like a large plane-leaf swept along by the
    torrent
of the sun
with the ancient monuments and the contemporary sorrow.

And the poet lingers, looking at the stones, and asks himself
does there really exist
among these ruined lines, edges, points, hollows, and curves
does there really exist
here where one meets the path of rain, wind, and ruin
does there exist the movement of the face, shape of
    the tenderness
of those who've shrunk so strangely in our lives,
those who remained the shadow of waves and thoughts with
    the sea's boundlessness
or perhaps no, nothing is left but the weight
the nostalgia for the weight of a living existence
there where we now remain unsubstantial, bending
like the branches of a terrible willow-tree heaped in
    permanent despair
while the yellow current slowly carries down rushes uprooted
    in the mud
image of a form that the sentence to everlasting bitterness
    has turned to marble:
the poet a void.

Shieldbearer, the sun climbed warring,
and from the depths of the cave a startled bat
hit the light as an arrow hits a shield:
Ἀσίνην τε ... Ἀσίνην τε. Could that be the king of Asine
we've been searching for so carefully on this acropolis
sometimes touching with our fingers his touch upon
    the stones.

George Seferis; translated by E. Keeley and P. Sherrard

Nafplion

The major port on this coast is Nafplion, formerly known as Nauplia or Napoli di Romagna. In the anarchic interregnum following
the War of Independence, the mountains of the Peloponnese were
the strongholds of numerous klephtic bands. Lamartine, in Nafplion in August 1831, described the situation:

Carl Heydeck, *Bortzi Fortress, Nafplion*. Städtische Galerie im Lenbach-
haus, Munich.

The most complete anarchy reigns at this moment over
all the Morea. Each day one faction triumphs over the other,
and we hear the musketry of the klephts, of the Colocotroni
faction, who are fighting on the other side of the gulf against
the troops of the government. We are informed, by every
courier that descends from the mountains, of the burning of
a town, the pillage of a valley, or the massacre of a population, by one of the parties that are ravaging their native country. One cannot go beyond the gates of Nauplia without being
exposed to musket shots. Prince Karadja had the goodness to
propose to me an escort of his palikars to go and visit the tomb
of Agamemnon; and General Corbet, who commands the
French forces, politely offered to add to them a detachment
of his soldiers. I refused, because I did not wish, for the
gratification of a vain curiosity, to expose the lives of several
men, for which I should eternally reproach myself.

A. de Lamartine, *Travels in the East*;
translated by TWR (Edinburgh, 1850)

Argos

It was not long thereafter that Julia Ward Howe, the authoress of
"The Battle Hymn of the Republic," and one of the first American travelers in Greece, saw at Argos further evidence of the bloody
war against the bandits.

The evening of our sojourn in Argos saw an excitement much like that which blocked the street at Nauplia. The occasion was the same—the bringing home of a brigand's head; but this the very head and fount of all the brigands, Kitzos himself, upon whose head had been set a price of several thousand drachmas. Our veteran with difficulty obtained a view of the same, and reported accordingly. The robber chief of Edmond About's 'Hadji Stauros', had been shot while sighting at his gun. He had fallen with one eye shut and one open, and in this form of feature his dissevered head remained. The soldier who was its fortunate captor carried it concealed in a bag, with its long elf-locks lying loose about it. He showed it with some unwillingness, fearing to have the prize wrested from him. It was, however, taken on board of our steamer, and carried to Athens, there to be identified and buried.

All this imported to us that Mycenae, which we desired to visit, had for some time been considered unsafe on account of the presence of this very Kitzos and his band. But at this moment the band were closely besieged in the mountains. They wanted their head, and so did Kitzos. We, in consequence, were fully able to visit the treasure of Atreus and the ruins of Mycenae without fear or risk from those acephalous enemies.

Julia Ward Howe, *From the Oak to the Olive* (1868)

The ancient city of Argos was the center of Agamemnon's kingdom, though his palace was at Mycenae. Agamemnon was far from William Lithgow's thoughts when he spent one of his more uncomfortable and philosophical nights there, *au bel air*.

Here in Argos I had the ground to be a pillow, and the world's wide fields to be a chamber, the whirling windy skies, to be a roof to my winter-blasted lodging, and the humid vapours of cold Nocturna, to accompany the unwished-for bed of my repose. What shall I say then, the solid and sad man is not troubled with the floods and ebbs of fortune, the ill employed power of greatness, nor the fluctuating motions of the humourous multitude; or, at least, if he be sensible of his own, or their irregularities or confusions, yet his thoughts are not written in his face, his countenance is not significant, nor his miseries further seen than in his own private suffering; whereas the face and disposition of the feeble one, ever resembleth his last thoughts, and upon every touch, or taste of that which is displeasant, and follows not the streams of his appetite, his countenance deformeth itself, and, like the moon, is in as many changes as his fortune: but the noble resolution must follow Aeneas' advice in all his adventures.

> Per varios casus, et tot discrimina rerum,
> Tendimus in Latium, etc.

> By divers ways, and dangers great, we mind
> To visit Latium, and Latinus kind.

In all this country of Greece, I could find nothing to answer the famous relations given by ancient authors of the excellency of that land, but the name only; the barbarousness of Turks and time having defaced all the monuments of antiquity. No shew of honour, no habitation of men in an honest fashion, nor professors of the country in a principality; but rather prisoners shut up in prisons, or addicted slaves to cruel and tyrannical masters; so deformed is the state of that once worthy realm, and so miserable is the burden of that afflicted people; which, and the appearance of that permanency, grieved my heart to behold the sinister workings of blind Fortune, which always plungeth the most renowned champions, and their memory, in the profoundest pit of all extremities and oblivion.

William Lithgow, *Totall Discourse of the
Rare Adventures and Painefull Peregrinations*
(London, 1632)

Mycenae

The focus of the Argolid must inevitably be Mycenae. To Mycenae came, on Troy's fall, the news of victory signaled by a chain of beacons from Trojan Ida to Agamemnon's palace. Aeschylus' Clytemnestra describes this vivid telegraph:

> Hephaistos, the lame God,
> And spriteliest of mortal messengers;
> Who, springing from the bed of burning Troy,
> Hither, by fore-devised Intelligence
> Agreed upon between my lord and me,
> Posted from dedicated height to height
> The reach of land and sea that lies between.
> And, first to catch him and begin the game,

Did Ida fire her forest pine, and, waving,
Handed him on to that Hermaean steep
Of Lemnos; Lemnos to the summit of
Zeus-consecrated Athos lifted; whence,
As by the giant taken, so despatched,
The torch of conquest, traversing the wide
Aegaean with a sunbeam-stretching stride,
Struck up the drowsy watchers on Makistos;
Who, flashing back the challenge, flash'd it on
To those who watch'd on the Messapian height.
With whose quick-kindling heather heap'd and fired
The meteor-bearded messenger refresh'd,
Clearing Asopus at a bound, struck fire
From old Kithaeron; and, so little tired
As waxing even wanton with the sport,
Over the sleeping water of Gorgopis
Sprung to the Rock of Corinth; thence to the cliffs
Which stare down the Saronic Gulf, that now
Began to shiver in the creeping dawn;
Whence, for a moment on the neighbouring top
Of Arachnaeum lighting, one last bound
Brought him to Agamemnon's battlements.
By such gigantic strides in such a race
Where first and last alike are conquerors,
Posted the travelling fire, whose father-light
Ida conceived of burning Troy tonight.

Aeschylus, *Agamemnon*, 281–316;
translated by Edward Fitzgerald

Already ruined in antiquity, Mycenae drew from the pen of the poet Alpheus of Mytilene (fl. circa A.D. 0) an epigram of somewhat conventional melancholy.

The cities of the hero age thine eyes may seek in vain,
Save where some wrecks of ruin still break the level plain,
So once I saw Mycenae, the ill-starred, a barren height
Too bleak for goats to pasture,—the goat-herds point
    the site.
And as I passed a grey-beard said, 'Here used to stand of old
A city built by giants, and passing rich in gold.'

Alpheus, in *Anthologia Palatina*, IX, 101;
translated by Rennell Rodd

For centuries nothing was visible on these windswept hills. But since the excavation by Heinrich Schliemann in 1874–76, capped by his famous telegram announcing the discovery of the golden masks, "I have gazed on the face of Agamemnon," Mycenae has been a cynosure for most travelers in Greece.

All is degradation in the chambers of dead bones,
Nor marble, nor porphyry, but make it worse
For the mind sees, inside it, to the stained wet shroud
Where all else is dry, and only that is fluid,
So are carven tombs in the core to their cool marble,
The hollowed out heart of it, the inner cell,
All is degradation in the halls of the dead;
I never thought other things of death, until
The climb to Mycenae, when the wind and rain
Stormed at the tombs, when the rocks were as clouds
Struck still in the hurricane, driven to the hillside,
And rain poured in torrents, all the air was water.
The wet grey Argolide wept below,
The winds wailed and tore their hair,
The plain of Argos mourned and was in mist,
In mist tossed and shaken, in a sea of wrack;
This was the place of weeping, the day of tears,
As if all the dead were here, in all their pain,
Not stilled, nor assuaged, but aching to the bone:
It was their hell, they had no other hope than this,
But not alone, it was not nothingness:
The wind shrieked, the rain poured, the steep wet stones
Were a cliff in a whirlwind, by a raging sea,
Hidden by the rainstorm pelting down from heaven
To that hollow valley loud with melancholy;
But the dark hill opened. And it was the tomb.

A passage led into it, cut through the hill,
Echoing, rebounding with the million ringing rain,
With walls, ever higher, till the giant lintel
Of huge stone, jagged and immense, rough hewn
That held up the mountain: it was night within:
Silence and peace, nor sound of wind nor rain,
But a huge dome, glowing with the day from out
Let in by the narrow door, diffused by that,
More like some cavern under ocean's lips,
Fine and incredible, diminished in its stones,
For the hand of man had fitted them, of dwindling size,
Row after row, round all the hollow dome,

Ludwig Lange, *Mycenae*. Staatliche Graphische Sammlung, Munich.

As scales of fish, as of the ocean's fins,
Pinned with bronze flowers that were, now, all fallen,
But the stones kept their symmetry, their separate shape
To the dome's high cupola of giant stone:
All was high and solemn in the cavern tomb:
If this was death, then death was poetry,
First architecture of the man made years,
This was peace for the accursed Atridae:
Here lay Agamemnon in a cell beyond,
A little room of death, behind the solemn dome
Not burnt, nor coffined, but laid upon the soil
With a golden mask upon his dead man's face
For a little realm of light within that shadowed room:
And ever the sun came, every day of life,
Though less than starpoint in that starry sky,
To the shadowed meridian, and sloped again,
Nor lit his armour, nor the mask upon his face,
For they burned in eternal night, they smouldered in it.
Season followed season, there was summer in the tomb
Through hidden crevice, down that point of light,
Summer of loud wings and of the ghosts of blossom.
One by one, as harvesters, all heavy laden,
The bees sought their corridor into the dome

With honey of the asphodel, the flower of death.
Or thyme, rain sodden, and more sweet for that;
Here was their honeycomb, high in the roof,
I heard sweet summer from their drumming wings,
Though it wept and rained and was the time of tears;
They made low music, they murmured in the tomb,
As droning nuns through all a shuttered noon,
Who prayed in this place of death, and knew it not.

Sacheverell Sitwell, Agamemnon's Tomb

MYCENE [sic]

Time's filial beast
To make his mockery of life
Planted the pale cyclamen aridly: here
Where the nosing goat
Presses an indifferent hoof.

If I might have spoken
I would have said: Pride has no power
To sever the fiery knot
That gathers within the blue stain
Of eyes that might be trembling waters
Were lust to be provoked. I saw you then
Iphigeneia or some legendary girl
Crouched over a fire of withered thyme
In Agamemnon's tomb. The flames
Were brief: and left a darkness
Deeper than the night: into which we walked
Strangers to our separate doom.

Herbert Read

AT MYCENAE

Orestes, running out of the back door
    Felt the wall's shadow lighten on his back,
    Where blood and milk, mingled, seeped on the floor.

He looked one last time on that town the sack
    Of Troy made famous, then forgot, and ran.
    Free in the hills, no one could fetch him back.

'I am alone, free from the ties of men:
    Odysseus drifts among the bladder wrack,
    And swift Achilles lies as still as stone.

Behind the summit now my trodden track.'
That year the blood-red poppies did not bloom.
The land seemed dead, the rocks of Lethe cracked.

'And I was glad to see the Furies come.'

Richard Stoneman

Nemea

Just off the northward route out of the Argolid lie the little ancient townships of Phlious, Nemea (site of the third of the great Pan-hellenic Games, dedicated to Zeus), and Kleonae, which provided the judges of the Nemean Games. The latter were founded, according to legend, by the members of the second Argive expedition against Thebes, at the grave-mound of the child Opheltes.

Pindar celebrates a victory here and also at the Isthmus (where the games were dedicated to Poseidon).

> The causeway of the tireless sea honoured Alcimidas' victory among the Amphictyons, at the precinct of Poseidon, during the biennial bull-sacrifice; and the grassy pasture of the Lion shaded the head of the victor, there beneath the shady mountains of Phlious.
>
> Pindar, *Nemean*, 6, 39–44; translated by RS

It was here that Heracles strangled the otherwise invulnerable Nemean Lion, whose pelt he ever afterwards wore. The Lion was a familiar legend even in the nineteenth century.

> In about two hours we deviated from the direct road in the direction of Nemea, leaving Antonietti and the tchocodar to make the best of their way to Corinth. We very soon observed a large cave at the end of a long mountain on our right hand, which is supposed to have been the retreat of the Nemean lion whose destruction afforded one of the twelve labours to the Grecian Hercules: winding round this hill (the ancient Tretus) we entered upon the spacious plain, that scene of animated contests and tumultuous passions, now solitary as the desert and silent as the grave. Three lofty Doric columns, remains of the great temple of Jupiter, cast as it were a melancholy charm over its solitude, seeming as if they were spared but to impress upon man the awful moral lesson, 'that all his pomp is vanity.' Turning through a chasm amongst the hills behind this temple, we passed a fountain of delicious water, probably that mentioned by Pausanias under the name

of Adrastéa: soon afterwards we discovered the ancient road by which the chariots passed to Nemea, the rock being in many places indented to the depth of more than a foot by the constant attrition of the wheels: there is nothing to detain the traveller upon the site of Cleonae, for that ancient city—*ingenti turritae mole Cleonae*—has been long swept away by the besom of destruction.

Thomas S. Hughes, *Travels in Sicily, Greece and Albania*
(London, 1820)

The site, where excavations during the 1970s uncovered the ancient running track complete with incised starting line, remains one of the most peaceful and picturesque in the Peloponnese.

NEMEA

A song in the valley of Nemea:
Sing quiet, quite quiet here.

Song for the brides of Argos
Combing the swarms of golden hair:
Quite quiet, quiet there.

Under the rolling comb of grass,
The sword outrusts the golden helm.

Agamemnon under tumulus serene
Outsmiles the jury of skeletons:
Cool under cumulus the lion queen:

Only the drum can celebrate,
Only the adjective outlive them.

A song in the valley of Nemea:
Sing quiet, quiet, quiet here.

Tone of the frog in the empty well,
Drone of the bald bee on the cold skull,

Quiet, Quiet, Quiet.

Lawrence Durrell

Corinth

Corinth's place in literature has been almost exclusively that of a synonym for departed glory. Surveying those busy, much-frequented ruins, bright with poppy and chrysanthemum, under the solid rock of Acrocorinth, you would think it not so very different

Carl Rottmann, *Nemea*. Staatliche Antikensammlungen und Glyptothek, Munich (detail).

from other sites of comparable splendid ruin. But Corinth met its destruction many centuries before the other cities of Greece, at the hands of Rome in 146 B.C. So it is not inappropriate that the plangent note is first sounded by the Roman, Servius Sulpicius, in a letter to Cicero in March 45 B.C.

> When the report reached me of the death of your daughter Tullia, I was indeed duly and deeply and grievously sorry . . .
>
> I want to tell you of something which has brought me no slight comfort, in the hope that perhaps it may have some power to lighten your sorrow too. As I was on my way back from Asia, sailing from Aegina to Megara, I began to gaze at the landscape around me. There behind me was Aegina, in front of me Megara, to the right Piraeus, to the left Corinth; once flourishing towns, now lying low in ruins before one's eyes. I began to think to myself: 'Ah! how can we manikins wax indignant if one of us dies or is killed, ephemeral creatures as we are, when the corpses of so many towns lie abandoned in

a single spot? Check yourself, Servius, and remember that you were born a mortal man.' That thought, I do assure you, strengthened me not a little . . .

Cicero, *Letters to his Friends*, IV, 5;
translated by D. R. Shackleton Bailey

Antipater sounds the same strain, a strain he uttered over many cities of Greece. To picture Greece through Antipater's eyes is to see a desolation almost total. How he would have wept over Ottoman Greece!

> O Corinth, Dorian Corinth, where is thy beauty now?
> So fair it was: and where the crown that shone upon
>   thy brow?
> A coronet of towers and countless wealth was thine,
> With many a noble palace, and many a holy shrine.
> What of thy myriad warriors, thy dames of high estate?
> O daughter of a thousand woes, thy place is desolate!
> Nay, thou hast left no footprint, that future men may say
> 'Here Corinth stood!'—the tide of war hath swept them
>   all away.
> Yet we the deathless Nereids, the halcyons of the sea,
> In loneliness are faithful yet to wail thy woe for thee.

Antipater, in *Anthologia Palatina*, IX, 151;
translated by J. A. Pott

As an example of ruined greatness, a Tintern Abbey of the Ottoman Empire, Corinth aroused powerful sentiments in philhellenic breasts like that of William Haygarth, and the urge to regenerate Greece was fueled with special force in Byron by its ruins. Richard Monckton Milnes and Walter Savage Landor also wrote poems looking forward to a future return to glory for Corinth.

> What scenes of beauty deck Achaia's shores!
> The long extended line of rugged coast;
> The woody headland; the retiring bay;
> The river pouring its impetuous foam
> From mountain-cliff; the wide expanded gulph
> Spread like a silv'ry lake, with lateen sail
> Of boat, white gleaming 'gainst its purple banks;
> Parnassus' snow-wreath'd bosom shading dark
> The ocean's yellow wave, and Helicon
> In softer lines descending to the plain,
> Successive charm, whilst Corinth's rocky height,
> Half-veil'd in distance, bounds the spacious view.

Hard is his heart, O Corinth! who beholds
Thee bow'd to dust, nor sheds one pitying tear.
William Haygarth, *Greece: A Poem*
(London, 1814)

Wandering in youth, I traced the path of him,
The Roman friend of Rome's least mortal mind,
The friend of Tully: as my bark did skim
The bright blue waters with a fanning wind,
Came Megara before me, and behind
Aegina lay, Piraeus on the right,
And Corinth on the left; I lay reclined
Along the prow, and saw all these unite
In ruin, even as he had seen the desolate sight;

For Time hath not rebuilt them, but uprear'd
Barbaric dwellings on their shatter'd site,
Which only make more mourn'd and more endear'd
The few last rays of their far-scatter'd light,
And the crush'd relics of their vanish'd might.
Lord Byron, *Childe Harold's Pilgrimage*, IV, 44–45

Many a vanish'd year and age,
And tempest's breath, and battle's rage,
Have swept o'er Corinth; yet she stands,
A fortress form'd to Freedom's hands.
The whirlwind's wrath, the earthquake's shock,
Have left untouch'd her hoary rock,
The keystone of a land, which still,
Though fall'n, looks proudly on that hill,
The landmark to the double tide
That purpling rolls on either side,
As if their waters chafed to meet,
Yet pause and crouch beneath her feet.
But could the blood before her shed
Since first Timoleon's brother bled,
Or baffled Persia's despot fled,
Arise from out the earth which drank
The stream of slaughter as it sank,
That sanguine ocean would o'erflow
Her isthmus idly spread below:
Or could the bones of all the slain,
Who perish'd there, be piled again,
That rival pyramid would rise

More mountain-like, through those clear skies,
Than yon tower-capp'd Acropolis,
Which seems the very clouds to kiss.

Lord Byron, The Siege of Corinth

CORINTH
ON LEAVING GREECE

I stood upon that great Acropolis,
The turret-gate of Nature's citadel,
Where once again, from slavery's thick abyss
Strangely delivered, Grecian warriors dwell.
I watcht the bosom of Parnassus swell,
I traced Eleusis, Athens, Salamis,
And that rude fane below, which lives to tell
Where reigned the City of luxurious bliss.
Within the maze of great Antiquity
My spirit wandered tremblingly along;—
As one who with rapt ears to a wild song
Hearkens some while,—then knows not, whether he
Has comprehended all its melody,
So in that parting hour was it with Greece and me.

Richard Monckton Milnes, Memorials of a Tour
in Greece, Chiefly Poetical (London, 1834)

TO CORINTH

Queen of the double sea, beloved of him
Who shakes the world's foundations, thou hast seen
Glory in all her beauty, all her forms;
Seen her walk back with Theseus when he left
The bones of Sciron[2] bleaching to the wind,
Above the ocean's roar and cormorant's flight,
So high that vastest billows from above
Shew but like herbage waving in the mead;
Seen generations throng thine Isthmian games,
And pass away . . . the beautiful, the brave,
And them who sang their praises.
      But, O Queen,
Audible still (and far beyond thy cliffs)
As when they first were uttered, are those words

---

2. A legendary bandit; Theseus hurled him from a cliff into the sea.

Divine which praised the valiant and the just,
And tears have often stopt, upon that ridge
So perilous, him who brought before his eye
The Colchian babes.[3]

      'Stay! spare him! save the last!
Medea! . . . is that blood? again! it drops
From my imploring hand upon my feet . . .
I will invoke the Eumenides no more,
I will forgive thee, bless thee, bend to thee
In all thy wishes . . . do but thou, Medea,
Tell me, one lives.'

      'And shall I too deceive?'
Cries from the fiery car an angry voice;
And swifter than two falling stars descend
Two breathless bodies: warm, soft, motionless,
As flowers in stillest noon before the sun,
They lie three paces from him: such they lie
As when he left them sleeping side by side,
A mother's arm round each, a mother's cheeks
Between them, flushed with happiness and love.
He was more changed than they were . . . doomed to shew
Thee and the stranger, how defaced and scarred
Grief hunts us down the precipice of years,
And whom the faithless prey upon the last.

    To give the inertest masses of our Earth
Her loveliest forms was thine, to fix the Gods
Within thy walls, and hang their tripods round
With fruits and foliage knowing not decay.
A noble work remains: thy citadel
Invites all Greece: o'er lands and floods remote
Many are the hearts that still beat high for thee:
Confide then in thy strength, and unappalled
Look down upon the plain, while yokemate kings
Run bellowing, where their herdsmen goad them on:
Instinct is sharp in them and terror true,
They smell the floor whereon their necks must lie.

Walter Savage Landor

For modern Greek authors, on the other hand, the city seems to
typify much that is strongest and most alive in the Greek tradition.

---

3. The sons of Jason and Medea, whom Medea, the witch from Colchis, murdered as revenge on Jason for his infidelity.

Drinking the Sun of Corinth

Drinking the sun of Corinth
Reading the marble ruins
Striding across vineyards and seas
Sighting along the harpoon
A votive fish that slips away
I found the leaves that the psalm of the sun memorizes
The living land that desire opens joyously.

I drink water, cut fruit,
Thrust my hand into the wind's foliage
The lemon trees irrigate the pollen of summer
The green birds tear my dreams
I leave with a glance
A wide glance in which the world is recreated
Beautiful from the beginning to the dimensions of the heart!

Odysseus Elytis;
translated by E. Keeley and P. Sherrard

On Acrocorinth

The sun set over Acrocorinth
burning the rock red. From the sea
a fragrant smell of seaweed now began
to intoxicate my slender stallion.

Foam on the bit, the white of his eye
bared fully, he struggled to break
my grip, tight on his reins,
to leap free into open space.

Was it the hour? The rich odors?
Was it the sea's deep saltiness?
The forest's breathing far away?
O had the meltemi[4] held strong
a little longer, I'd have known how to grip
the reins and flanks of mythic Pegasus!

Angelos Sikelianos;
translated by E. Keeley and P. Sherrard

4. The fierce wind which blows across the Aegean in the summer months.

7

Attica
(from the Isthmus to Aulis)
and Euboea

Megara

The first town of any size after crossing the Isthmus is Megara, the home in the sixth century B.C. of the aristocratic poet Theognis, author of a series of elegiac poems for singing at parties, many of them lamenting the increasing power of the common people. This did not lessen his affection for the city itself, as this poem shows (translation by Douglas Young of St. Andrews University, who made the major modern edition of Theognis):

> I've been a gangrel bodie, I've been to Sicilie,
> and owre til Euboia wi the vines upon its howe,
> bonnie Sparta on Eurotas where the rashes grow;
> and aa the fowk in ilka place were guid to me.
> But I'd nae rowth o pleisure for aa that I micht see.
> Och, I'd suner be at hame in my ain countrie.
>
> Theognis, 783–88.

Aigina

On the right as you follow the coast road into Athens, Salamis sprawls, soon succeeded by the distinctive peak of the island of Aigina. Aigina was a prosperous city in classical times, earning its wealth largely from its sea trading (which made it a rival to Athens). Many of the island's aristocracy commissioned Pindar to celebrate their athletic victories; he seems to have reciprocated with a genuine fondness for the pleasant island.

> Alcimedon . . .
>
> won in the wrestling and proclaimed
> His fatherland, long-oared Aigina.
> There Saviour Right is honoured
> At the side of Zeus, the strangers' God
>
> Most among men . . .

Charles Cockerell, *Excavations at Aigina*. From Fani-Maria Tsigakou,
Rediscovery of Greece: Travellers and Painters of the Romantic Era (1862)
(detail).

An ordinance of the Immortals
Placed this sea-girt land
As a holy pillar for strangers from everywhere,
—May Time rising ahead
Not weary of doing this—

A Dorian people watch over it
From Aiakos' time.

Pindar, *Olympian*, 8, 20–31;
translated by C. M. Bowra

The island retained its fertility and prosperity during the Turkish period.

> Aegina hath great plenty of corn, cotton, honey and wax;
> also abundance of almonds, and keratia, or carobs. It abounds
> also with a sort of red-legged partridges, that by order of the
> epitropi, or the chief magistrates of the town, all, both young
> and old, women and children, go out yearly, as the pigmies of
> old did against the cranes, to war with them, and to break their
> eggs before they be hatch'd; otherwise, by their multitudes,

they would so destroy, and eat up the corn, that they would inevitably bring a famine every year upon the place. But they say, there are no hares at all in this island.

George Wheeler, *Journey into Greece* (1682)

In April 1811 the young artist C. R. Cockerell, later to achieve fame as one of the foremost, if most idiosyncratic, architects of the Greek Revival (his masterpiece is the Ashmolean Museum in Oxford), was making the Grand Tour in Greece, accompanied by an English friend, John Foster, and two Germans whom he had met in Athens, Jakob Linckh and Karl Haller von Hallerstein. Apparently on an impulse, he chose to excavate at the Temple of Aphaia on Aigina (it was then supposed to be the Temple of Zeus Panhellenius, more famous in the literary sources, but now a shattered ruin on the highest peak of the island). His good fortune was remarkable.

But meanwhile a startling incident had occurred which wrought us all to the highest pitch of excitement. On the second day one of the excavators, working in the interior portico, struck on a piece of Parian marble which, as the building itself is of stone, arrested his attention. It turned out to be the head of a helmeted warrior, perfect in every feature. It lay with the face turned upwards, and as the features came out by degrees you can imagine nothing like the state of rapture and excitement to which we were wrought. Here was an altogether new interest, which set us to work with a will. Soon another head was turned up, then a leg and a foot, and finally, to make a long story short, we found under the fallen portions of the tympanum and the cornice of the eastern and western pediments no less than sixteen statues and thirteen heads, legs, arms, &c. (another account says seventeen and fragments of at least ten more), all in the highest preservation, not 3 feet below the surface of the ground. It seems incredible, considering the number of travellers who have visited the temple, that they should have remained so long undisturbed.

C. R. Cockerell, *Travels in Southern Europe and the Levant* (ed. S. P. Cockerell, London, 1903)

Soon the entire frieze was unearthed, late archaic work of a style hitherto scarcely known. The English and German friends naturally vied as to whose country should have the honor of possessing the marbles. An auction was eventually held at Zante, but owing to a confusion over the venue, the English agent failed to arrive, and the bid of Martin von Wagner, representing Prince Ludwig, secured the marbles for Bavaria. Cockerell redeemed himself some months later, by a second remarkable discovery, of the frieze of the Temple of Apollo Epikourios at Vassai, now in the British Museum.

The beautiful Temple of Aphaia, commanding a matchless view over the Saronic Gulf, inspired the pen of the American poet G. Hill.

The Ruins of the Temple of Jupiter Panhellenius in the Island of Aegina

Lone, from the summit of a lofty isle,
The columns of a ruined temple lift
Their shattered fronts, each with its diadem
Of crumbling architrave and withered weeds.
Nor scroll nor monument records their birth.
A gray fraternity! rough with the dints
Of scars inflicted by the elements—
So old, indeed, and weather-stained they seem
More ancient than the pinnacle they crown.
Their tenants are the rook, vexing the air
With her still ceaseless clamor, the wild bee,
Feeding upon the myrtle-flowers they shade,
And the small martlet, that delights to build
And sport, as 't were in mockery of man,
Where desolation has usurped his seat . . .

G. Hill, *The Ruins of Athens,*
and Other Poems (Boston, 1831)

Eleusis

Eleusis was the home of the great cult of Demeter and her daughter Persephone—the Eleusinian Mysteries—a rite so secret that the efforts of scholars have scarcely been able to unravel its exact nature. Here Demeter sat by the Maiden Well, mourning for her lost Persephone, and was offered hospitality by the women who came to draw water. In the Homeric Hymn to Demeter, the goddess herself explains by a prophecy the origin of the Mysteries:

Demeter: 'At regular seasons, as the years turn, the children of the Eleusinians shall have war and strife between them, for ever. I am Demeter great in honour, who have created the greatest joy and blessing for mortals and immortals. Come now, let the whole people build me a great temple in the city, and an altar within it, and a high wall, on the jutting hill above the spring Callichoron. And I will institute ceremonies, by performing which correctly you shall placate my spirit.'

So speaking the goddess changed her stature and appearance, casting off old age; and beauty poured over her. A delightful scent arose from her spicy garments, and a bright light shone from the immortal flesh of the goddess; her blond hair tumbled over her shoulders, and the stout building was filled with luminescence as if by lightning.

All night they honoured the goddess, trembling with fear . . . and when they had completed their work, each went to his own home. But fair Demeter remained sitting there, pining with longing for her deep-girdled daughter. She made the year most wretched for men on the fruitful earth, for no seeds came up. Demeter of the fair garland hid them all.

Homeric Hymn to Demeter, 265–307 (excerpts); translated by RS

A statue of Demeter herself was perhaps one of the longest continually worshiped objects in human history, as the tale of its recovery shows. Edward Daniel Clarke, who traveled extensively "through Europe, Asia and Africa" in the early years of the nineteenth century, was another figure not averse to Elginian despoliation of antiquities in the cause of science. The story of the discovery of the statue is a typical case, and perhaps also an object lesson.

To heighten the interest with which we regarded the reliques of the Eleusinian fane, and to fulfil the sanguine expectations we had formed, the fragment of a colossal statue, mentioned by many authors as that of the Goddess herself, appeared in colossal majesty among the mouldering vestiges of her once splendid sanctuary. We found it, exactly as it had been described to us by the Consul at Nauplia, on the side of the road, immediately before entering the village, and in the midst of a heap of dung, buried as high as the neck, a little beyond the farther extremity of the pavement of the temple. The inhabitants of the small village which is now situated among the ruins of Eleusis still regarded this statue with a very high degree of superstitious veneration. They attributed to its presence the fertility of their land; and it was for this reason that they heaped around it the manure intended for their fields.

Clarke and his companions, wishing to purchase the statue, made inquiries of the priest, who sent them back to Athens to obtain a firman[1] from the woywode.[2] This done, they made their own dragging frame, which in due course was put into action.

But the superstition of the inhabitants of Eleusis, respecting an idol which they all regarded as the protectress of their fields, was not the least obstacle to be overcome. In the evening, soon after our arrival with the firman, an accident happened which had nearly put an end to the undertaking. While the inhabitants were conversing with the Tchohodar, as to the means of its removal, an ox, loosed from its yoke, came and placed itself before the statue; and, after butting with its horns for some time against the marble, ran off with considerable speed, into the Plain of Eleusis. Instantly a general rumour prevailed: and several women joining in the clamour, it was with difficulty any proposal could be made.

'They had been always', they said, 'famous for their corn; and the fertility of the land would cease when the statue was removed.' Such were exactly the words of Cicero with respect to the Sicilians, when Verres removed the statue of Ceres: quod, Cerere violata, omnes cultus fructusque Cereris in his locis interiisse arbitrantur. It was late at night before these scruples were removed.

Further hindrances, among them the fear of the Eleusinians that anyone who touched the statue would instantly lose his arm, and the need to bridge gaps in the quay, further delayed the transport of the statue, which the following day, 23 November, was eventually put on board a Casiot ship bound for Smyrna to begin its journey to England. The story receives its fitting conclusion in a remark Clarke adds in a footnote:

They predicted the wreck of the ship which should convey it; and it is a curious circumstance, that their augury was completely fulfilled, in the loss of the Princessa merchantman, off Beachy Head, having the statue on board.

E. D. Clarke, *Travels in Various Countries* (London, 1810–23)

The cargo was, however, recovered, and the statue now stands, but little regarded, in the Fitzwilliam Museum at Cambridge.

1. A letter of authority.

2. A provincial governor.

Henry Miller's response to Eleusis is a characteristic passage of his larger-than-life vision of Greece, which has something in common with Kazantzakis. Even words take on new dimensions to cope with the intensity of the vision. (What, after all, is a coryphant? Something between a corybant and a hierophant. . .)

. . . Along the Sacred Way, from Daphni to the sea, I was on the point of madness several times. I actually did start running up the hillside only to stop midway, terror-stricken, wondering what had taken possession of me. On one side are stones and shrubs which stand out with microscopic clarity; on the other are trees such as one sees in Japanese prints, trees flooded with light, intoxicated, coryphantic trees which must have been planted by the gods in moments of drunken exaltation. One should not race along the Sacred Way in a motorcar—it is sacrilege. One should walk, walk as the men of old walked, and allow one's whole being to become flooded with light. This is not a Christian highway: it was made by the feet of devout pagans on their way to initiation at Eleusis. There is no suffering, no martyrdom, no flagellation of the flesh connected with this processional artery. Everything here speaks now, as it did centuries ago, of illumination, of blinding, joyous illumination. Light acquires a transcendental quality: it is not the light of the Mediterranean alone, it is something more, something unfathomable, something holy. Here the light penetrates directly to the soul, opens the doors and windows of the heart, makes one naked, exposed, isolated in a metaphysical bliss which makes everything clear without being known. No analysis can go on in this light: here the neurotic is either instantly healed or goes mad. The rocks themselves are quite mad: they have been lying for centuries exposed to this divine illumination: they lie very still and quiet, nestling amid dancing coloured shrubs in a blood-stained soil, but they are mad, I say, and to touch them is to risk losing one's grip on everything which once seemed firm, solid and unshakeable. One must glide through this gully with extreme caution, naked, alone, and devoid of all Christian humbug. One must throw off two thousand years of ignorance and superstition, of morbid, sickly subterranean living and lying. One must come to Eleusis stripped of the barnacles which have accumulated from centuries of lying in stagnant waters. At Eleusis one realizes, if never before, that there is no salvation in becoming adapted to a world which is crazy. At Eleusis one becomes adapted to the cosmos. Outwardly Eleusis may seem broken, disinte-

grated with the crumbled past; actually Eleusis is still intact
and it is we who are broken, dispersed, crumbling to dust.
Eleusis lives, lives eternally in the midst of a dying world.

Henry Miller*, *The Colossus of Maroussi* (1941)

Mount Hymettus

Skirting Athens, we reach Hymettus, deliciously described by Ovid:

> Near, where his purple head Hymettus shows
> And flow'ring hills, a sacred fountain flows,
> With soft and verdant turf the soil is spread,
> And sweetly-smelling shrubs the ground o'ershade.
> There rosemary and bays their odours join,
> And with the fragrant myrtle's scent combine.
> There tamarisks with thick-leav'd box are found,
> And cytisus and garden-pines abound.
> While through the boughs, soft winds of Zephyr pass,
> Tremble the leaves and tender tops of grass.
> Hither would Cephalus[3] retreat to rest,
> When tir'd with hunting, or with heat opprest;
> And, thus, to Air, the panting youth would pray;
> 'Come, gentle Aura, come, this heat allay.'

Ovid, *Art of Love*, III, 687–99;
translated by William Congreve

Theocritus is hard to catch napping; but Ovid, for example, tells us that buxus grows on Mount Hymettus. There is no
box on Hymettus, though it prospers in certain gardens in
Athens (e.g. the Crown Prince's); Ovid was thinking of the
dwarf holly. It is the worst of writing poetry that you are apt to
be torn between respect for truth and the exigencies of scan-
sion. What would the painfully correct Lucretius have done
with buxus?

Norman Douglas, *Together* (London, 1923)

3. When out hunting, Cephalus would lie down on the grass, saying "come, gentle Aura
[breeze]; come, this heat allay." When his wife, Procris, heard of this she was jealous,
thinking that Aura was his mistress, so she followed him and hid in some bushes to
watch him; he heard a rustling and, supposing that it was a wild animal, threw his spear
in the bushes and killed her.

Sounion (Sunium)

The southern tip of Attica is adorned by the marble temple of Poseidon, a landmark for sailors in the Gulf and a regular place of excursion from Athens ever since tourism began. The central scene of William Falconer's *The Shipwreck* (1762) is set off Cape Colonna, as it was then called:

> But now Athenian mountains they descry,
> And o'er the surge Colonna frowns on high;
> Where marble columns, long by time defaced,
> Moss-covered on the lofty Cape are placed;
> There reared by fair devotion to sustain
> In elder times Tritonia's sacred fane;
> The circling beach in murderous form appears,
> Decisive goal of all their hopes and fears:
> The seamen now in wild amazement see
> The scene of ruin rise beneath their lee;
> Swift from their minds elapsed all dangers past,
> As dumb with terror they behold the last.

>   ·⤳

> Roused by the blustering tempest of the night,
> A troop of Grecians mount Colonna's height;
> When gazing down with horror on the flood,
> Full to their view the scene of ruin stood—
> The surf with mangled bodies strewed around,
> And those yet-breathing on the sea-washed ground:
> Though lost to science and nobler arts,
> Yet nature's lore informed their feeling hearts;
> Straight down the vale with hastening steps they hied,
> The unhappy sufferers to assist, and guide.

> William Falconer, The Shipwreck, III

Byron had an equally exciting visit to Sounion, which he describes in a letter to his traveling companion, John Cam Hobhouse:

> *P.S.—Decr. 5th. 1810.*
> Dear Cam, —I open my letter to mention an escape; Graham, Cockerell, Lusieri, myself, and a Bavarian Baron, went to Cape Colonna where we spent a day.—At that time five and twenty Mainnotes (pirates) were in the caves at the foot of the cliff with some Greek boatmen their prisoners.—They demanded of these who were the Franks above? one of the Greeks knew me, and they were preparing to attack us, when seeing my Albanians and conjecturing there were others in

William Pars, *Sunium*. Copyright British Museum, London.

the vicinity, they were seized with a panic and marched off.—
We were all armed (about 12 with our attendants) some with
fusils & all with pistols and ataghans, but though we were prepared for resistance, I am inclined to think we are rather better
without a battle.—Some of the Greeks whom they had taken,
told me afterwards they saw me with my double barrell
mounted on a chestnut horse, and described the rest of our
party very accurately.—Two of them arrived yesterday,
released, but stripped of every thing by the Mainnotes.—
These last deliberated some time, but as we were in a very
advantageous position among the columns, ignorant of our
numbers, and alarmed by some balls which whizzed over their
heads by accident, they kept to the shore, and permitted us to
depart in peace.—The Albanians, my Turkish bandy legged
Cook, a servant of Lusieri's & myself had guns and pistols,
the rest side arms and pistols, but how we should have carried
on the war is very doubtful, I rather think we should have been
taen like Billy Taylor and carried off to Sea.—We are all snug
in our winter quarters after the same tour we made last year.—
Graham and myself got drunk at Keratia, the former in his
Bacchanism decapitated a large pig with a Highland
Broadsword to the horror of Lusieri, and after all we could not
eat him.—Good bye, Yani,

yrs. a second time
BxxxxxxxxxxxxxxxxxxxxxxxN.—

Things had not changed at the end of the century, when a group
of English tourists were abducted by bandits at this precise spot.

The story has been told by Romilly Jenkins in *The Dilessi Murders*, and was in 1981 the theme of Angelopoulos's film, *Alexander the Great*.

H. W. Williams visited the temple not long after Byron, and also left his impressions (including a severe comment on such barbarisms as the prominently carved "BYRON" on one of the columns).

> You may be sure we did not tarry long before we proceeded to the temple. All was wild and desolate, impressing the mind with melancholy thoughts. The place where Plato and his scholars once assembled is now a trackless waste. Only fourteen columns of the temple now remain, of the whitest Parian marble, some of them greatly corroded by time, and dislocated by lightning. As seen by us they were relieved against the sky; but when the white clouds appeared behind them, the temple was just perceptible, and looked like a faint vision of a thing that had been! All was still as death, save the murmuring of the waves below, polishing the fallen marbles into pebbles on the shore, and degrading them into dust, to be blown before the winds of heaven! Pure as this temple is, like a mild and decaying beauty, yet it has not escaped from the rude hands of British sailors, being besmeared with black paint or pitch, and names written in letters at least two feet in height all round the architrave. Centuries (if the temple shall stand so long) will be required to eradicate the mischief. I shall forbear mentioning the name of the ship which occupies the whole of the front next the sea, nor shall I give the names of those who have been so barbarous; but I advise our Scotish youths to reflect a little, before they again proceed to such wantonness. They, of all others, should be grateful for the stream of light which has flowed from Greece, and accordingly should respect her few remains.
>
> H. W. Williams, *Travels in Italy, Greece and the Ionian Islands*
> (London, 1840)

The Abbé Barthélemy makes Anacharsis, the hero of his turgid and encyclopaedic novel, visit Sounion in the company of Plato, amid a thunderstorm of copybook sublimity. Sounion seems to have appealed to the taste for the Sublime. Herman Melville was as enthusiastic as his predecessors.

OFF CAPE COLONNA

Aloof they crown the foreland lone,
    From aloft they loftier rise—

Fair columns, in the aureola rolled
    From sunned Greek seas and skies.
They wax, sublimed to fancy's view,
A god-like group against the blue.
Over much like gods! Serene they saw
    The wolf-waves board the deck,
And headlong hull of Falconer,
    And many a deadlier wreck.

                     Herman Melville

Marathon

North of Sounion lies the plain of Marathon, with its massive mound covering the bodies of the Greeks killed resisting the Persian invasion in 490 B.C. According to Pausanias (1, 32, 3) the site echoes every night with the sound of horses whinnying and men fighting.

The news of the victory of Marathon was brought to Athens by the runner Pheidippides, who crossed Mt. Parnes without stopping, and was met by the god Pan as he went. Browning's Pheidippides describes the occasion:

Athens,— except for that sparkle,—thy name, I had
    mouldered to ash!
That sent a blaze through my blood; off, off and away was
    I back,
—Not one word to waste, one look to lose on the false and
    the vile!
Yet 'O Gods of my land!' I cried, as each hillock and plain,
Wood and stream, I knew, I named, rushing past them again,
'Have ye kept faith, proved mindful of honours we paid you
    ere-while?
Vain was the filleted victim, the fulsome libation! Too rash
Love in its choice, paid you so largely service so slack!

'Oak and olive and bay,—I bid you cease to enwreathe
Brows made bold by your leaf! Fade at the Persian's foot,
You that, our patrons were pledged, should never adorn
    a slave!
Rather I hail thee, Parnes,—trust to thy wild waste tract!
Treeless, herbless, lifeless mountain! What matter if slacked
My speed may hardly be, for homage to crag and to cave
No deity deigns to drape with verdure? at least I can breathe,
Fear in thee no fraud from the blind, no lie from the mute!'

Such my cry as, rapid, I ran over Parnes' ridge;
Gully and gap I clambered and cleared till, sudden, a bar
Jutted, a stoppage of stone against me, blocking the way.
Right! for I minded the hollow to traverse, the fissure across:
'Where I could enter, there I depart by! Night in the fosse?
Athens to aid? Though the dive were through Erebos, thus
　　　I obey—
Out of the day dive, into the day as bravely arise! No bridge
Better!'—when—ha! what was it I came on, of wonders
　　　that are?

There, in the cool of a cleft, sat he—majestical Pan!
Ivy drooped wanton, kissed his head, moss cushioned
　　　his hoof:
All the great God was good in the eyes grave-kindly—
　　　the curl
Carved on the bearded cheek, amused at a mortal's awe,
As, under the human trunk, the goat-thighs grand I saw.
'Halt, Pheidippides!'—halt I did, my brain of a whirl:
'Hither to me! Why pale in my presence?' he gracious began:
'How is it,—Athens, only in Hellas, holds me aloof?

'Athens, she only, rears me no fane, makes me no feast!
Wherefore? Than I what godship to Athens more helpful
　　　of old?
Ay, and still, and forever her friend! Test Pan, trust me!
Go, bid Athens take heart, laugh Persia to scorn, have faith
In the temples and tombs! Go, say to Athens, "The Goat-
　　　God saith:
When Persia—so much as strews not the soil—is cast in
　　　the sea,
Then praise Pan who fought in the ranks with your most
　　　and least,
Goat-thigh to greaved-thigh, made one cause with the free
　　　and the bold!"

'Say Pan saith: "Let this, foreshowing the place, be
　　　the pledge!"'
(Gay, the liberal hand held out the herbage I bear
—Fennel—I grasped it a-tremble with dew—whatever
　　　it bode)
'While, as for thee . . .' But enough! He was gone. If I
　　　ran hitherto—
Be sure that, the rest of my journey, I ran no longer, but flew.
Parnes to Athens—earth no more, the air was my road:

Here am I back. Praise Pan, we stand no more on the
    razor's edge!
Pan for Athens, Pan for me! I too have a guerdon rare!
                Robert Browning, *Pheidippides*

Colonus

Circling back to the north of Athens we reach Colonus, in antiquity
the birthplace of Sophocles and, according to legend, the place
where Oedipus was translated to heaven. It is now a suburb of
Athens. Sophocles' chorus describing the place is one of his loveliest set pieces, and Yeats's translation is its equal:

Colonus' Praise

Come praise Colonus' horses, and come praise
The wine-dark of the wood's intricacies,
The nightingale that deafens daylight there,
If daylight ever visit where,
Unvisited by tempest or by sun,
Immortal ladies tread the ground
Dizzy with harmonious sound,
Semele's lad[4] a gay companion.

And yonder in the gymnasts' garden thrives
The self-sown, self-begotten shape that gives
Athenian intellect its mastery,
Even the grey-leaved olive-tree
Miracle-bred out of the living stone;
Nor accident of peace nor war
Shall wither that old marvel, for
The great grey-eyed Athene stares thereon.

Who comes into this country, and has come
Where golden crocus and narcissus bloom,
Where the Great Mother, mourning for her daughter
And beauty-drunken by the water
Glittering among grey-leaved olive-trees,
Has plucked a flower and sung her loss;
Who finds abounding Cephisus[5]
Has found the loveliest spectacle there is.

4. The god Dionysus.
5. River of Athens.

Because this country has a pious mind
And so remembers that when all mankind
But trod the road, or splashed about the shore,
Poseidon gave it bit and oar,
Every Colonus lad or lass discourses
Of that oar and of that bit;
Summer and winter, day and night,
Of horses and horses of the sea, white horses.

> Sophocles, *Oedipus at Colonus*, 668–719;
> translated by W. B. Yeats

Oropos

Heracleides (second or first century B.C.) describes the road out of
Athens to the sanctuary of Amphiaraus at Oropos. The seer
Amphiaraus fought with the Seven against Thebes; when defeat was
unavoidable, he was saved from death as the earth swallowed him
up. He reemerged, a hero, at Oropos.

> From Athens to Oropos by Psaphides and the sanctuary of Zeus
> Amphiaraus is a day's journey for a good walker. It is all up-hill,[6]
> but the abundance and good cheer of the inns prevent the trav-
> eller from feeling the fatigue. Oropos is a nest of hucksters. The
> greed of the custom-house officers here is unsurpassed, their
> roguery inveterate and bred in the bone. Most of the people
> are coarse and truculent in their manners, for they have
> knocked the decent members of the community on the head.
> They deny they are Boeotians, standing out for it that they are
> Athenians living in Boeotia. To quote the poet Xeno:

> All are custom-house officers, all are robbers.
> A plague on the Oropians!

> > Heracleides; translated by J. G. Frazer
> > in *Pausanias and other Greek Sketches*
> > (London, 1900)

6. This is an odd mistake. In point of fact half of the way is uphill and the other half is
downhill. The road rises first gently and then steeply to the summit of the pass over
Mount Parnes not far from the ancient Decelea; thence it descends, at first rapidly in
sharp serpentine curves, then gradually through a rolling woodland country to the sea
at Oropos. [Frazer's note.]

Aulis

It was at Aulis that the fleet gathered for the expedition to Troy, and was becalmed until Agamemnon propitiated Artemis with the sacrifice of his daughter Iphigeneia. The story was the theme of Euripides' *Iphigeneia at Aulis;* the chorus of this play consists of women of Chalcis, who describe the encampment:

CHORUS OF THE WOMEN OF CHALKIS

I crossed sand-hills.
I stand among the sea-drift before Aulis.

I crossed Euripos' strait—
Foam hissed after my boat.

I left Chalkis,
My city and the rock-ledges.
Arethusa twists among the boulders,
Increases—cuts into the surf.

I come to see the battle-line
And the ships rowed here
By these spirits—
The Greeks are but half-man.

Golden Menelaus
And Agamemnon of proud birth
Direct the thousand ships.

They have cut pine-trees
For their oars.
They have gathered the ships for one purpose:
Helen shall return.

There are clumps of marsh-reed
And spear-grass about the strait.
Paris the herdsman passed through them
When he took Helen—Aphrodite's gift.

For he had judged the goddess
More beautiful than Hera.
Pallas was no longer radiant
As the three stood
Among the fresh-shallows of the strait.

I crept through the woods
Between the altars:
Artemis haunts the place.

Shame, scarlet, fresh-opened—a flower,
Strikes across my face.
And sudden—light upon shields,
Low huts—the armed Greeks,
Circles of horses . . .

Euripides, Iphigeneia at Aulis, 164–91;
translated by HD

Euboea

Between Aulis and Chalcis lies the Euripus, a uniquely tidal stretch of the Mediterranean, where the direction of flow of the water in the narrow passage between the mainland and the island of Euboea changes every hour or so. This made the short crossing treacherous, especially for a landlubber like the poet Hesiod.

I'll set before thee all the trim and dress
Of those still-roaring-noise-resounding seas,
Though neither skill'd in either ship or sail,
Nor ever was at sea; or, least I fail,
But for Euboea once from Aulis, where
The Greeks, with tempest driv'n, for shore did stere
Their mighty navy, gather'd to employ
For sacred Greece 'gainst fair-dame-breeding Troy;
To Chalcis there I made by sea my pass,
And to the Games of great Amphidamas,
Where many a fore-studied exercise
Was instituted, with exciteful prize,
For great-and-good and able-minded men;
And where I won, at the Pierian Pen,
A three-ear'd tripod, which I offer'd on
The altars of the Maids of Helicon;
Where first their loves initiated me
In skill of their unworldly harmony.

Hesiod, Works and Days, 648–62;
translated by George Chapman

William Lithgow did not enjoy his visit to Euboea (then called Negropont).

Hoysing saile from Dalamede, we set over to Nigroponti, being sixty miles distant, and bearing up eastward to double the south cape, we straight discovered two Turkish galleots pursuing us: whereupon with both sailes and oars, we sought in to the bottome of a long creeke, on the west side of the cape, called Bajo di piscatori; whither also fled nine fisher-boats for refuge: the galleots fearing to follow us in, went to ankor, at a rocky isolet in the mouth of the bay, and then within night were resolved to assail us. But night come, and every night of sixe (for there six days they expected us) we made such bon-fires, that so affrighted them (being two miles from any village) they durst never adventure it: yet I being a stranger was exposed by the untoward Greekes to stand centinel every night, on the top of a high promontore, it being the dead time of a snowy and frosty winter; which did invite my Muse to bewaile the tossing of my toylesome life, my solitary wandring, and the long distance of my native soyle:

> Carmina secessum scribantis, & otia quaerunt
> Me mare, me venti, me fera jactat hyems.

I wander in exile,
 As though my pilgrimage
Were sweete comedian scaenes of love
 Upon a golden stage.
Ah I, poore I, distres'd,
 Oft changing to and fro,
Am forc'd to sing sad obsequies
 Of this my swan-like wo.
A vagabonding guest,
 Transported here and there,
Let with the mercy-wanting winds
 Of feare, griefe, and dispaire.
Thus ever-moving I,
 To restlesse journeys thrald,
Obtaines by Times triumphing frownes
 A calling, unrecal'd:
Was I praeordain'd so
 Like Tholos Ghost to stand
Three times foure houres, in twenty foure
 With musket in my hand.
Ore-blasted with the stormes
 Of winter-beating snow,
And frosty pointed jaile-stones hard
 On me poore wretch to blow.
No architecture lo
 But whirling windy skies.
O'er-syl'd with thundring claps of clouds,
 Earths center to surprise.

I, I, it is my fate,
    Allots this fatall crosse,
And reckons up in characters,
    The time of my times losse.
My destiny is such,
    Which doth predestine me,
To be a mirrour of mishaps,
    A mappe of misery.
Extreamely doe I live,
    Extreames are all my joy,
I find in deepe extreamities,
    Extreames, extreame annoy.
Now all alone I watch,
    With Argoes eyes and wit.
A cypher twixt the Greekes and Turkes
    Upon this rock I sit.
A constrain'd captive I,
    Mongst incompassionate Greekes,
Bare-headed, downeward bowes my head,
    And liberty still seekes.
But all my sutes are vaine,
    Heaven sees my wofull state:
Which makes me say, my world's eye-sight
    Is bought at too high rate.
Would God I might but live,
    To see my native soyle:

[The poem concludes in reminiscences and praise of Lanarkshire.]

William Lithgow, *Totall Discourse of the
Rare Adventures and Painefull Peregrinations*
(London, 1632)

A final anecdote from Euboea.

To the south of the castle is a new plattforme with several very large gunns, which carry stoneshot of about eighteen inches diameter. When I was there in the year 1676 a Renegado was taken; he was a Greek born on the island of Candy; afterwards he married at Scio, and lived very well; but upon some discontent he made his escape from Scio, and got to the privateers of Malta, with whom he lived for some years;

and landing on this island, he with some others were surprized, and taken. His companions were condemned to the gallys, but his sentence was to be shott away, out of one of these great gunns, which was accordingly effected.

Bernard Randolph, *The Present State of the Islands in the Archipelago* (London, 1687)

8

Athens

Ludwig Lange, *Reconstruction View of the Acropolis from the East*. Staatliche
Graphische Sammlung, Munich (detail).

Athens arose: a city such as vision
  Builds from the purple crags and silver towers
Of battlemented cloud, as in derision
  Of kingliest masonry: the ocean-floors
Pave it; the evening sky pavilions it;
    Its portals are inhabited
    By thunder-zoned winds, each head
Within its cloudy wings with sun-fire garlanded,—
  A divine work! Athens, diviner yet,
    Gleamed with its crest of columns, on the will
Of man, as on a mount of diamond, set;
    For thou wert, and thine all-creative skill
Peopled, with forms that mock the eternal dead
    In marble immortality, that hill
    Which was thine earliest throne and latest oracle.
                    P. B. Shelley, *Ode to Liberty*

Few cities have attracted more encomium, more descriptive and historical writing, more laments for their past glories, than Athens. Athens has stood as a symbol of Greece, the quintessence of Greece's power to arouse emotion, as the barometer of feeling has swayed across the centuries. Shelley's lines are one peak of that continuous chain of sentiment. The tradition goes back at least to Euripides' chorus in praise of Athens in *Medea;* before that, Pindar, in a poem now largely lost, praises Athens in terms more succinct than Shelley's but no less flattering:

> O shining, violet-crowned, song-famed
> bulwark of Greece,
> illustrious Athens,
> city of the gods . . .
>
> Pindar, fragment 76;
> translated by RS

According to tradition, this praise of a rival city, with a political constitution so at variance with its own, was too much for the authorities in Pindar's native Thebes, who had him fined a sum variously given as 1,000 and 10,000 drachmas (C. M. Bowra, *Pindar*, 143). Clearly the Athenians at any rate lapped up the praise: Aristophanes mocks at the popularity of the lines:

> For before, when an embassy came from the states,
> intriguing your favour to gain,
> And called you the town of the violet crown,
> so grand and exalted ye grew,
> That at once on your tiptails erect ye would sit,
> those crowns were so pleasant to you.
> And then, if they added the shiny, they got
> whatever they asked for their praises,
> Though apter, I ween, for an oily sardine
> than for you and your city the phrase is.
>
> Aristophanes, *Acharnians,* 636–40,
> translated by B. B. Rogers

A more measured and rational, but no less wholehearted celebration of the achievements of classical Athens are the famous lines spoken by Satan to Christ in Milton's *Paradise Regain'd*, offering him dominion there—the greatest of temptations for a classic soul:

Look once more e're we leave this specular Mount
Westward, much nearer by Southwest, behold
Where on the Aegean shore a City stands
Built nobly, pure the air, and light the soil,
Athens the eye of Greece, Mother of Arts
And Eloquence, native to famous wits
Or Hospitable, in her sweet recess,
City or Suburban, studious walks and shades;
See there the Olive Grove of Academe,
Plato's retirement, where the Attic Bird
Trills her thick-warbl'd notes the summer long,
There flowrie hill Hymettus with the sound
Of Bees industrious murmur oft invites
To studious musing; there Ilissus rouls
His whispering stream; within the walls then view
The schools of antient Sages; his who bred
Great Alexander to subdue the world,
Lyceum there, and painted Stoa next:
There thou shalt hear and learn the secret power
Of harmony in tones and numbers hit
By voice or hand, and various-measur'd verse,
Aeolian charms and Dorian Lyric Odes,
And his who gave them breath, but higher sung,
Blind Melesigenes thence Homer call'd,
Whose poem Phoebus challeng'd for his own.
Thence what the lofty grave Tragedians taught
In chorus or Iambic, teachers best
Of moral prudence, with delight receiv'd
In brief sententious precepts, while they treat
Of fate, and chance, and change in human life;
High actions, and high passions best describing:
Thence to the famous Orators repair,
Those antient, whose resistless eloquence
Wielded at will that fierce Democratie,
Shook the Arsenal and fulmin'd over Greece,
To Macedon, and Artaxerxes' Throne;
To sage Philosophy next lend thine ear,
From Heaven descended to the low-rooft house
Of Socrates, see there his Tenement,
Whom well-inspir'd the Oracle pronounc'd
Wisest of men; from whose mouth issu'd forth
Mellifluous streams that water'd all the schools

Of Academics old and new, with those
Sirnam'd Peripatetics, and the Sect
Epicurean, and the Stoic severe;
These here revolve, or, as thou lik'st, at home,
Till time mature thee to a Kingdom's waight;
These rules will render thee a King compleat
Within thy self, much more with Empire joyn'd.

John Milton, *Paradise Regain'd*, IV, 236–84

Among the present-day traffic and turmoil of Athens, it is difficult
to picture any haven of peace, a pleasance; but such in former times
was the land around the river Ilissus, which trickled past the Temple
of Olympian Zeus and the Hill of the Muses, and where
Socrates was once induced by his pupil Phaedrus to walk, straying
from his usual territory in the agora, and the proximity of the
human race.

> **Soc.** Let us turn aside and go by the Ilissus; we will sit
> down at some quiet spot.
> **Phaedr.** I am fortunate in not having my sandals, and as
> you never have any, I think that we may go along the brook
> and cool our feet in the water; this will be the easiest way, and
> at midday and in the summer is far from being unpleasant.
> **Soc.** Lead on, and look out for a place in which we can
> sit down.
> **Phaedr.** Do you see that tallest plane-tree in the distance?
> **Soc.** Yes.
> **Phaedr.** There are shade and gentle breezes, and grass on
> which we may either sit or lie down.
> **Soc.** Move forward.
> **Phaedr.** I should like to know, Socrates, whether the
> place is not somewhere here at which Boreas is said to have
> carried off Orithyia from the banks of the Ilissus?
> **Soc.** Such is the tradition.
> **Phaedr.** And is this the exact spot? The little stream is
> delightfully clear and bright; I can fancy that there might be
> maidens playing near.
> **Soc.** I believe that the spot is not exactly here, but about
> a quarter of a mile lower down, where you cross to the shrine
> of Agra, and there is, I think, some sort of an altar of Boreas
> at the place.
> **Phaedr.** I have never noticed it; but I beseech you to tell
> me, Socrates, do you believe this tale?
> **Soc.** The wise are doubtful, and I should not be singular

Carl Rottmann, *Athens from the Temple of the Olympian Zeus.* Staatliche Graphische Sammlung, Munich (detail).

if, like them, I too doubted. I might have a rational explanation that Orithyia was playing with Pharmacia, when a northern gust carried her over the neighbouring rocks; and this being the manner of her death, she was said to have been carried away by Boreas. There is a discrepancy, however, about the locality; according to another version of the story she was taken from the Areopagus, and not from this place. Now I quite acknowledge that these allegories are very nice, but he is not to be envied who has to invent them; much labour and ingenuity will be required of him; and when he has once begun, he must go on and rehabilitate Hippocentaurs and chimeras dire. Gorgons and winged steeds flow in apace, and numberless other inconceivable and portentous natures. And if he is sceptical about them, and would fain reduce them one after another to the rules of probability, this sort of crude philosophy will take up a great deal of time. Now I have no leisure for such inquiries; shall I tell you why? I must first know myself, as the Delphian inscription says; to be curious about that which is not my concern, while I am still in ignorance of my own self, would be ridiculous. And therefore I bid farewell to all this; the common opinion is enough for me. For, as I was saying, I want to know not about this, but about myself: am I a monster more complicated and swollen with passion than Typho, or a creature of a gentler and simpler sort, possessing, by divine grace, a nature devoid of pride? But meanwhile let me ask you, friend: have we not reached the plane-tree to which you were conducting us?

Phaedr. Yes, this is the tree.

Soc. By Hera, a fair resting-place, full of summer sounds and scents. Here is this lofty and spreading plane-tree, and the agnus castus high and clustering, in the fullest blossom and the greatest fragrance; and the stream which flows beneath the plane-tree is deliciously cold to the feet. Judging from the ornaments and images, this must be a spot sacred to Achelous and the Nymphs. How delightful is the breeze; so very sweet; and there is a sound in the air shrill and summerlike which makes answer to the chorus of the cicadae. But the greatest charm of all is the grass, like a pillow gently sloping to the head. My dear Phaedrus, you have been an admirable guide.

Soc. Should we not offer up a prayer first of all to the local deities?

Phaedr. By all means.

Soc. Beloved Pan, and all ye other gods who haunt this place, give me beauty in the inward soul; and may the outward and inward man be at one. May I reckon the wise to be the wealthy, and may I have such a quantity of gold as a temperate man and he only can bear and carry.

Plato, *Phaedrus*, 229a–230c, 279bc;
translated by B. Jowett

Heracleides of Crete, who wrote a description of Greece in the second or first century B.C., which was formerly attributed to Dicaearchus of Messene, describes the Athenian scene at that time:

The road to Athens is a pleasant one, running between cultivated fields the whole way. The city itself is dry and ill supplied with water. The streets are nothing but miserable old lanes, the houses mean, with a few better ones among them. On his first arrival a stranger could hardly believe that this is the Athens of which he has heard so much. Yet he will soon come to believe that it is Athens indeed. A Music Hall, the most beautiful in the world, a large and stately theatre, a costly, remarkable, and far-seen temple of Athena called the Parthenon rising above the theatre, strike the beholder with

Dmitri Constantin, *The Acropolis from the Southwest, Athens.* The J. Paul Getty Museum, Malibu, California.

admiration. A temple of Olympian Zeus, unfinished but planned on an astonishing scale; three gymnasiums, the Academy, Lyceum, and Cynosarges, shaded with trees that spring from greensward; verdant gardens of philosophers; amusements and recreations; many holidays and a constant succession of spectacles—all these the visitor will find in Athens.

The products of the country are priceless in quality but not too plentiful. However, the frequency of the spectacles and holidays makes up for the scarcity to the poorer sort, who forget the pangs of hunger in gazing at the shows and pageants. Every artist is sure of being welcomed with applause and of making a name; hence the city is crowded with statues.

Of the inhabitants some are Attic and some are Athenian. The former are gossiping, slanderous, given to prying into the business of strangers, fair and false. The Athenians are high-minded, straight-forward, and staunch in friendship. The city is infested by a set of scribblers who worry visitors and rich strangers. When the people catches the rascals, it makes an example of them. The true-born Athenians are keen and critical auditors, constant in their attendance at plays and spectacles. In short, Athens as far surpasses all other cities in the pleasures and conveniences of life as they surpass the country. But a man must be aware of the courtesans, lest they lure him to ruin. The verses of Lysippus run thus:

> If you have not seen Athens, you're a stock;
> If you have seen it and are not taken with it, you're
>> an ass;
> If you are glad to leave it, you're a pack-ass.
>> Heracleides; translated by J. G. Frazer in *Pausanias*
>> *and Other Greek Sketches* (London, 1900)

Athens under Roman rule remained the university of the Empire, a cultural magnet for educated Romans. The poet, Propertius, was not the first or the last to try to evade a *grande passion* by a Grand Tour, in defiance of Horace's advice, *caelum non animum mutant qui trans mare currunt* ("They change their sky, not heart, who cross the sea").

> To break this hard passion
>> I must make the great journey,
>> Take the long road
>>> To erudite Athens,
> And perhaps the flame
>>> Constantly arising
>> As I gaze at her raptly
>> Will then subside.
> The fire feeds on itself and grows;
>> I have tried all the patent medicines,
>>> But desire stays lodged in my heart,
>> Eros oppresses me.
> Her invitations are now few, refusals frequent,
>> and when she condescends to lie with me
>> she sleeps on the far edge of the bed,
>>> in her clothes.
> One remedy remains: to leave
>> to shift my ground.
> The road that removes me from her sight
>> may remove her from my heart.
> Come now, my fellow wayfarers,
>>> pull the ship into the sea,
>>> draw lots for our duty,
>>> draw the auspicious sail to mast top
>>>> and weigh anchor
>>> when the overslung sky
>>>> favors the course of mariners
>>>>> on the glassy sea.

Farewell my friends,
  and farewell to the proud walls of Rome,
  and goodbye my beloved
   for what you were to me.
I will now be floated through rumbling breakers
    to the tune of my prayers to the sea
     roaring gods
  through the Ionian Sea to the calm port of Lechaeum,
and the sails will be hauled down
   the small ship's mast.
From there, where the Corinthian isthmus
  cleaves the two seas,
I will foot the remainder of the road
  to Piraeus
  and I will mount the ramp of Theseus,
  slanting through the long walls up to Athens.
In Plato's school and Epicurus' garden
  I may begin to enlarge my wisdom
   and reap learned Menander's fruit,
and I will undertake rhetoric, the sword of Demosthenes.
  Of course I will take in the great paintings
   and please my eyes with the bronzework and
   the ivory.
Either the interval of years, or the long seas rolling
  between us,
  shall erase the scar in my heart;
If I die, it will be fate's work, not Aphrodite's,
  and I will not die in dishonor.

Propertius, III, 21;
translated by J. P. McCulloch

With the decline of the Roman Empire, Athens, like other cities of Greece, shrank and fell into ignominy and poverty. One stage in the decline is described by Synesius of Cyrene, the bishop of Ptolemais in Egypt, who visited the city in A.D. 395 and described his reactions to his brother:

> May the sailor who brought me here die miserably: Athens contains nothing magnificent except its place names. When a sacrificial victim is burnt, only the skin remains as an indication of what animal that once was: just so, now that philosophy has deserted Athens, all that remains is to wander and wonder at the Academy and the Lyceum; and that colourful portico, from which the sect of Chrysippus took its name (not

that there is much colour in it now. The proconsul has removed the panels on which Polygnotus of Thasos had expended all his art). In our day, Egypt nourishes the seeds of wisdom taken from Hypatia; Athens was indeed once a city, the home of the wise; now it is inhabited by bee-keepers. The Plutarchean philosophers are very conscious of this, and they attract the young to the theatres, not by the reputation of their rhetoric, but by amphoras of Hymettian honey.

Synesius, Letters, 135 (Migne); translated by RS

The silence of the Dark Ages falls on Athens under the Byzantine Empire, that great civilization notable for the extraordinary paucity of literary work of merit it produced after the age of Justinian (which is not to deny its value to us in the preservation and organization of the works of classical literature). The charming and scurrilous novel of Emanuel Royidis, *Pope Joan*, of the eighteenth century, evokes a vivid imaginary picture of Athens in the ninth century, when no contemporary voice is recorded for our information.

Deprived of its idols and altars Athens resembled nothing so much as a blind Polyphemus. In every niche where once a statue had stood they found a cross; instead of temples they now found small ugly domed churches resembling stone periwigs. These had been built by the Athenian Eudocia, who, wishing to honour every saint with a private residence, had been compelled to undertake this horde of chapels, giving more honour, it would seem, to the industry of the beaver than to the dignity of the 'Unknown God'. At the porches of these chapels were seated the monks and anchorites of the town, scratching at old parchments or at ulcers and weaving rush baskets as they breakfasted on onions. Only the classic beauty of the Athenian girls was left for the two strangers to admire. In that age, of course, Athens was the harem of the Byzantine emperors. They gathered the loveliest girls from the town as later the Sultans did from Circassia. The improvement of the standard of Attic beauty began, as a matter of fact, with the Iconomachy: for when the Byzantine images were cast down the women of Athens, instead of being forced to gaze upon gaunt Panagias and rachitic saints, were able to lift their eyes to the bas reliefs of the Parthenon, and bring forth their children in their image. From this point of view, and for the good of the children, it would seem almost advisable to reform our ecclesiastical iconography—for who can deny this sort of influence, for example, in the wives of the Jewish bankers of

Prussia? Their children bear so close a resemblance to King William as justly to be called his subjects; and this comes about from the incessant counting of thalers and florins bearing the stamp of the king's head.

Lawrence Durrell, *Pope Joan* (London, 1948);
adapted from the Greek of Emanuel Royidis

At the end of the twelfth century, the cultured Michael Acominatus of Chonae in Asia Minor (elder brother of the historian Nicetas), who had been educated in Constantinople under the great Eustathius, the commentator on Homer, was made bishop of Athens. Gregorovius calls him "the last great citizen and the last glory of that city of the sage," a ray of sunlight that flashed in the darkness of medieval Athens. After the Frankish conquest of Constantinople in 1204, he retired to Ceos where he died about 1220.

He provides us with the fullest account of Athens at this period, which is quoted at length in Kevin Andrews's fascinating anthology, *Athens Alive!* (Athens, 1979). Ruined buildings, corrupt priests, attacks by pirates, and abuse of the praetor's powers, are the leitmotifs of his description. Like many later writers, he cannot forbear to contrast its present state with the former glory of Athens, and the anguish of the paradox moves him to verse:

Love for once-famous Athens wrote these words:
It plays with shadows, cools the fever heat
Of vain desire: nowhere was to be seen—
Alas—one vestige of that song-famed city,
Drowned in the abysses of unnumbered years
And deep oblivion. I suffer like a lover
Unable to bring the loved presence back,
Consoling passion's flames with images.
How unhappy am I, a new Ixion,
Loving Athens as Ixion loved Hera,
Embracing, in the end, a melting cloud.
Alas for what I suffer, speak and write!
Coming to Athens, I see Athens nowhere,
But humble, hollow yet still hallowed dust.
Where are your glories, wretchedest of cities?
How all is gone as if it had been a legend—
The courts, the juries, platforms, votes and laws,
Harangues and festivals and generalships
Of infantry and fleet, the power of words:
The ubiquitous Muse herself is vanished now.
All Athens' glory is dead. Not even a trace

Can be picked out. Forgive me then, no vestige
Of Athens' former fame being visible,
If I set up an image with my pen.

Michael Acominatus, in C. A. Trypanis, ed.,
Penguin Book of Greek Verse, no. 242;
translated by RS

With Michael Acominatus is established the second leitmotif of writing about Athens (and Greece), the theme of departed glory. At the risk of monotony, I include several variations on the theme by travelers of different periods. The first is William Lithgow, whom we have met before in Zante, in Argos, and on Euboea, this time in full flood in his poem, *The Gushing Teares of Godlie Sorrow:*

Have I, said Athens, been the mother nurse!
Of lib'rall arts, and science, natures light;
And now my carcase beares the vulgar curse
Of Sparta's scorn, and Lacedemon spight:
  Shall malice tread on virtue? shall disgrace
  Of neighbours hate, on my gold tresses trace?

Though thirty one invaders on me prey,
Each one triumphing in another's ill,
Yet flexe I not, though forc'd for to obey,
No pride shall presse my patience; nor good will
  Gaine me to flatter; nor puff'd tyrants shall
  Bruise me in pieces, though I suffer thrall.

Yet was her virgin body made a whore
To ev'ry proud insulter; and her fame
A strumpet's voice; whom Mars did once deflow'r,
And turning harlot, robb'd her vestal name;
  The victors glutting, on her vanquish'd spoiles,
  Made grief guide sorrow; Fortune fix'd her foils.

In this digression take a moral note,
From slaughter'd Athens now a village left;
That all beginnings (not their endings) quote,
Have flourish'd faces from their spring-tide reft;
  Their medium is not long, the morn is all,
  And then their end, in lumps of fragments fall.

The cheerful Thomas Lisle (1709–67), who recorded his journey across the Aegean in his verse, *Letter from Smyrna*, addressed to his sisters (published in Dodsley's Collection of Poems in 1766), did not come close enough to shore to perceive the state of Athens, and is content with rapture at his proximity to classic scenes.

> How did my heart with joy run o'er,
> When to the fam'd Cecropian shore,
> Wafted by gentle breezes, we
> Came gliding through the smooth still sea!
> While backward rov'd my busy thought
> On deeds in distant ages wrought;
> On tyrants gloriously withstood;
> On seas distain'd with Persian blood;
> On trophies rais'd o'er hills of slain
> In Marathon's unrival'd plain.
> Then, as around I cast my eye,
> And view'd the pleasing prospect nigh,
> The land for arms and arts renown'd,
> Where wit was honour'd, poets crown'd;
> Whose manners and whose rules refin'd
> Our souls, and civiliz'd mankind;
> Or (yet a loftier pitch to raise
> Our wonder, and compleat its praise)
> The land that Plato's master bore—
> How did my heart with joy run o'er!
>
> Thomas Lisle, *Letter from Smyrna*

A sterner vision is that of Edward Gibbon, who never visited Athens, but constructed his picture of the city's decline on the model of his experience of Rome, where "on the 15th of October 1764, as I sat musing amidst the ruins of the Capitol, while the barefooted friars were singing Vespers in the temple of Jupiter . . . the idea of writing the decline and fall of the city first started to my mind." The scheme was one in tune with the fledgling Romanticism of the age. His harsh picture of the contemporary Athenians is perhaps not unallowable.

> Athens, though no more than the shadow of her former self, still contains about eight or ten thousand inhabitants: of these, three-fourths are Greeks in religion and language; and the Turks, who compose the remainder, have relaxed, in their intercourse with the citizens, somewhat of the pride and gravity of their national character. The olive-tree, the gift of Minerva, flourishes in Attica; nor has the honey of Mount Hymettus lost any part of its exquisite flavour: but the languid trade is monopolised by strangers, and the agriculture of a barren land is abandoned to the vagrant Wallachians. The

Athenians are still distinguished by the subtlety and acuteness of their understandings; but these qualities, unless ennobled by freedom and enlightened by study, will degenerate into a low and selfish cunning: and it is a proverbial saying of the country, 'From the Jews of Thessalonica, the Turks of Negropont, and the Greeks of Athens, Good Lord deliver us!' This artful people has eluded the tyranny of the Turkish bashaws by an expedient which alleviates their servitude and aggravates their shame. About the middle of the last century the Athenians chose for their protector the Kislar Aga, or chief black eunuch of the Seraglio. This Aethiopian slave, who possesses the sultan's ear, condescends to accept the tribute of thirty thousand crowns: his lieutenant, the Waywode, whom he annually confirms, may reserve for his own about five or six thousand more; and such is the policy of the citizens, that they seldom fail to remove and punish an oppressive governor. Their private differences are decided by the archbishop, one of the richest prelates of the Greek church, since he possesses a revenue of one thousand pounds sterling; and by a tribunal of the eight *geronti* or elders, chosen in the eight quarters of the city: the noble families cannot trace their pedigree above three hundred years; but their principal members are distinguished by a grave demeanour, a fur cap, and the lofty appellation of *archon*. By some, who delight in the contrast, the modern language of Athens is represented as the most corrupt and barbarous of the seventy dialects of the vulgar Greek: this picture is too darkly coloured; but it would not be easy, in the country of Plato and Demosthenes, to find a reader or a copy of their works. The Athenians walk with supine indifference among the glorious ruins of antiquity; and such is the debasement of their character, that they are incapable of admiring the genius of their predecessors.

Edward Gibbon, Decline and Fall of the Roman Empire,
chapter 42

Soon after this was written, the flood of English Grand Tourists, their usual routes to southern Europe barred by the armies of Napoleon, began their descent on Athens. Some of the most entertaining of their adventures are recounted in Hugh Tregaskis, *Beyond the Grand Tour* (1979). Foremost among these was the predatory Lord Elgin, who, like many a traveler before him, was anxious to enrich his country with a piece of antiquity. "I don't name Athens and my Artists," he wrote in a letter in May 1802. "It would be a sacrilege to speak hastily of such wonders, and the justice done them. All I can say is to express a belief that the object has been attained, and that when all arrives safe in England, I shall be able to shew a compleat representation of Athens." His lively wife participated enthusiastically in the spoliation of the Acropolis, though her appreciation of her trophies was clearly vague, as is clear from her comments toward the end of this letter to her husband (24/25 May 1802):

> *11 o'clock at night.*—Now for some news that will please you. I have got another large case packed up this day—a long piece of the Basso Relievo from the Temple of Minerva—I forget the proper term. So I have by my management, got on board four immense long heavy packages, and tomorrow the Horse's Head, etc. etc. is to be carefully packed up and sent on board; this is all that is ready for going. If there were twenty ships here, nothing more could be sent for some time—the last two cases is entirely my doing, and I feel proud, Elgin! . . .
>
> *Tuesday 25th May.*—Know that, besides the five cases I have already told you of, I have prevaled on Captain Hoste to take three more; two are already on board, and the third will be taken when he returns from Corinth. How I have faged to get all this done, do you love me better for it, Elgin?
>
> And how I have pushed Lusieri to get cases made for these last three packages!
>
> I beg you will shew delight (lay aside the Diplomatic character) to Captain Hoste for taking so much on board. I am now satisfied of what I always thought—which is how much more Women can do if they set about it, than Men. I will lay any bet that had you been here, you would not have got half so much on board as I have.
>
> As for getting the other things you wished for, down from the Acropolis, it is quite *impossible* before you return. Lusieri says Captain Lacy was, upon his first coming here, against the things being taken down, but at last he was keener than anybody, and, absolutely wished you to have the whole Temple of the Cari—something, where the Statues of the Women are.

Byron, like many another philhellene, had no patience with the deeds of Elgin, though he ridiculed the Earl's pursuits in *English Bards and Scotch Reviewers:*

> Let Aberdeen and Elgin still pursue
> The shade of fame through regions of Virtu;
> Waste useless thousands on their Phidian freaks,
> Misshapen monuments and maimed antiques;

And make their grand saloons a general mart
For all the mutilated blocks of art,

a fiery rage appears in his lines on Elgin in *The Curse of Minerva*
(Pallas speaks):

Survey this vacant, violated fane;
Recount the relics torn that yet remain:
These Cecrops placed, this Pericles adorned,
That Adrian reared when drooping Science mourned.
What more I owe let gratitude attest—
Know, Alaric and Elgin did the rest.
That all may learn from whence the plunderer came,
The insulted wall sustains his hated name:
For Elgin's fame thus grateful Pallas pleads,
Below, his name—above, behold his deeds!
Be ever hailed with equal honour here
The Gothic monarch and the Pictish peer:
Arms gave the first his right, the last had none,
But basely stole what less barbarians won.

Robert Byron remarks with scorn on the recompense Elgin made
to the Athenians for their loss, an iron clock:

The English tradition is more firmly rooted in Athens
than in any other European capital. This perhaps is not surprising when it is remembered that Lord Elgin presented the
municipality with an iron clock in lieu of the Parthenon frieze.
Unfortunately this incomparable object perished by fire on
August 8th, 1884. One can picture the cuspidals and pinna-
cles of its airy Gothic fretwork, wrought by a hand inspired
as Phidas' own—more so, perhaps, since the latter was outside the Church of England—and one regrets the passing of
the old English 'Milor' and all that he embodied in the eyes
of an impoverished continent. There remains, however, right-
eously erect, the English church; and the Athenian can indeed
count himself lucky in this Gothic masterpiece. It stands on a
small railed mound on the further side of the tramlines from
the Zappeion Gardens, and is built of granite, imported at
immense expense into the finest marble country in the world.
There is no salvation in marble.

Robert Byron, *Europe in the Looking Glass* (London, 1926)

The question of returning the marbles arises perennially, but it
is indubitably true that the sculptures now in London are in a bet-

ter state of preservation than their fellows which have remained in the polluted atmosphere of Athens. Their presence in London drew from the first scores of enthusiasts, such as the painter Henry Fuseli, who, as Benjamin Robert Haydon recalls, scampered about in front of them exclaiming "De Greeks were godes! De Greeks were godes!" Another admirer was John Keats; he visited the marbles—

> again and again, and would sit for an hour or more at a time, rapt in revery. Severn, the great painter, came upon him on one such occasion. Keats' eyes were shining so brightly and his face was so lit up by some visionary rapture that Severn quietly stole away.
>
> William Sharp, *Life and Letters of Joseph Severn* (London, 1892)

Keats enshrined his response to the marbles in his sonnet, *On Seeing the Elgin Marbles:*

> My spirit is too weak; mortality
>   Weighs heavily on me like unwilling sleep,
>   And each imagined pinnacle and steep
> Of godlike hardship tells me I must die
> Like a sick eagle looking at the sky.
>   Yet 'tis a gentle luxury to weep,
>   That I have not the cloudy winds to keep
> Fresh for the opening of the morning's eye.
> Such dim-conceived glories of the brain
>   Bring round the heart an indescribable feud;
> So do these wonders a most dizzy pain,
>   That mingles Grecian grandeur with the rude
> Wasting of old time—with a billowy main,
>   A sun, a shadow of a magnitude.

The artist Edward Dodwell (1767–1832) arrived in Athens in 1801. He had some difficulty in getting access to the Acropolis to draw, owing to the rapacity for frequent bribes of the disdar in charge of the Acropolis. In the end the instrument he had invented to ensure accurate reproduction of architectural proportion, the camera obscura, came to his aid.

> After experiencing numerous vexations from this mercenary Turk, a ridiculous circumstance at length released us from the continuance of his importunities. I was one day engaged in drawing the Parthenon with the aid of my camera obscura, when the Disdar, whose surprise was excited by the

novelty of the sight, asked with a sort of fretful inquietude, what new conjuration I was performing with that extraordinary machine? I endeavoured to explain it by putting in a clean sheet of paper, and making him look into the camera obscura; he no sooner saw the temple instantly reflected on the paper, in all its lines and colours, than he imagined that I had produced the effect by some magical process; his astonishment appeared mingled with alarm, and stroking his long black beard, he repeated the words 'Allah, masch Allah,—made by God' several times. He again looked into the camera obscura with a kind of diffidence, and at that moment some of his soldiers happening to pass before the reflecting glass, were beheld by the astonished disdar walking upon the paper: he now became outrageous, and after calling me a pig, devil and Buonaparte (at that time in Turkey meaning one endowed with supernatural talents), he told me that if I chose I might take away the temple and all the stones in the citadel, but that he would never permit me to conjure his soldiers into my box. When I found that it was in vain to reason with his ignorance, I changed my tone, and told him that if he did not leave me unmolested, I would put him into my box; and that he should find it a very difficult matter to get out again. His alarm was now visible; he immediately retired, and ever after stared at me with a mixture of apprehension and amazement. When he saw me come to the Acropolis, he carefully avoided my approach; and never afterwards gave me any further molestation.

Edward Dodwell, *A Classical and
Topographical Tour through Greece* (London, 1819)

William Haygarth, the author of *Greece: A Poem* (1814), naturally devotes much of his space to the Attic scene. Pastoral pleasance and departed glory mingle inextricably in his description:

Let me recline where yonder olives spread
Their antique arms, emboss'd with moss-grown knots
O'er cool Cephissus' stream; let me repose
And listen to the shrill cicada's note,
And distant water's melancholy sound,
Falling at intervals upon the ear.
How solemn this unruffled breath of shade,
Like the wide ocean slumb'ring in a calm!
How graceful this umbrageous canopy
Dimly recedes into a lengthen'd aisle
Of mingling boughs! How firm each massive trunk

William James Stillman, *View of the Acropolis from the East, Athens.* The
J. Paul Getty Museum, Malibu, California.

Props on the basement of its pillared strength
This sylvan temple . . .

Ilissus flows no more—its stream has pass'd
Like Greece's glory; it has pour'd its tide
And mingled with the ocean. Seek not now
The fane of Ceres, or the huntress Queen
That glitter'd on its banks; hope not to roam
Midst platane trees, waving their arms above
Its limpid waters, nor expecting stand
In glory's school, to view the dusty throng
Of foot and horsemen, steeds and winged cars
Rounding the course; but in their stead behold,
Where yonder columns on their ruined shafts
Bear the deep shades of age, a motley group
Of Greece's lords and slaves. There at their base,
Unconscious of the majesty which frowns
Above their heads, and raising heavily
The sleepy eye, repose a Moslem band,
Rob'd in their gaudy vests, and breathing far
Volumes of fragrance from their taper pipes,
Which rest upon the ground.

The composition of descriptive poems on particular monuments of Athens became something of a craze, or at least a popular theme for prize poems, like this Oxford one by the obscure Samuel Rickards (1816):

TEMPLE OF THESEUS

Amid the wrecks of age, o'er wasted lands,
Fix'd as his fame, the Hero's Temple stands:
Though many a pile, wide mould'ring on the plain,
Mark the dread scene of Desolation's reign;
Though desert fields, and rifted towers declare
The shocks of nature, or the waste of war;
Yet rear'd in monarch state that fane appears,
Proud o'er the lapse of twice ten hundred years,
And seems to live an emblem to the brave,
How Time reveres the Patriot Hero's grave.

Such the fair pile, where, shrin'd in holy cell,
The slumb'ring ashes of the mighty dwell,
Where Tweddell, youthful shade, to classic rest
Sinks, like a wearied child, on Science' breast,
And in the sacred scenes he lov'd to roam,
Finds the last honors of a kindred home,
While Muses, mourning whom they could not save,
Still guard his fame; for Athens is his grave.

The Tweddell of the final lines was a young Grand Tourist who had become acquainted with Lord Elgin in Hamburg on his way to Athens, and devoted his time in Greece to making a fine collection of drawings, as well as buying others from Fauvel. He died in Fauvel's arms on 25 July 1799 from a fever no doubt induced by his vegetarian diet and aggravated by his refusal to accept any treatment. His grave became something of a pilgrimage spot for other English Tourists.

Thomas S. Hughes, who was in Athens in the early years of the nineteenth century, records, like several other travelers, the remarkable exhibition of the whirling dervishes in the Temple of the Winds:

> During the General's sojourn at Athens we accompanied him to that extraordinary exhibition which is displayed every Friday in the ancient tower of Andronicus, called the Temple of the Winds, and converted now into a college of howling dervishes. The frantic gestures, horrible outcries, and incon-

ceivable exertions of these fanatics, urged on by superstitious enthusiasm and stimulated by emulation, made us absolutely shudder at such a degradation of human nature. A sheik or priest presided over the orgies who stood upon a raised step and appeared to limit the time of operation by counting the beads of a rosary; but the movements were regulated by the deafening noise of three small kettle-drums which were beat violently with short elastic sticks. A single person first gets up and goes hopping or jumping round the room, throwing his head backwards and forwards or twirling it like a harlequin, uttering every now and then a hideous noise like the loud grunting of a pig. After a little time another starts up and catching him round the waist accompanies him in his revolutions which soon become most vehemently accelerated; then another and another succeeds until the first is quite surrounded and almost suffocated by the throng; in this manner holding each other with a tight grasp they go round and round leaping up and crying out, as if engaged in a trial of lungs, hoo hoo, ullah ullah, hoo ullah. To this they are excited by a beating of the drums more violent than the cymbals of the Corybantes, as well as by the voice of the sheik who at this time runs over his beads with an astonishing rapidity: their exclamations appear as if uttered by persons in the excruciating tortures of the rack, or even bring to imagination the place of accursed souls: in the mean time their looks become wild, the foam starts from their mouths, their turbans fall to the ground, their hair floats about in disorder, their garments collapse, and some of the performers sink down in a state of perfect insensibility: these, after recovering, generally boast that they have been favoured with celestial visions. When the tumult has at length subsided, a different set of devotees commence that curious, beautiful, and mysterious dance which consists in twirling the body round rapidly like a top, or as upon a pivot, whilst they are moving in a circular orbit with their flowing robes distended like a parachute by the velocity of the motion: nothing but long and constant practice could enable them to perform these giddy revolutions: they seem to feel no fatigue, to make no exertions; but with the head inclined towards the shoulder, and the utmost placidity of countenance they float along as if they were in the enjoyment of a delightful trance. The contrast of this soothing harmony, as it might be called, this graceful ἐμμέλεια, with the horrid uproar of the preceding scene, is extremely pleasing. The mind pictures to itself order and beauty produced out of chaos, or the harmonic revolutions of the planetary system. At the conclusion of these ceremonies some poor sick children were brought before the sheik who put his hand upon their heads and tied a bit of black silk round their arms, for the purpose of charming away their complaints. He received our donations for the exhibition we had witnessed with great condescension, and politely invited us into his apartments adjoining the temple, where we took coffee and pipes with the actors in this extraordinary pantomime.

Thomas S. Hughes, *Travels in Sicily, Greece and Albania* (London, 1820)

From such incidental anecdotes, we return to the gloomy notes of the poets. Winthrop Mackworth Praed (1802–39), a precocious poet and admirer of the philhellenic statesman, George Canning, became, after some essays in teaching and journalism, Member of Parliament for the English seaside town of Great Yarmouth in 1834; five years later he was dead of consumption. His verses on Athens reflect the youthful philhellenism of the man:

ATHENS

Desolate Athens! though thy gods are fled,
Thy temples silent, and thy glory dead,
Though all thou hadst of beautiful and brave
Sleep in the tomb, or moulder in the wave,
Though power and praise forsake thee, and forget,
Desolate Athens, thou art lovely yet!
Around thy walls, in every wood and vale,
Thine own sweet bird, the lonely nightingale,
Still makes her home; and, when the moonlight hour
Flings its soft magic over brake and bower,
Murmurs her sorrows from her ivy shrine,
Or the thick foliage of the deathless vine.
Where erst Megaera chose her fearful crown,
The bright narcissus hangs his clusters down;
And the gay crocus decks with glittering dew
The yellow radiance of his golden hue.
Still thine own olive haunts its native earth,
Green, as when Pallas smiled upon its birth;
And still Cephisus pours his sleepless tide,
So clear and calm, along the meadow side,
That you may gaze long hours upon the stream,
And dream at last the poet's witching dream,
That the sweet Muses in the neighboring bowers

Sweep their wild harps, and wreathe their odorous flowers,
And laughing Venus o'er the level plains
Waves her light lash and shakes her gilded reins.

Winthrop Mackworth Praed
(prize poem, Cambridge, 1824)

The poet Thomas Kibble Hervey achieved a similar minor fame with his series of poems on Greek subjects, of which this is one:

THE TEMPLE OF JUPITER OLYMPIUS AT ATHENS. AFTER A PICTURE BY WILLIAMS, IN HIS *VIEWS IN GREECE*

Thou art not silent!—oracles are thine
Which the mind utters, and the spirit hears,
Lingering, 'mid ruined fane and broken shrine,
O'er many a tale and trace of other years!
Bright as an ark, o'er all the flood of tears
That wraps thy cradle-land—thine earthly love,
Where hours of hope, 'mid centuries of fears,
Have gleamed, like lightnings through the gloom above,
Stands, roofless to the sky, thy home, Olympian Jove!

Thy columned aisles with whispers of the past
Are vocal,—and, along thine ivied walls,
While Elian echoes murmur on the blast,
And wild-flowers hang, like victor-coronals,
In vain the turbaned tyrant rears his halls,
And plants the symbol of his faith and slaughters;
Now, even now, the beam of promise falls
Bright upon Hellas, as her own bright daughters,
And a Greek Ararat is rising o'er the waters!

Thou are not silent!—when the southern fair—
Ionia's moon—looks down upon thy breast,
Smiling as pity smiles above despair,
Soft as young beauty soothing age to rest,—
Sings the night-spirit in thy weedy crest,
And she—the minstrel of the moonlight hours
Breathes—like some lone one, sighing to be blest,—
Her lay—half hope, half sorrow,—from the flowers,
And hoots the prophet owl, amid his tangled bowers!

And, round thine altar's mouldering stones are born
Mysterious harpings,—wild as ever crept
From him who waked Aurora, every morn,

William James Stillman, *The Acropolis, from the Hill above Illissus, Athens.*
The J. Paul Getty Museum, Malibu, California.

And sad as those he sang her, till she slept!
A thousand and a thousand years have swept
O'er thee, who wert a mortal from thy spring,
A wreck in youth!—nor vainly hast thou kept
Thy lyre,—Olympia's soul is on the wing
And a new Iphitus has waked, beneath its string!

Thomas Kibble Hervey,
The Poetical Sketchbook (London, 1829)

Lamartine, too, was moved to an outburst of verse by the fallen
splendor of Athens:

DAWN IN ATHENS

From high Cytheron's top the day comes down,
And strikes of many a height the arched crown;
From flank to base, from plain to sea, the ray
Passes, but tinges nothing by the way;
No cities in the distance, bright with fires;
No smoke by morning's breath sent up in spires;
No hamlets perched upon the sloping hill;
No towers the vale—the seas no vessels fill;
In passing o'er each liveless height and plain,

The rays fall dead, and never rise again.
But one, the loftiest shot from morning's bow,
Bends from the gilded Parthenon on my brow,
Then, glancing sadly o'er the stones, time-scarred,
Where dozes o'er his pipe the Moslem guard,
Turns down, as if to weep its ruined grace,
And dies on Theseus' lofty temple-base!
Two rays, disporting on two wrecks!—this pair
Are all that shine and say, Athens is there!

Alphonse de Lamartine, *Travels in the East*;
translated by TWR (Edinburgh, 1850)

Herman Melville visited Greece in 1856–57, and recorded his impressions both in a journal and in a handful of crystalline poems. Here he is on the Parthenon:

THE PARTHENON

1. Seen aloft from afar

Estranged in site,
Aerial gleaming, warmly white,
You look a suncloud motionless
In noon of day divine;
Your beauty charmed enhancement takes
In Art's long after-shine.

2. Nearer viewed

Like Lais, fairest of her kind,
In subtlety your form's defined—
The cornice curved, each shaft inclined,
While yet, to eyes that do but revel
    And take the sweeping view,
Erect this seems, and that a level,
    To line and plummet true.

Spinoza gazes; and in mind
Dreams that one architect designed
    Lais—and you!

3. The frieze

What happy musings genial went
With airiest touch the chisel lent
    To frisk and curvet light
Of horses gay—their riders grave—
Contrasting so in action brave

With virgins meekly bright,
Clear filing on in even tone
With pitcher each, one after one
Like water-fowl in flight.

4. The last tile

When the last marble tile was laid
The winds died down on all the seas;
    Hushed were the birds, and swooned the glade;
    Ictinus sat; Aspasia said
'Hist!—Art's meridian, Pericles!'

Herman Melville

Gustave Flaubert also included Greece in the itinerary of his oriental tour in 1850, his eye ever open to oddity, grotesquerie, or romantic potential. The major fruit of his oriental travels was the novel, *Salammbô*. Here he describes his last visit to the Acropolis, with that dry tone that but half-conceals romantic sentiment:

> Today, 23 January, Thursday, I went to say farewell to the Acropolis.
>
> In the Parthenon, at the foot of one of the tablets, a battered thigh bone, all grey.
>
> The wind was strong, the sun was setting, the sky was all red above Aegina; behind the columns of the Propylaea, it spread out in egg-yellow.
>
> As I was coming away from the Temple of Neptune, two large birds flew out from behind the facade and departed for the East, the direction of Smyrna, of Asia.
>
> When I pushed the gate of the Acropolis, I noticed that it shrieked painfully, like that of a barn.
>
> I had come out and was looking at the Theatre of Herodes, when a soldier came up to sell me, for two drachmas, a small female figurine with hair pulled up on top of the head.
>
> A ragged woman, of whom I had only seen the back, was climbing to the citadel.
>
> As I went to the Parthenon, and as I returned, I looked for a long time at that bosom with its round breasts, which was made to drive you mad with love.
>
> Adieu, Athens! Now, elsewhere!
>
> 10.30 p.m.
>
> Gustave Flaubert, *Voyage en Orient* (1849–51);
>
> translated by RS

In the face of the combined laments and encomia of so many literate persons, it is perhaps not surprising that W. M. Thackeray, who traveled through Greece en route to Cairo in 1846, was moved to direct his world-weary irony also on the Attic past.

> Not feeling any enthusiasm myself about Athens, my bounden duty of course is clear, to sneer and laugh heartily at all who have . . .
>
> So in coming in sight of the promontory of Sunium, where the Greek muse, in an awful vision, came to me, and said in a patronizing way, 'Why, my dear,' (she always, the old spinster, adopts this high and mighty tone), 'Why, my dear, are you not charmed to be in this famous neighbourhood, in this land of poets and heroes, of whose history your classical education ought to have made you a master; if it did not, you have wofully neglected your opportunities, and your dear parents have wasted their money in sending you to school.' I replied, 'Madam, your company in youth was made so laboriously disagreeable to me, that I can't at present reconcile myself to you in age. I read your poets, but it was in fear and trembling; and a cold sweat is but an ill accompaniment to poetry. I blundered through your histories; but history is so dull (saving your presence) of herself, that when the brutal dulness of a schoolmaster is superadded to her own slow conversation, the union becomes intolerable: hence I have not the slightest pleasure in renewing my acquaintance with a lady who has been the source of so much bodily and mental discomfort to me.'
>
> W. M. Thackeray, *Notes of a Journey from Cornhill to Grand Cairo* (London, 1846)

As Grand Tourism gave way to tourism, American visitors, too, began to proliferate, complaining, like Julia Ward Howe, of the rough stones of the paths, and the food, or, like Samuel S. Cox, of the general dilapidation. Cox was born in Ohio in 1824, and devoted much of his early years to oriental tourism. He does not seem to have enjoyed it much. When, at the age of sixty-one, he was appointed minister to Turkey, he resigned after a year. Seeing the Temple of Zeus Olympius, he could not refrain from odious comparisons with his own country.

> Now as I look at its remains, the eye finds its area covered by great stacks of wheat, in the process of threshing. Men are superintending. This process was peculiar. Imagine three cultivators, or corn harrows, with teeth turned backward; these

chained together, and a man on each; drawn by horses trampling the straw, while men were engaged in stirring it up, and you have a very unscientific description of the threshing process. Women were riding the horses, and stirring the straw, assessing the work. A motley group that, in the Temple of Jupiter! Why so much straw *here?* It is a ridiculous law, that every farmer shall bring his wheat or grain into the point fixed by the officer, there to be threshed in his presence, so that *government may take its toll!* American farmers! how would you like that? Jupiter Olympus! would you not upset such a government in a jiffy?

S. S. Cox, *A Buckeye Abroad* (New York, 1852)

The prevailing attitude is nicely satirized in an anonymous poem of 1857:

A Fashionable New Yorker Abroad

. . . we reached Athens—a sizable place,
    Some three or four miles from the Gulf of Aegina;
It contains a cathedral not equal to Grace
    Church in New York, which I think is much finer.
Went up to the top of the famous Acropolis,
    Which is visited daily by hundreds of people,
But can't say I think that the view from the top o' this
    Is equal to that from our Trinity steeple.
The houses are mostly unsightly and small;
    In Minerva and Hermes' street noticed a few
Which will do very well, but are nothing at all
    Compared with our mansion in Fifth-Avenue.
The piles of old ruins one sees here and there
    I consider a perfect disgrace to the town;
If they had an efficient and competent Mayor,
    Like our Mayor Wood, he would soon have them down.

Nothing to Do: A Tilt at Our Best Society (Boston, 1857)

Mark Twain, who some ten years later made the journey to the East, the account of which first established his reputation, revels in his own philistinism and his delight in bad architecture, bad painting, etc., etc.; his main aim is to have fun, and to make fun, and his account of a clandestine visit to the Acropolis by night, evading the quarantine restrictions, is typical of this engaging book:

As we marched along we began to get over our fears and ceased to care much about quarantine scouts or anybody else.

We grew bold and reckless; and once, in a sudden burst of courage, I even threw a stone at a dog. It was a pleasant reflection, though, that I did not hit him, because his master might just possibly have been a policeman. Inspired by this happy failure, my valor became utterly uncontrollable, and at intervals I absolutely whistled, though on a moderate key. But boldness breeds boldness, and shortly I plunged into a vineyard, in the full light of the moon, and captured a gallon of superb grapes, not even minding the presence of a peasant who rode by on a mule. Denny and Birch followed my example. Now I had grapes enough for a dozen, but then Jackson was all swollen up with courage, too, and he was obliged to enter a vineyard presently. The first bunch he seized brought trouble. A frowzy, bearded brigand sprang into the road with a shout and flourished a musket in the light of the moon! We sidled towards the Pireaus—not running, you understand, but only advancing with celerity. The brigand shouted again, but still we advanced. It was getting late, and we had no time to fool away on every ass that wanted to drivel Greek platitudes to us. We would just as soon have talked with him if we had not been in a hurry. Presently Denny said, 'Those fellows are following us!'

We turned, and sure enough, there they were—three fantastic pirates armed with guns. We slackened our pace to let them come up, and in the meantime I got out my cargo of grapes and dropped them firmly but reluctantly into the shadows by the wayside. But I was not afraid. I only felt that it was not right to steal grapes. And all the more so when the owner was around—and not only around, but with his friends around also. The villains came up and searched a bundle Dr Birch had in his hand and scowled upon him when they found it had nothing in it but some holy rocks from Mars Hill, and these were not contraband. They evidently suspected him of playing some wretched fraud upon them and seemed half inclined to scalp the party. But finally they dismissed us with a warning, couched in excellent Greek, I suppose, and dropped tranquilly in our wake. When they had gone three hundred yards they stopped, and we went on rejoiced. But behold, another armed rascal came out of the shadows and took their place and followed us two hundred yards. Then he delivered us over to another miscreant, who emerged from some mysterious place, and he in turn to another! For a mile and a half our rear was guarded all the while by armed men. I never traveled in so much state before in all my life.

It was a good while after that before we ventured to steal any more grapes, and when we did we stirred up another troublesome brigand, and then we ceased all further speculation in that line. I suppose that fellow that rode by on the mule posted all the sentinels, from Athens to the Piraeus, about us . . .

Just as the earliest tinges of the dawn flushed the eastern sky and turned the pillared Parthenon to a broken harp hung in the pearly horizon, we closed our thirteenth mile of weary, roundabout marching and emerged upon the seashore abreast the ships, with our usual escort of fifteen hundred Piraean dogs howling at our heels. We hailed a boat that was two or three hundred yards from shore and discovered in a moment that it was a police boat on the lookout for any quarantine-breakers that might chance to be abroad. So we dodged—we were used to that by this time—and when the scouts reached the spot we had so lately occupied, we were absent. They cruised along the shore, but in the right direction, and shortly our own boat issued from the gloom and took us aboard. They had heard our signal on the ship. We rowed noiselessly away, and before the police boat came in sight again, we were safe at home once more.

Mark Twain, *The Innocents Abroad*
(Connecticut, 1869), chapter 32

In the high summer of 1904, Sigmund Freud made a long dreamed-of visit to Athens. His reaction to the experience of his first sight of the Acropolis was characteristically complex:

When, finally, on the afternoon after our arrival, I stood on the Acropolis and cast my eyes around upon the landscape, a surprising thought suddenly entered my mind: 'So all this really *does* exist, just as we learnt at school!' To describe the situation more accurately, the person who gave expression to the remark was divided, far more sharply than was usually noticeable, from another person who took cognizance of the remark; and both were astonished, though not by the same thing. The first behaved as though he were obliged, under the impact of an unequivocal observation, to believe in something the reality of which had hitherto seemed doubtful. If I may make a slight exaggeration, it was as if someone, walking beside Loch Ness, suddenly caught sight of the form of the famous Monster stranded upon the shore and found himself driven to the admission: 'So it really *does* exist—the sea-serpent we've never believed in!' The second person, on the other hand, was justifiably astonished, because he had been unaware that the real existence of Athens, the Acropolis, and the landscape around it had ever been objects of doubt. What he had been expecting was rather some expression of delight or admiration.

Now it would be easy to argue that this strange thought that occurred to me on the Acropolis only serves to emphasize the fact that seeing something with one's own eyes is after all quite a different thing from hearing or reading about it. But it would remain a very strange way of clothing an uninteresting common-place. Or it would be possible to maintain that it was true that when I was a schoolboy I had *thought* I was convinced of the historical reality of the city of Athens and its history, but that the occurrence of this idea on the Acropolis had precisely shown that in my unconscious I had *not* believed in it, and that I was only now acquiring a conviction that 'reached down to the unconscious'. An explanation of this sort sounds very profound, but it is easier to assert than to prove; moreover, it is very much open to attack upon theoretical grounds. No. I believe that the two phenomena, the depression at Trieste and the idea on the Acropolis, were intimately connected. And the first of these is more easily intelligible and may help us towards an explanation of the second.

The experience at Trieste was, it will be noticed, also no more than an expression of incredulity: 'We're going to see Athens? Out of the question!—it will be far too difficult!' The accompanying depression corresponded to a regret that it *was* out of the question: it would have been so lovely. And now we know where we are. It is one of those cases of 'too good to be true' that we come across so often. It is an example of the incredulity that arises so often when we are surprised by a piece of good news, when we hear we have won a prize, for instance, or drawn a winner, or when a girl learns that the man whom she has secretly loved has asked her parents for leave to pay his addresses to her.

. . . It is not true that in my schooldays I ever doubted the real existence of Athens. I only doubted whether I should ever see Athens. It seemed to me beyond the realms of possibility that I should travel so far—that I should 'go such a long way'. This was linked up with the limitations and poverty of our conditions of life in my youth. My longing to travel was no doubt also the expression of a wish to escape from that pressure, like the force which drives so many adolescent children to run away from home. I had long seen clearly that a great part of the pleasure of travel lies in the fulfilment of these early wishes—that it is rooted, that is, in dissatisfaction with home and family. When first one catches sight of the sea, crosses the ocean and experiences as realities cities and lands which for so long had been distant, unattainable things of desire—one feels oneself like a hero who has performed deeds of improbable greatness . . .

But here we come upon the solution of the little problem of why it was that already at Trieste we interfered with our enjoyment of the voyage to Athens. It must be that a sense of guilt was attached to the satisfaction in having gone such a long way: there was something about it that was wrong, that from earliest times had been forbidden. It was something to do with a child's criticism of his father, with the undervaluation which took the place of the overvaluation of earlier childhood. It seems as though the essence of success was to have got further than one's father, and as though to excel one's father was still something forbidden.

As an addition to this generally valid motive there was a special factor present in our particular case. The very theme of Athens and the Acropolis in itself contained evidence of the son's superiority. Our father had been in business, he had had no secondary education, and Athens could not have meant much to him. Thus what interfered with our enjoyment of the journey to Athens was a feeling of *filial piety*. And now you will no longer wonder that the recollection of this incident on the Acropolis should have troubled me so often since I myself have grown old and stand in need of forbearance and can travel no more.

Sigmund Freud, *A Disturbance of Memory on the Acropolis* (1936)

The first book of Robert Byron, whom we have encountered before, was an account of a journey through Europe, *Europe in the Looking Glass* (London, 1926). His interest was studiously averted from classical antiquity, as his main interest was in Byzantine architecture, on which he later wrote a book, as well as many observations on the same subject in his description of travels on Mt. Athos, *The Station*. His masterpiece is *The Road to Oxiana*, an account of an architectural pilgrimage through Persia and Afghanistan, as brilliant and as funny as it is seminal in its revaluation of Safavid and Abbasid architecture. It is a tragedy that he was killed on a ship which was torpedoed during the Second World War. Here he bends his incisive eye and lush powers of description to the Parthenon:

There have occurred, since the invention of photography, moments in the life of everyone, when the actual materialisation of objects familiar in monochrome since the earliest days of the nursery, somehow produces a sensation of such unreality that the eyes of the beholder seem to play him false, as if imposed on by a mirage. Such a feeling, I must confess, obtruded itself upon my common sense, as our cab gradually approached the foot of the mountainous platform on which the Parthenon stands. I felt that I was the victim of a delusion.

᠂᠊

Looking into a shop window later in the day, I was unable to help noticing some typical water-colour sketches of the Russell Flint school, which depicted the Parthenon as a row of grooved cinnamon ninepins against a sky the colour of a faded butcher's apron. It is pictures such as these, reacting on minds already sickened by those yellowed photographs that invariably adorn the dining-rooms of British pedagogy—photographs enlarged to accentuate every scratch and chip into a deep and crumbling abrasion—it is these that are responsible for the loathing with which the artistically educated person of the twentieth century is growing to regard anything of the nature of a 'Greek Ruin'. Let me, for the benefit of posterity, pit my pen against the lens of the Victorian photographer.

The pillars of the Parthenon are Doric, plain, massive and fluted from top to bottom. They are composed of separate blocks of marble, three and a half feet deep and five in diameter, which, at the time of construction, were forcibly ground to fit one another, only the topmost having previously been fluted. Then, when the succession of blocks had become a pillar, the whole fluting was carried out by hand. The marble is still as smooth as vellum, its surface hard as basalt, its edges sharp as steel. And for all the chips and flakes and holes, there is that certain quality about this handwork, by which handwork can always be distinguished, be it on metal, wood or stone—a textural quality that renders every imperfection not only superfluous, but invisible. Picture these pillars then, with their surface of vellum and their colour of sun-kissed satin, rising massive and radiant from the marble plinth of the whole building, against the brazen turquoise of the sky behind. At their feet the grey slabs of rock and the wreck of the innumerable statues and monuments with which the whole Acropolis was once adorned; behind, the tall spike of Lykabettus rising from the white blocks of the town beneath its veil of dust; in front, the chimneys and promontory of Piraeus; finally the sea and the islands. Immediately below, the Roman amphitheatre, a trellis-work of heavy brown stone arches one upon another, calls to mind the efficient vulgarity of the civilization that displaced the Greek, a relic infinitely more incongruous than the tramlines and the factory chimneys. Even antique dealers in the Levant despise Roman remains.

Robert Byron, *Europe in the Looking Glass* (London, 1926)

To the present-day traveler to Athens, where the monuments and exhibits in the museums are so firmly protected and so neatly arrayed for his benefit, it comes as a shock to realize how recently in this century it has become so. Two accounts of Athens' museums, scarcely sixty years ago, give a very different picture:

> The museums at Athens were a sore temptation to collectors, when I first went there more than forty years ago. There were a dozen of these museums scattered about the town: some of them mere sheds, and hardly any with glass cases for the smaller things, but only wire netting. And there were such beautiful little things that would so easily come through the mesh and go into a collector's pocket, and they could not possibly be reclaimed, as they were not marked or numbered, and the inventories were vague. In my innocence I bought a vase from a distinguished man (a Greek) and paid him rather a high price for it, forgetting that he probably had stolen it, and I might just as well have stolen it myself.

Cecil Torr, *Small Talk at Wreyland*, II (London, 1921)

D. in the following extract is Norman Douglas, best known for his books on southern Italy, *Old Calabria* and *South Wind*, here deflected from his beaten path to accompany his old friend Edward Hutton to Greece:

> **H.** Now tell me about that stupidity of yours.
>
> **D.** I know I can count on your sympathy, else I should prefer to say nothing about it. Well, Athens then was a much more easy-going place than it is now, and the Natural History Museum, where I spent most of my time, was so easy-going that, after becoming firm friends with the delightful old Curator, I could have done pretty well what I pleased with his collections. What a chance I missed! It makes me perfectly furious to think of it even now. I noticed over and over again, among a pile of books in the corner, that wonderful volume by Rösel von Rosenhof . . .

H. My dear boy, before you go any further, let me explain what you are going to do. You are going to tell me about one of your imaginary authors; you have invented that man, as you invented a good many others whom you quote in your books. I quite realize that this system gives your writings a fine veneer of scholarship, but, believe me, you'll be found out one of these days. Rösel von Rosenhof—that name is too good to be authentic.

D. I wish you were right; it would have saved me thirty-five years' remorse. Unfortunately, the fellow was born in Nürnberg and wrote an amazing volume on amphibians in 1758; the coloured illustrations are a marvel. Now how did a book of this kind get to Athens, and what business had it in the Natural History Museum? And why on earth didn't I pick it up and walk away with it?

H. *What?*

D. Day after day it lay there, asking to be removed by some enthusiast like myself. Day after day I thought: why not carry it off? And day after day I left it alone. I wanted it badly, you understand; I not only wanted it, I needed it for my studies, and my library to this hour is incomplete without it. The criminal folly of youth! Nobody would have noticed its absence; if they had, nobody would have cared; and if the Curator had caught me in the very act of absconding with it, do you know what he would have said?

H. I know perfectly well what I should have said.

D. He would have said: 'Stop, my charming young friend, and let me have it properly packed for you and sent to your hotel. I cannot let you be seen about the streets with such an unbecoming load under your arm. So you relish these musty German folios? Is it possible? What an astonishing young man you are! I will have the place carefully searched, and if we find any more of them, they shall be sent along. As to this one, pray have no hesitation—indeed, I am glad to see you have none— about accepting it as a little memento of the pleasure which your visit to Athens has given me; I only wish I could offer you something worthier! It might be as well, by the way, not to mention this matter to our mutual friend Mr Tricoupi. He is an admirable person, we all admit, but a little—how shall I put it?—a little obsessed with the duties of his exalted position. He has laid it down, for reasons which none of us have yet grasped, that Museums such as this one are public institutions, and there exists, I believe, some absurd rule about keeping the library books of such institutions within the precincts of the building itself. I feel sure I can count on your discretion!' Ah, where is now the Curator who talks like that?

Edward Hutton, *A Glimpse of Greece* (London, 1928)

Kostis Palamas (1859–1943) is one of the foremost Greek poets of the last hundred years. Much of his poetry is influenced by folk song. The vivid language of this sonnet evokes an Athens still familiar at the present day:

> Here sky is everywhere, everywhere the sun's
> Rays, all around the honey breath of Hymettus.
> Unwithering lilies grow from the marble;
> Flashing, begetter of Olympus, stands divine Pendeli.[1]
>
> The plunging pickaxe falls on Beauty,
> Cybele[2] contains gods, not mortals, in her entrails
> Athena gushes streams of violet blood
> When evening's arrows strike her.
>
> Temples are here, groves of the sacred olive:
> Among the crowd here that writhes and shifts,
> Like a caterpillar on a white flower
> The nation of relics lives and kings it
> Thousand-souled: its breath glows even in the earth.
> I sense it: it wrestles with the dark in me.
>
> Kostis Palamas; translated by RS

The Cerameicus is one of the most effectively restored parts of Athens. The classical cemetery, though its tomb-stelae are now in the National Museum, has been adorned with casts of the stelae which, standing as they do in a quiet and overgrown spot beside a trickling stream, recall the atmosphere that must have belonged to it two thousand years ago. The tomb stelae are some of the most touching remains of classical antiquity, eloquent in their understatement, and have provided the theme of poems by both Rilke and Spender:

> On Attic stelae, did not the circumspection
> of human gesture amaze you? Were not love and farewell
> so lightly laid upon shoulders, they seemed to be made
> of other stuff than with us? Oh, think of the hands,

---

1. Mountain northeast of Athens.

2. The mother-goddess of Anatolia, associated with Demeter. Here she stands for the earth.

how they rest without pressure, though power is there in
    the torsos.
The wisdom of those self-masters was this: hitherto it's us;
ours is to touch one another like this; the gods
may press more strongly upon us. But that is the gods' affair.
If only we too could discover some pure, contained
narrow, human, own little strip of corn-land
in between river and rock! For our own heart still
    transcends us
even as theirs did. And we can no longer gaze
after it now into pacifying image, or godlike
body, wherein it achieves a grander restraint.

R. M. Rilke, from the second Duino Elegy;
translated by J. B. Leishman

In Attica

Again, again, I see this form repeated:
The bare shadow of a rock outlined
Against the sky; declining gently to
An elbow; then the scooped descent
From the elbow to the wrist of a hand that rests
On the plain.
    Again, again,
That arm outstretched from the high shoulder
And leaning on the land.
      As though the torsoed
Gods, with heads and lower limbs broken off,
Plunged in the sky, or buried under earth,
Had left fingers here as pointers
Between the sun and plain:
      had made this landscape
Human, like Greek steles, where the dying
Are changed to stone on a gesture of curved air,
Lingering in their infinite departure.

Stephen Spender

9

Boeotia and Phocis

Thebes

Herakleides (see page 130) takes us west from Athens as far as Thebes.

From Plataea to Thebes is eighty furlongs. The road is through a flat the whole way. The city stands in the middle of Boeotia. Its circumference is seventy furlongs, its shape circular. The soil is dark. In spite of its antiquity the streets are new, because, as the histories tell us, the city has been thrice razed to the ground on account of the morose and overbearing character of the inhabitants. It is excellent for the breeding of horses; it is all well-watered and green, and has more gardens than any other city in Greece. For two rivers flow through it, irrigating the plain below the city; and water is brought from the Cadmea in underground conduits which were made of old, they say, by Cadmus. So much for the city. The inhabitants are high-spirited and wonderfully sanguine, but rash, insolent, and overbearing, ready to come to blows with any man, be he citizen or stranger. As for justice they set their face against it. Business disputes are settled not by reason but by fisticuffs, and the methods of the prize-ring are transferred to courts of justice. Hence lawsuits here last thirty years at the very least. For if a man opens his lips in public on the law's delay and does not thereupon take hasty leave of Boeotia, he is waylaid by night and murdered by the persons who have no wish that lawsuits should come to an end. Murders are perpetrated on the most trifling pretexts. Such are the men as a whole, though some worthy, high-minded, respectable persons are also to be found among them. The women are the tallest, prettiest, and most graceful in all Greece. Their faces are so muffled up that only the eyes are seen. All of them dress in white and wear low purple shoes laced so as to show the bare feet. Their yellow hair is tied up in a knot on the top of the head. In society their manners are Sicyonian rather than Boeotian. They have pleasing voices, while the voices of the men are harsh and deep. The city is one of the best places to pass the summer in, for it has gardens and plenty of cool water. Besides it is breezy, its aspect is verdant, and fruit and flowers abound. But it lacks timber, and is one of the worst places to winter in by reason of the rivers and the winds; for snow falls and there is much mud. The poet Laon writes in praise of the Boeotians, but he does not speak the truth, the fact being that he was caught in adultery and let off lightly by the injured husband. He says:

> Love the Boeotian, and fly not Boeotia;
> For the man is a good fellow, and the land is delightful.

Heracleides; translated by J. G. Frazer
in *Pausanias and Other Greek Sketches* (London, 1900)

The home of Pindar, Thebes has few other literary associations. The Roman epigrammatist, Honestus, recalls the legend of its building by the musician Amphion:

> Lyre-music built me, pipe-skirls brought me low.
> Bewail Thebes, cursed by an inconstant Muse.
> My lyre-enchanted walls hear no sound now,
> Those stones that leapt to build my mighty towers:
> Amphion worked this gift: his seven-stringed lyre
> Built my seven gates: at each, a hero's pyre.

Honestus, epigram 6,
in A. S. F. Gow and D. L. Page, eds.,
The Garland of Philip (Cambridge, 1968);
translated by RS

Orchomenos

Nearby Orchomenos was the site of a cult of the Graces (probably goddesses of agricultural significance, like the Demeter of Eleusis), finely celebrated by Pindar in their more literary role as patronesses of song and festal joy, in a poem for an Orchomenian:

> Ye pow'rs, o'er all the flow'ry meads,
> Where deep Cephissus rolls his lucid tide,
>   Allotted to preside,
> And haunt the plains renown'd for beauteous steeds,
>   Queens of Orchomenus the fair,
> And sacred guardians of the ancient line
>   Of Minyas divine,
> Hear, O ye Graces, and regard my pray'r!
>   All that's sweet and pleasing here
>   Mortals from your hands receive:

Splendour ye and fame confer,
 Genius, wit, and beauty give.
Nor, without your shining train,
Ever on the aethereal plain
In harmonious measures move
The celestial choirs above;
When the figur'd dance they lead,
Or the nectar'd banquet spread.
But with thrones immortal grac'd,
 And by Pythian Phoebus plac'd,
Ordering through the blest abodes
All the splendid works of gods,
Sit the sisters in a ring,
Round the golden-shafted king:
And with reverential love
 Worshipping the Olympian throne,
The majestick brow of love
 With unfading honours crown.

Pindar, *Olympian* xiv;
translated by Gilbert West
(London, 1749)

Nineteen centuries after Herakleides, Gustave Flaubert followed the same route north west from Athens. Here he describes the landscape that unfolds after Thebes is past:

After Zagora, a plain, a few sparse poplars, spaced infrequently along a little stream; their trunk resembles that of pollards, and the branches rise directly perpendicularly from it. Soon one enters a little oak wood, the trees come up to flank level, one can ride between them. The land here makes a large but gentle curve, with the result that the surface of the wood, exposed variously to the light, is clad in many tints: dark to the right, clear ahead, while on the left a violet sheen begins to undulate like a transparent nap over the iron hue of the leaves.

Before the wood, between two ravines, we perceive, very far off, a mountain entirely white, as white as orris root, on which there plays a slight pink tinge: these are the mountains of Corinth.

No one, complete silence, no wind, only at times the noise of the water. Still climbing; and suddenly there opens before you a great wave of land which curves rapidly, rises up before you a little to the right, and begins to roll away at once to the right, towards the plain of Orchomenos which is coming into view. To the left, grandiose motion, carrying its wood of red-brown oaks, now purpled. Between them, broad lawns descend. The tranquil light, falling abruptly from above like that in a studio, gave to the rocks and to the whole countryside something of statuary, an eternal smile analogous to that of the statues.

Gustave Flaubert, *Voyage en Orient* (1849–57);
translated by RS

Ascra

In the Boeotian plain below Mt. Helicon lies Ascra, the home of Hesiod, perhaps the earliest of Greek poets, who received his calling, like Caedmon, while he watched his sheep on the mountain.

Begin we from the Muses, O my song!
Whose dwelling is the vast and holy hill
Of Helicon; where aye, with delicate feet,
Fast by Jove's altar, and the fountain, dark
From azure depth, they tread the measured round;
And bathing their soft bodies in the brook
Permessus, or in that divinest spring
Olmius, or the well of Hippocrene,
O'er Helicon's smooth topmost height they wont
To thread their dances, graceful, kindling love,
And, with fast feet rebounding, smite the earth.
Thence rushing forth tumultuous, and enwrapt
In air's deep mist, they pass, with all their train,
On through the mount by night, and send abroad
A voice, in stilly darkness beautiful.

They to Hesiod erst
Have taught their stately song, the while he fed
His lambs beneath the heavenly Helicon.
And thus the goddesses, th' Olympian maids,
Whose sire is Jove, first hail'd me in their speech:
'Shepherds! that tend the fold afield, base lives,
Mere fleshly appetites, the Muses hear!
We know to utter fictions, veil'd like truths,
Or, an we list, speak truths without a veil.'
So spake the daughters of great Jove, whose speech
Is undisguis'd; and gave unto my hand
A rod, a bough of laurel blooming fresh,

Of goodly growth; and in me breathed a voice
Divine; that I might know, with listening ears,
Things past and future; and enjoin'd me praise
The race of blessed ones, that live for aye,
And first and last sing ever of themselves.

Hesiod, *Theogony*, 1–10, 22–34;
translated by C. A. Elton

James Gates Percival was born in 1795 in Connecticut. He was
hailed as America's Byron on the publication of his first poems in
1821, but did not build on his early promise. He was state geolo-
gist for Connecticut; he lived as a melancholy recluse, surrounded
by a huge collection of books, and was described on his death by the
Atlantic Monthly as "an inexhaustible, undemonstrative, noiseless,
passionless man, . . . impressing you, for the most part, as a creature
of pure intellect." His long poem, *Greece*, is an accomplished piece
of descriptive writing. Here his far-reaching eye looks down eastward from Mt. Parnassus:

> Down through a gloomy gorge,
> Walled in by rifted rocks, the vale of Ascra
> Lies, like a nook withdrawn beyond the reach
> Of violence; and yet the crescent crowns
> A minaret, and tells a startling tale
> Of woe and fear. Beyond, the Theban plain
> Stretches to airy distance, till it seems
> Lifted in air,—green cornfields, olive groves
> Blue as their heaven, and lakes, and winding rivers,
> And towns whose white walls catch the amber light,
> That burns, then dies away, and leaves them pale
> And glimmering, while a floating vapor spreads
> From marsh and stream, till all is like a sea,
> Rolling to Œta, and the Eubœan chain,
> Stretching, in purple dimness, on the verge
> Of this unclouded heaven.

The poet, Tony Harrison, while president of the Classical Association of Great Britain, visited Hesiod's country in the company of a
distinguished classical scholar and, in his lecture, "Facing up to
the Muses," delivered during the Association's proceedings in 1990,
drew from the landscape a poet's humorous response:

> . . . not too long afterwards we passed a sign reading
> ASKRI. 'That must be the ancient Askra where Hesiod was
> born,' said Dr. Taplin, and braked. 'Let's go there!' cried

Philomusus and Studioso together, and we turned left into a dusty side road. The drive to Askri took us longer than we expected, but we passed by timeless Greek images that gave me a sense of happiness 'without qualification,' that sort of 'unalloyed satisfaction' that E. R. Dodds derived from his wild cyclamen and sun-filled retsina: the blue bee boxes, the tins strapped to the pine trees catching the oozed resin to flavour the retsina, four goats on their hind legs stretching their necks to gobble figs from the tree, an image I'd seen on a fifth century vase. But then, as if to remind us that happiness without qualification can only exist in Golden Ages, that are mythical or locked in Hesiod, we were suddenly jolted out of our Boiotian well-being back into our times by a vast untended smouldering pile of rubbish and old lorry tyres giving off a foul Phlegraean smell. The fire had obviously been burning for days. It was probably that jolt into mephitic modernity and because we were making our new pilgrimage to the birthplace of Hesiod that made Dr. Taplin quote those lines from the poet's *Works and Days* (180–81) about the fifth age of mankind, the Age of Iron, when Zeus would destroy the whole race of meropon anthropon, 'men gifted with speech' . . .

We both fell quiet, I remember, our 'unalloyed satisfactions' somehow undermined by these thoughts, and I think we were both thinking the same thing, that even if it hadn't been the fifth age, the age of iron, for poor old Hesiod, then we of the late terrible twentieth century would certainly have to say . . .

'this really is the age of iron' (176). After some moments of this brooding, suddenly troubled silence, Oliver turned to me and said did I know there had been *poliokrotaphoi*, babies born *literally* with their hair already grey in Japan as a result of the A-bombs dropped on Hiroshima and Nagasaki. And with these chilling thoughts we arrived at a village with three *kapheneia*, all facing outwards towards the square, all full of men drinking coffee, clicking their worry beads and reading the newspapers (the two activities go together in the age of iron!) and looking out and watching life passing by which now happened to be Philomusus and Studioso. The village sign had said Panaghia so I leaned out of the car and said 'Where is Askri, please?' 'It's here,' said one old man. There was little evidence of poor old Hesiod, and in any case, come to think of it, didn't the poet himself write pretty grudgingly and dismissively about his birthplace . . .

'Askri, lousy in winter, terrible in summer and not much good at any time' (639-40). Scarcely approvable by the local tourist board. It was probably the remembered curmudgeonly, grousing voice of old Hesiod that induced Dr. Taplin to turn the car round and begin to head back the way we came. At that point the man I'd asked directions of made one of those eloquently economical Greek gestures that managed to convey with a slight movement of the wrist, 'Why the hell have you come to Askri only to turn your car round?' His gesture rather shamed us into stopping, and we got out and ordered a coffee and maybe (though still mindful of the blandishments of Madido), *maybe* an *ouzaki* and began talking to the men. 'Why had we come to Askri? Had we lost our way?' Dr. Taplin, whose modern Greek puts mine to shame, explained that he was a teacher of ancient Greek at Oxford and that I was a poet, and that we had wanted to pay homage to the birthplace of Hesiod. One of the men pointed to me and said, 'He is a *synadelphos Hesiodou*, a brother of Hesiod.' 'Of course,' said another, 'Hesiod's actual brother, Perses, he was a lazy bugger like me. Spent all his time in the *kapheneion!*' Then they said, like a chorus, if we'd come so far, and were really making a pilgrimage to Hesiod, we should go a little further still to the Valley of the Muses, and the Mouseion. They began to draw maps of various complicated tracks on cigarette packets, until finally, unable to transfer the directions to paper, one of the men said he'd come with us. We all got into the car and went along a very rough road for quite some time until we came almost to the end of the valley and could make out on the left a hollowed-out space covered with vegetation and thorns but with the unmistakable shape of an ancient theatre.

It turned out to be the Mouseion where the ancient *Mouseia*, the poetry festivals in honour of the Muses, were held. . . I was trying to imagine what it would have been like to read my poems in that place when it had been a theatre with an audience looking over my head towards Boiotia. I tried to cover the sweep of the auditorium now bristling with the thorns that had scourged our feet, and I raised my head to take in what would have been the very back row, and found myself facing up to the ridge of a mountain, and my hair literally began to stand on end. The mountain was, of course, Helicon and the spectators on the ridge none other than the Muses. They looked down on the poet performing his work. And the poet had to face up to the Muses.

Ludwig Lange, *Levadhia*. Staatliche Graphische Sammlung, Munich.

Levadia

Above Levadia was the ancient oracle of Trophonius, the remarkable method of consulting which is described in fascinating detail by Pausanias. It is one of our fullest records of Greek religious practice.

> With respect to what pertains to this oracle, when any one desires to descend into the cave of Trophonius, he must first take up his residence for a certain number of days in a building destined to this purpose. This building is a temple of *The Good Dæmon*, and of *Good Fortune*. While he stays here he purifies himself in other respects, and abstains from hot baths. The river Hercyna is used by him for a bath: and he is well supplied with animal food from the victims which are sacrificed. For he who descends hither sacrifices to Trophonius and his sons; to Apollo, Saturn, and Jupiter the king; to Juno *The Chariot Driver*, and to Ceres, whom they call Europa,

and who they say was the nurse of Trophonius. A diviner is present to each of the sacrifices, who inspects the entrails of the victims, and while he beholds them, prophesies whether or not Trophonius will propitiously receive the person who consults him. The other victims do not in a similar manner disclose the mind of Trophonius: but each person who descends to him sacrifices, on the night in which he descends, a ram in a ditch, invoking at the same time Agamedes. They pay no regard to the former entrails, even though they should be favourable, unless the entrails of this ram are likewise auspicious. And when it happens that the entrails thus correspond in signification, then the person that wishes to consult Trophonius, descends with good hope, and in the following manner: The sacrificers bring him by night to the river Hercyna; there they anoint him with oil; and two boys belonging to the city, each about thirteen years old, and whom they call Mercuries, wash him, and supply him with every thing necessary.

He is not immediately after this led by the sacrificers to the oracle, but is first brought to the fountains of the river, which are very near to each other. Here he is obliged to drink of that which is called the water of Lethe, that he may become oblivious of all the former objects of his pursuit. Afterwards he must drink of another water, which is called the water of *Mnemosyne*, or *memory*, that he may remember the objects which will present themselves to his view on descending into the grove. Having therefore beheld the statue, which they say was made by Dædalus (and which the priests never show to any but those who desire to consult Trophonius), performed certain religious ceremonies, and prayed, he proceeds to the oracle clothed in white linen, begirt with fillets, and having on his feet such slippers as are worn by the natives of this place. The oracle is above the grove in a mountain, and is inclosed with a wall of white stone, whose circumference is very small, and whose altitude is not more than two cubits. Two obelisks are raised on this wall, which, as well as the zones that hold them together, are of brass. Between these there are doors: and within the inclosure there is a chasm of the earth, which was not formed by nature, but was made by art, and is excavated in according proportion with consummate accuracy and skill. The shape of this chasm resembles that of an oven. Its breadth, measured diametrically, may be conjectured to be about four cubits. Its depth does not appear to me more than eight cubits. There are not steps to its bottom: but when any one designs to descend to Trophonius, they give him a ladder, which is both narrow and light. On descending into this chasm, between its bottom and summit there is a small cavern, the breadth of which is about two spans, and its altitude appears to be about one span.

He, therefore, who descends to the bottom of this chasm lays himself down on the ground, and holding in his hand sops mingled with honey, first of all places his feet in the small cavern, then hastens to join his knees to his feet; and immediately after the rest of his body contracted to his knees, is drawn within the cavern, just as if he was hurried away by the vortex of the largest and most rapid river. But those that have descended to the adytum of this place are not all instructed in the secrets of futurity in the same manner. For one obtains this knowledge by his sight, and another by his hearing; but all return through the same opening, and walk backwards as they return. They say no one that descended here ever died in the chasm, except one of the spear-bearers of Demetrius, who would not perform any of the established religious ceremonies, and who did not come hither for the purpose of consulting divinity, but that he might enrich himself by carrying the gold and silver from the adytum. It is also said, that his dead body was thrown up by a different avenue, and not through the sacred opening. Other reports are circulated about this man, but those which I have mentioned appear to me to be the most remarkable. When the person that descended to Trophonius returns, the sacrificers immediately place him on a throne, which they call the throne of Mnemosyne, and which stands not far from the adytum. Then they ask him what he has either seen or heard, and afterwards deliver him to certain persons appointed for this purpose, who bring him to the temple of Good Fortune, and the Good Dæmon, while he is yet full of terror, and without any knowledge either of himself, or of those that are near him. Afterwards, however, he recovers the use of his reason, and laughs just the same as before. *I write this, not from hearsay, but from what I have seen happen to others, and from what I experienced myself, when I consulted the oracle of Trophonius.* All, too, that return from Trophonius are obliged to write in a table whatever they have either heard or seen: and even at present the shield of Aristomenes remains in this place, the particulars respecting which I have already related.

Pausanias, *Description of Greece*, ix, 39;
translated by Thomas Taylor

Soon after Levadia is the "place where three roads meet," where Oedipus unwittingly killed his own father. The nearby village of Distomo was decimated by the occupying German forces in the Second World War in requital for resistance: a song came out of the event:

> A bird spoke up beside the river of Levadia
> And looked (my sons) toward Distomo.
> It keened (my sons) and spoke, it keens and it speaks out
> —At Distomo (my sons) they are killing.
>
> Anonymous song, in Beaton;* translated by RS

Mt. Parnassus

Parnassus, home of Apollo and the Muses, was a natural theme of celebration for romantic poets like Falconer and Byron.

> Contiguous here, with hallowed woods o'erspread,
> Renowned Parnassus lifts its honoured head;
> There roses blossom in eternal spring,
> And strains celestial feathered warblers sing:
> Apollo, here, bestows the unfading wreath;
> Here zephyrs aromatic odours breathe;
> They o'er Castalian plains diffuse perfume,
> Where round the scene perennial laurels bloom . . .
>
> William Falconer, *The Shipwreck*, III

> Oh, thou Parnassus! whom I now survey,
> Not in the phrensy of a dreamer's eye,
> Not in the fabled landscape of a lay,
> But soaring snow-clad through thy native sky,
> In the wild pomp of mountain majesty!
> What marvel if I thus essay to sing?
> The humblest of thy pilgrims passing by
> Would gladly woo thine echoes with his string,
> Though from thy heights no more one Muse will wave
>   her wing.

> Oft have I dream'd of thee! whose glorious name
> Who knows not, knows not man's divinest lore,
> And now I view thee, 'tis, alas, with shame
> That I in feeblest accents must adore.
> When I recount thy worshippers of yore
> I tremble, and can only bend the knee;

Nor raise my voice, nor vainly dare to soar,
But gaze beneath thy cloudy canopy
In silent joy to think at last I look on Thee!

Happier in this than mightiest bards have been,
Whose fate to distant homes confined their lot,
Shall I unmov'd behold the hallow'd scene,
Which others rave of, though they know it not?
Though here no more Apollo haunts his grot,
And thou, the Muses' seat, art now their grave,
Some gentle spirit still pervades the spot,
Sighs in the gale, keeps silence in the cave,
And glides with glassy foot o'er yon melodious wave.

Lord Byron, *Childe Harold's Pilgrimage*, I, 60–62

The naturalist John Sibthorp toured this part of Greece in summer 1794, finding the locals, as well as the monks of Ossios Loukas,
obliging in the provision of information.

July 6 (1794)
A monk of the cloister, famous for his knowledge in simples,
arrived the preceding evening. I had been told of his reputation at Delphi. I walked out into the wood with him at day-
break, a venerable octagenarian. I learnt from him more than
one hundred names of the plants growing in the environs of
the monastery; many of them were barbarous, yet most of
them were significative; some remained unaltered and uncor-
rupted; the ancient names of Theophrastus and Dioscorides.
To all he attributed some medical virtue, some superstitious
use. I regret much that the infirmities of his age would not permit me to carry him along with me to Livadea. I had offered
rewards on my arrival at the convent for procuring different
birds. A short time before my departure a Caloyer arrived,
making a triumphant entrance, followed by two men support-
ing an immense vulture. I do not find it mentioned by Lin-
næus, though frequent in the Greek mountains. It is called
ὀρνευ and λυκόρνεο; it measured, the wings expanded from
tip to tip, eight feet, and from the tip of the beak to the
extremity of the tail three feet nine inches, and weighed nine
okes, or twenty-two pounds and a half.

John Sibthorp, in *Walpole**

The fastnesses of Parnassus provided an effective retreat for the
rebels in the War of Independence. One of the local klephtic

leaders, Odysseus Androutsos, had secured a cave high on the mountain. E. J. Trelawny, that dashing soldier of fortune, describes the place:

> In one of the precipices of Mount Parnassus, in Livadia, the highest mountain in Greece, there is a cavern at an elevation of a thousand feet above the plain. This cavern Odysseus had, with great ingenuity, managed to ascend, and convert into a place of safety for his family and effects during the war. The only access to it was by ladders, bolted to the rock. The first ladder, forty-five or fifty feet in length, was placed against the face of the rock, and steadied by braces; a second, resting on a projecting crag, crossed the first; and a third, lighter and shorter, stood on its heel on a natural shelf in the fractured stone. This third ladder led to a trap-door; the bolts and bars of which being removed, you entered a vaulted guard-room, pierced with lancet-holes of musketry. This opened on a broad terrace, sixty feet in length, screened by a substantial parapet-wall, breast-high, with embrasures mounted with cannon. The height of the natural arch spanning the cave is thirty feet above this lower terrace, so that it is particularly light, airy, and cheerful, commanding extensive and magnificent views. Ascending by steps to a yet higher terrace of solid rock, the breadth and height of the cave diminishes, until the end is reached. On the right of the great cave there is a smaller one; besides which there are many small grottoes, the size of chambers, connected by galleries. They are perfectly dry, and were used for store-rooms and magazines. One of them I converted into a chapel for an old priest, covering the rugged walls with gaudy hangings, flaming paintings, and holy relics of saints, saved from the desecrated churches in the neighbourhood.
>
> The interior of this magnificent cavern often reminded me, with its grottoes, galleries, and vaulted roof, of a cathedral, particularly when the softened light of the evening obscured its ruggedness, or by moonlight. The towering mass of rock above the cave projected boldly over its base. To make it perfect, there was a never-failing supply of the purest water, which found its way through subterranean channels from the regions of perpetual snow, filtering through fractures in the rock above into a capacious cistern built on the upper terrace.
>
> This cavern was our citadel, and by removing the upper ladder became impregnable without the aid of a garrison. We built boarded houses within it, and stored it with all the

necessaries and many of the luxuries of life, besides immense
supplies of arms and ammunition.

E. J. Trelawny, *Records of Shelley,*
Byron and the Author (London, 1878)

Delphi

Delphi was one of the holiest sites of ancient Greece, which fact
alone should be enough to dispel the view that the ancients had
no feeling for the natural beauty of landscape. Regarded as the center of the earth—and marked as such by the navel stone still to be
seen in the museum—it was the chief sanctuary of Apollo and the
site of the Pythian Games, second only to the Olympic Games in
antiquity and prestige. The *Homeric Hymn to Apollo* describes the
legendary foundation of the sanctuary by the god himself:

> From hence [Delphusa], O Phoebus, first thou
>   mad'st retreat,
> And of the Phlegians reached the walled seat,
> Inhabited with contumelious men,
> Who, slighting Jove, took up their dwellings then
> Within a large cave, near Cephissus' lake.
> Hence, swiftly moving, thou all speed didst make
> Up to the tops intended, and the ground
> Of Crissa, under the-with-snow-still-crown'd
> Parnassus, reach'd, whose face affects the West;
> Above which hangs a rock, that still seems prest
> To fall upon it, through whose breast doth run
> A rocky cave, near which the King the Sun
> Cast to contrive a temple to his mind,
> And said, 'Now here stands my conceit inclin'd
> To build a famous fane, where still shall be
> An oracle to men, that still to me
> Shall offer absolute hecatombs, as well
> Those that in rich Peloponnesus dwell
> As those of Europe, and the isles that lie
> Wall'd with the sea, that all their pains apply
> T' employ my counsels. To all which will I
> True secrets tell, by way of prophecy,
> In my rich temple, that shall ever be
> An oracle to all posterity.'
> This said, the fane's form he did straight present,
> Ample, and of a length of great extent;
> In which Trophonius and Agamede,

Who of Erginus were the famous seed,
Impos'd the stony entry, and the heart
Of every God had for their excellent art.
    About the temple dwelt of human name
Unnumber'd nations, it acquir'd such fame,
Being all of stone, built for eternal date.
And near it did a fountain propagate
A fair stream far away . . .

Homeric Hymn to Apollo;
translated by George Chapman

A series of temples were, according to legend, built at Delphi, including one made of wax and feathers; the first was said to have been constructed by the heroes Trophonius and Agamedes. Pindar describes how the Olympian gods ("the children of Cronus") destroyed this temple because the female figures which adorned it, perhaps sirens like those who tempted Odysseus, killed pilgrims with the sweetness of their singing:

> Six golden enchantresses sang above the acroterion. But the children of Cronus, opening the earth with a thunderbolt, hid that thing, the most holy of all creations, in anger at their sweet voice, because strangers wasted away far from their children and wives, hanging their hearts on that honey-minded song.

Pindar, *Paean*, VIII, 70–79; translated by RS

The Delphians were proud of the beauty of their architecture and sculpture, which, in classical times, rivaled that of Athens. The temple-servant Ion in Euripides' play tends devoutly the façade of the temple of Apollo, and describes to the chorus of Athenian women what may have been the sculptures of the eastern pediment:

Ion: But see, the early birds have left their nests,
And this way from Parnassus wing their flight.
Come not, I charge you, near the battlements,
Nor near the golden dome. Herald of Jove,
Strong though thy beak beyond the feather'd kind,
My bow shall reach thee. Towards the altar, see,
A swan comes sailing: elsewhere wilt thou move
Thy scarlet-tinctured foot? or from my bow
The lyre of Phoebus to thy notes attuned
Will not protect thee; farther stretch thy wings;
Go, wanton, skim along the Delian lake,
Or thou wilt steep thy melody in blood.

Ludwig Lange, *Delphi*. Staatliche Graphische Sammlung, Munich.

Look, what strange bird comes onwards; wouldst thou fix
Beneath the battlements thy straw-built nest?
My singing bow shall drive thee hence; begone,
Or to the banks of Alpheus, gulfy stream,
Or to the Isthmian grove; there hatch thy young;
Mar not these pendent ornaments, nor soil
The temple of the god . . .

Chorus:
The stately column, and the gorgeous dome
Rais'd to the gods are not the boast alone
Of our magnificent Athens; nor the statues
That grace her streets: this temple of the god,
Son of Latona, beauteous to behold,
Beams the resplendent light of both her children.
Ion: Turn thine eyes this way: look, the son of Jove
Lops with his golden scimitar the heads
Of the Lernean Hydra: view it well.
Cho.: I see him.
Ion: And this other standing nigh,
Who snatches from the fire the blazing brand.

Cho.: What is his name? The subject, on the web
Design'd, these hands have wrought in ductile gold.
Ion: The shield-supporting Iolaus, who bears
The toils in common with the son of Jove.
View now this hero; on his winged steed
The triple-bodied monster's dreadful force
He conquers through the flames his jaws emit.
Cho.: I view it all attentively.
Ion: Observe
The battle of the giants, on the walls
Sculptur'd in stone.
Cho.:   Let us note this, my friends.
Ion: See where against Enceladus she shakes
Her gorgon shield.
Cho.:   I see my goddess, Pallas.
Ion: Mark the tempestuous thunder's flaming bolt
Launch'd by the hand of Jove.
Cho.:   The furious Mimas
Here blazes in the vollied fires; and there
Another earth-born monster falls beneath
The wand of Bacchus wreath'd with ivy round,
No martial spear. But, as 'tis thine to tend
This temple, let me ask thee, is it lawful,
Leaving our sandals, its interior parts
To visit?
Ion: Strangers, this is not permitted.
Cho.: Yet may we make inquiries of thee?
Ion: Speak;
What wou'dst thou know?
Cho.:   Whether this temple's site
Be the earth's centre.
Ion: Ay; with garlands hung,
And Gorgons all around.

> Euripides, *Ion;* translated by Robert Potter
>
> (London, 1781)

The oracle of Delphi was a significant power in both politics and private affairs for many centuries, foretelling in ambiguous verses the downfall of empires and the successes of Athens as well as the outcome of speculations and journeys. Its decline was a subject of comment already in antiquity. Plutarch, a priest at Delphi, devoted an essay to the subject; and the oracle itself is said to have given the following reply to the Emperor Julian in about A.D. 350:

Go tell the king—the carven hall is felled,
Apollo has no cell, prophetic bay
Nor talking spring; his cadenced well is stilled.

Oxford Book of Greek Verse, 627;
translated by Peter Jay in Peter Jay, ed.,
The Greek Anthology (London, 1973)

Milton identified its decline with the moment when Pan also died, at the birth of Christianity in the reign of Tiberius.

The Oracles are dumm,
No voice or hideous humm
    Runs through the arched roof in words deceiving.
Apollo from his shrine
Can no more divine,
    With hollow shriek the steep of Delphos leaving.
No nightly trance, or breathed spell,
Inspire's the pale-ey'd priest from the prophetic cell.

The lonely mountains o'er,
And the resounding shore,
    A voice of weeping heard, and loud lament;
From haunted spring, and dale
Edg'd with poplar pale,
    The parting Genius is with sighing sent,
With flowre-inwov'n tresses torn
The Nimphs in twilight shade of tangled thickets mourn.

John Milton, Hymn on
the Morning of Christ's Nativity

The water of Castalia, the spring of the Muses, was even in antiquity a desirable drink for the aspiring poet. Leigh Hunt recalled this in the following poem:

From EPISTLE TO LORD BYRON
ON HIS DEPARTURE FOR ITALY AND GREECE

. . . But I must finish, and shall chatter less
On Greece, for reasons which yourself may guess.
Only remember what you promised me
About the flask from dark-welled Castaly,—
A draught, which but to think of, as I sit,
Makes the room round me almost turn with wit.
Gods! What may not come true, what dream divine,
If thus we are to drink the Delphic wine!

The awesome beauty of Delphi has inspired more than one poet to verse. Here is a miscellany, the first by the traveler Aubrey de Vere, whose industrious explorations earned him the commendation of Landor:

From LINES WRITTEN UNDER DELPHI

A still, black glen—below, a stream-like copse
Of hoary olives—rocks like walls beside,
Never by Centaur trod, though these fresh gales
Give man the Centaur's strength! Again I mount,
From cliff to cliff, from height to ascending—
Glitters Castalia's fount; I see, I touch it!—
That rift once more I reach, the oracular seat,
Whose arching rocks half meet in air suspended—
Between them one blue streak of heaven; hard by
Dim Temples hollowed in the stone, for rites
Mysterious scooped, or mansions of the dead—
Released, I turn, and see, far, far below,
A vale so rich in floral garniture,
And odours from the orange and the sea,
So girt with white peaks flashing from sky chasms,
So lighted with the vast blue lamp of Heaven,
So lulled with music from the winds and waves,
The guest of Phoebus claps his hands and shouts,
'There is but one such spot: from Heaven Apollo
Beheld;—and chose it for his earthly shrine!'

Aubrey de Vere

DELFICA

Do you understand this ancient romance
at the foot of the sycamore, or under the white laurels,
the olive-tree, the myrtle, or the trembling willows,
This song of love, Daphne, which eternally recommences?

Do you recognise the temple, with its vast peristyle
and the bitter citrons in which your teeth plunged?
Or the cave, fatal to rash guests
Where the ancient seed of the conquered dragon sleeps?

They will return, these gods you always lament!
Time will bring back the ancient course of days;
The earth shuddered with a prophetic murmur . . .

Meanwhile, the sibyl with a Latin face
In sleeping still beneath Constantine's arch:
And nothing has disturbed the stern gateway.

Gérard de Nerval, *Tivoli*, 1843;
translated by RS

DELPHI

A plant, not laurel
Or myrtle, stem
and leaves united where spirit
and structure are grafted by metamorphosis
to prove that death
exists no less at Delphi.
And there is no laurel for the oracle,
no cave for its play. The sun blows
down from Parnassus and unhinges
the centre of the world. Castalia drips
warm on the tourist's lips
and the seller of sparkling water laughs
by the fountain with two votive
statuettes moist with mould. But at the first
step of the temple, if you know yourself,
Phoebus lifts his bow and shoots straight at the tendon,
hidden under the stone river-bed
where the sacred serpents give birth.
You know no longer if immobility is life
and death movement. Here on the stadium
from the chthonic cracks of the mountains,
razor-sharp and curved like the moon,
the plebeian charioteer with the low forehead
and the glazed eye of a grasshopper
Leaves eternally.

Salvatore Quasimodo; translated by RS

10

Northern Greece

Anonymous (Austro-Venetian School), *The Battle of Lepanto, October 7, 1571.* The National Maritime Museum, London.

I: Epirus
Nafpaktos/Lepanto

The narrows now guarded by Rhion and Andirrhion have been the site of two great battles in Greek history: the Battle of Naupactus between Athens (which held Naupactus) and Sparta in 429–28 B.C., at which Athens was victorious (Thucydides, 2, 86ff.), and the Battle of Lepanto in 1571 between the Crusaders and the Ottomans, which, like the first, was in fact fought outside the narrows in the Gulf of Patras, overlooked by the castle of Lepanto. Cervantes, the author of *Don Quixote*, fought in the battle and lost the use of his left hand: The experiences of the Captive in *Don Quixote* are based on Cervantes' own experiences in the war against the Turks. James I of England wrote a long and turgid poem on the battle, which was more memorably celebrated by G. K. Chesterton in his *Lepanto:*

> . . . The Pope was in his chapel before day or battle broke,
> *(Don John of Austria is hidden in the smoke.)*
> The hidden room in a man's house where God sits all
>   the year,

The secret window whence the world looks small and
 very dear.
He sees as in a mirror on the monstrous twilight sea
The crescent of the cruel ships whose name is mystery;
They fling great shadows foe-wards, making Cross and
 Castle dark;
They veil the plumèd lions on the galleys of St Mark;
And above the ships are palaces of brown, black-
 bearded chiefs,
And below the ships are prisons, where with multi-
 tudinous griefs
Christian captives sick and sunless, all a labouring
 race repines
Like a race in sunken cities, like a nation in the mines.
They are lost like slaves that swat, and in the skies of
 morning hung
The stairways of the tallest gods when tyranny was young.
They are countless, voiceless, hopeless as those fallen or
 fleeing on
Before the high Kings' horses in the granite of Babylon.
And many a one grows witless in his quiet room in hell,
Where a yellow face looks inward through the lattice
 of his cell,
And he finds his God forgotten, and he seeks no
 more a sign—
(But Don John of Austria has burst the battle line!)
Don John pounding from the slaughter-painted poop,
Purpling all the ocean like a bloody pirate's sloop,
Scarlet running over on the silvers and the golds,
Breaking of the hatches up and bursting of the holds,
Thronging of the thousands up that labour under sea,
White for bliss and blind for sun and stunned for liberty.
Vivat Hispania!
Domino Gloria!
Don John of Austria
Has set his people free!

Cervantes on his galley sets the sword back in the sheath.
(Don John of Austria rides homeward with a wreath)
And he sees across a weary land a straggling road in Spain,
Up which a lean and foolish knight for ever rides in vain,
And he smiles, but not as Sultans smile, and settles back
 the blade . . .
(But Don John of Austria rides home from the Crusade.)

The Lepanto of a century later is described by Bernard Randolph and by Sir George Wheeler:

> It is situated on the side of a high and steep hill, having six walls from the water-side to the castle, which cross the hills, all which and the castle are surrounded with a high wall, which runs up at each side of the city. The houses stand scattering between these several walls, but the greatest part are by the sea-side. The castle stands on the top of the hill. It is kept in very good repair. There are about twenty very good guns. The port is almost oval, having a very narrow entrance. There is a chain which passes from one side to the other. At each side of the entrance are places for many guns, though now they have not above three or four. The city is well peopled, being a nest of pyrats.
>
> Bernard Randolph, The Present State of the Morea
(London, 1686)

> There are not many Christians here, the greatest part being Turks and Jews; and hath been a very great harbour for pirats . . .
>
> The trade of this place consists of leather, oyl, tobacco, rice, barley, and wheat. Furrs also are good cheap here; and therefore, by the advice of our host, we lined our vests with good fox-skins; which was but needful: for the winter proved extream cold in these parts . . .
>
> We came in a very ill time to see this place: for the next day, so soon as it was light, all the barques were seized upon, to bring over the Basha of the Morea; who had received orders to come hither, and to Saint Mauro, to burn all the galliots, or small gallies of the pirates he should find there. But they staid not to be so complimented by him. The whole town was in a consternation at his coming; none stirred abroad, none opened their shops or doors. However we had the opportunity to see his reception, without stirring out of our chamber; it over-looking the harbour. The whole of his train was near five hundred persons; of which fifty Sclavonians were his guard. He crossed over from Vostitza, a town of the Morea, opposite to Lepanto. Before him in a boat came kettle-drums, others playing upon hautboys; and another string'd instrument, play'd on by a moor: between which we could conceive no manner of harmony. Before him also was carried upon a pole, two

horses tails, the marks of his dignity. At his arrival the port saluted him with five guns, and the Veivode, Caddi, and other chief officers of the town, came to the gate at his landing, to kiss his vest, and receive him with all the respect they were capable to give him. So soon as he was landed, he mounted on horse-back, and was conducted to the veivode's house; the rest accompanying him on foot. The next day he clapped the Emir in prison, instead of his brother, who had murdered one of the town a great while ago: but he came off again for a sum of money; which was all the Basha desir'd. The next day after he demanded fifty horses of the Turks, fifty of the Hebrews, and thirty of the Christians; these being the least part of the town.

George Wheeler, *Journey into Greece* (London, 1682)

Mesolonghi (Missolonghi):
Byron and the War of Independence

Further out from the narrows is the drear marsh town of Meso-longhi, immortal from its being the scene of the death of Lord Byron. Byron was one of many European philhellenes who went to the aid of Greece when the War of Independence broke out in 1821, offering their services as soldiers and, in Byron's case, con-siderable wealth in the service of the cause. The bitterness of the conflict and the passions it aroused are vividly described in William St. Clair's *That Greece Might Still Be Free*, and are also reflected in the oral poetry of the time. The following is a klephtic ballad from the locality of Yannina, which recalls the battle of Karpenisi in 1823:

> Three birds sat (ah! poor Kitzio Andoni mine)
> High up at Karpenisi, and lamented and said:
> 'What has happened to you, what has become of you?
> What has happened to you, what has become of you
>   this summer?
> Have they taken you alive?
> Have they taken you alive in the dark haunts of the klephts?
> Have the Albanians and the Mouhourdar Aga taken you?
> To Janina they brought you, to the Vizier's door.'
> The Vizier looked from the window.
> 'Greeting to you, Mouhourdar Aga, greeting to you, my lad.
> Mouhourdar, what word have you brought us? Is it
>   good news?'
> 'I have brought you Kitzio Andoni, with his hands bound
>   behind him.'

'Take him and bind him to the plane tree down there
And do not torture him hero that he is;
For it were a crime and a shame with such a hero;
Only take hammers and smite him on the arms and the legs,
Break his knees, and break his arms,
For he slew the Albanians, and Veli Ghekas himself.
With thirteen of his lads, and other bulu-bashis besides.
And do you torture him as much as you can,
And break him into pieces.'

Translated by John W. Baggally*

The Greek struggle inspired a number of European poets, among them Wilhelm Müller, the author of *Griechenlieder*, which range from translations of Greek folk poetry to free inventions, and Casimir Delavigne, who composed several lengthy odes on subjects such as the ruins of Greece and the death of Lord Byron. Felicia Hemans's *The Suliote Mother* is not untypical of the genre (the story it relates is also told by Thomas S. Hughes in his *Travels in Greece*, II, 67):

THE SULIOTE MOTHER

[It is related, in a French life of Ali Pasha, that several of the Suliote women, on the advance of the Turkish troops into the mountain fastnesses, assembled on a lofty summit, and, after chanting a wild song, precipitated themselves with their children into the chasm below, to avoid becoming the slaves of the enemy.]

She stood upon the loftiest peak,
   Amidst the clear blue sky;
A bitter smile was on her cheek,
   And a dark flash in her eye.

'Dost thou see them, boy?—through the dusky pines
Dost thou see where the foeman's armour shines?
Hast thou caught the gleam of the conquerer's crest?
My babe, that I cradled on my breast!
Wouldst thou spring from thy mother's arms with joy?
—That sight hath cost thee a father, boy!'

For in the rocky strait beneath,
   Lay Suliote sire and son:

Ari Scheffer, *Les Femmes Souliotes*. Musée du Louvre, Paris.

They had heaped high the piles of death
    Before the pass was won.

'They have crossed the torrent, and on they come:
Woe for the mountain hearth and home!
There, where the hunter laid by his spear,
There, where the lyre hath been sweet to hear,
There, where I sang thee, fair babe! to sleep,
Nought but the blood-stain our trace shall keep!'

And now the horn's loud blast was heard,
    And now the cymbal's clang,
Till even the upper air was stirred,
    As cliff and hollow rang.

'Hark! they bring music, my joyous child!
What saith the trumpet to Suli's wild?
Doth it light thine eye with so quick a fire,
As if at a glance of thine armèd sire?
Still!—be thou still!—there are brave men low:
Thou wouldst not smile couldst thou see him now!'

But nearer came the clash of steel,
    And louder swelled the horn,
And farther yet the tambour's peal
    Through the dark pass was borne.

'Hear'st thou the sound of their savage mirth?
Boy! thou wert free when I gave thee birth,—
Free, and how cherished, my warrior's son!
He too hath blessed thee, as I have done!
Ay, and unchained must his loved ones be—
Freedom, young Suliote! for thee and me!'

And from the arrowy peak she sprung,
    And fast the fair child bore:—
A veil upon the wind was flung,
    A cry—and all was o'er!

Another episode of the long war between Ali and the Suliotes provided the theme for S. L. Fairfield's lively poem of 1828, *The Suliote
Polemarque*: A party of Suliotes, led by a priest (Caloyer), take
refuge in a tower on Mt. Pindus:

—He fired the train!
The fire ran, leapt and burst and flew
    Through all the vaulted magazine,
And dark as fiends the Moslems grew—
    The Suliotes knelt and prayed serene,
Each for a moment—seas of flame
    Burst through vast rocks that had withstood
The skills of many a vaulted name,
    The earthquake and the boundless flood.
The mountain sprang asunder then,
    And mid a storm of shattered rocks,
The arms and limbs of thousand men
    Flew through the air in blackened flocks,
And, mid the glare and gloom—the roar,
    The reck, the ruin, upward rose,
Like the wind's glance o'er tower and shore,
    A form that triumph'd o'er his foes;
Blackened and rent, with hands outspread,
    And blood-shot eyes and lava lips,
And sword and torch, as when he said—
    'His hands in blood proud Ali dips—
Here is a stream and fire to dry!'
    O'er the haughty Pacha's head he rode
Like a quench'd meteor through the sky—
    The awful ruin of a god!
So Suli's cliffs and crags became
    A lurid mass of fire and blood,
The home of havoc and of flame,

> Where Freedom in her death hour stood,
> Where tyrants ne'er shall dare to stand,
>   While Suli's sons on earth draw breath,
> In that proud, holy, storied land
>   Where Glory lights the realms of Death.
>
>   S. L. Fairfield,
>   *Poetical Works* (Philadelphia, 1842)

Among the heroes of the war was Markos Botsaris, who died at the Battle of Karpenisi, about fifty miles from Mesolonghi. His epitaph is included in the collection of klephtic songs made by Charles Brinsley Sheridan, son of the playwright:

> Grecian stranger! pass not by!
> For beneath this tombstone lie
>   Blest remains.
> His—the bravest of the brave,
> Botzaris, who died to save
>   Greece from chains!
>
> Freedom was his idol still;
> His the unconquerable will
>   To *succeed:*
> To destroy our Moslem foes,
> To relieve our country's woes,
>   And be FREED.
>
> Here his ashes only rest,
> For his soul is with the blest,
>   With our sires,
> Those who nobly felt and fought,
> Kindling with each patriot thought
>   Freedom's fires.
>
> Tell the monarchs frowning round,
> That thy corse on Grecian ground,
>   And thy name,
> Bid us fight for equal laws,
> Nor elude in Freedom's cause
>   Death by shame.

Dionysios Solomos, the national poet of Greece and author of Greece's national anthem, in his long and self-indulgent *Lyrical poem on the Death of Lord Byron*, imagines his hero mourning and drawing inspiration from the grave of Botsaris. Byron himself laid bare the consideration that led him to give his life to the cause in the poem he wrote, at Mesolonghi, on the eve of his thirty-sixth birthday:

On This Day I Complete My Thirty-sixth Year

'Tis time this heart should be unmoved,
    Since others it hath ceased to move;
Yet, though I cannot be beloved,
    Still let me love!

My days are in the yellow leaf;
    The flowers and fruits of Love are gone;
The worm, the canker, and the grief
    Are mine alone!

The fire that on my bosom preys
    Is lone as some volcanic isle;
No torch is kindled at its blaze—
    A funeral pile.

The hope, the fear, the jealous care,
    The exalted portion of the pain
And power of love, I cannot share,
    But wear the chain.

But 'tis not *thus*—and 'tis not *here*—
    Such thoughts should shake my soul, nor *now*
Where Glory decks the hero's bier,
    Or binds his brow.

The Sword, the Banner, and the Field,
    Glory and Greece, around me see!
The Spartan, borne upon his shield,
    Was not more free.

Awake! (not Greece—she *is* awake!)
    Awake, my spirit! Think through *whom*
Thy life-blood tracks its parent lake,
    And then strike home!

Tread those reviving passions down,
    Unworthy manhood!—unto thee
Indifferent should the smile or frown
    Of Beauty be.

If thou regret'st thy youth, *why live?*
    The land of honourable death
Is here:—up to the Field, and give
    Away thy breath!

Seek out—less often sought than found—
  A soldier's grave, for thee the best;
Then look around, and choose thy ground,
  And take thy Rest.
                              Missolonghi, 22 January 1824

On 15 February he was taken ill, and from that illness he never fully recovered, but died on 19 April. Pietro Gamba, his doctor, gives an eyewitness's account:

> It was Easter day, on which holiday, after twelve o'clock, the Greeks are accustomed to discharge their fire-arms and artillery. Fearing that the noise might be injurious to my Lord, we thought of marching our artillery brigade out of the city, and by exercising our guns, to attract the crowd from the vicinity of his house. At the same time, the town guard patroled the streets, and informing the people of the danger of their benefactor, invited them to make as little noise as possible near the place where he lay. Our scheme succeeded perfectly; but, nevertheless, we should not have been induced to quit the house if we had been aware of the real state of our friend. I do not think that he suspected it himself, even so late as three in the afternoon . . .
>
> It was about six o'clock in the evening when he said, 'I want to go to sleep now'; and immediately turning round, he fell into that slumber, from which, alas! he never awoke. From that moment he seemed incapable of sense or motion: but there were occasional symptoms of suffocation, and a rattling in the throat, which induced his servants now and then to raise his head. Means were taken to rouse him from his lethargy, but in vain. He continued in this state for four-and-twenty hours; and it was just a quarter past six o'clock on the next day, the 19th, that he was seen to open his eyes, and immediately shut them again. The physicians felt his pulse—he was gone!
>
> Pietro Gamba, *Narrative of Lord Byron's Last Journey*
> *to Greece* (London, 1825)

The Provisional Government of Western Greece issued a proclamation, reported in the *Morning Chronicle* of Saturday, 15 May 1824:

> The present day of festivity and rejoicing has become one of sorrow and of mourning. The Lord Noel Byron departed this life at six o'clock in the afternoon, after an illness of ten days; his death being caused by an inflammatory fever. Such

J. Odevaere, *The Death of Lord Byron*. Groeningemuseum, Bruges.

was the effect of his Lordship's illness on the public mind, that all classes had forgotten their usual recreations of Easter, even before the afflicting event was apprehended.

The loss of this illustrious individual is undoubtedly to be deplored by all Greece; but it must be more especially a subject of lamentation at Missolonghi, where his generosity has been so conspicuously displayed, and of which he had even become a citizen, with the further determination of participating in all the dangers of war.

Everybody is acquainted with the beneficent acts of his Lordship, and none can cease to hail his name as that of a real benefactor.

Until, therefore, the final determination of the national government be known, and by virtue of the powers with which it has been pleased to invest me, I hereby decree,

1st. To-morrow morning, at daylight, thirty-seven minute guns will be fired from the Grand Battery, being the number which corresponds with the age of the illustrious deceased.

2d. All the public offices, even the tribunals, are to remain closed for three successive days.

3d. All the shops, except those in which provisions or medicines are sold, will also be shut; and it is strictly enjoined that every species of public amusement, and other demonstrations of festivity at Easter, shall be suspended.

4th. A general mourning will be observed for twenty-one days.

5th. Prayers and a funeral service are to be offered up in all the churches.

Given at Missolonghi,

this 19th day of April, 1824.

(Signed) A. Mavrocordato.
George Praidis, Secretary.

The effect of Byron's death was shattering and instantaneous: He immediately became a hero of Greece, and was celebrated in klephtic ballads as well as in the poetry of Delavigne and other Romantic poets. The following ballad, the original of which was first printed by J. A. Notopoulos in the *Keats-Shelley Journal*, 4 (London, 1955), is typical:

A golden eagle soared on high over Missolonghi;
He looks to the right, he looks to the left, he looks down on
    the castle.
He whets his talons on a frozen tomb.
Rise up, great Lord, rise up, for it is noon.
Rise up, put on your weapons and take up your pen,
Write to the East, tell it to the West.
Missolonghi is your grave, and you will rise one day
With the leap of a deer, with the pride of a lion,
With the voice of a nightingale, to write the songs
Which the enslaved sing, when they take up their weapons.

Translated by RS

A hundred and fifty years later, his memory remains green in the lament of Louis MacNeice, "Cock o' The North":

The flattest place, it seems, in Hellas. A bad dream.
The sea gets never deeper, nor is it sea;
A thin mud line coalesces with the horizon.
Whose name was writ in bilge . . . A stilted hovel
Like a sick bird 'stood hunched in the lagoon,
Its thatchy feathers moulting. Stepping stones through pus
But the next step was where? Across the gulf
The mountains of the Morea seemed a mirage; to the east
What there remained of a river flowing from Calydon
Wept stones for Meleager. The boar was black
Like the after-life of an Ethiop; his tusks
Flashed curving through the forest like the Milky Way
And his small eyes were death. But not Meleager's;

His death came through fire, in his hour of triumph,
Through a fire some miles away. And miles behind, away,
Byron while shooting duck felt groping at his liver
The flames in Six Mile Bottom. You would never guess
This from his statue in the Garden of Heroes
Among the arranged trees and the marble clichés
And the small memorial cannon like staring infants
With lollipops in their mouths. You would never guess
From Greece who Veeron was. Across the gulf—
'*Hier stand, hier sass* Their Royal Highnesses . . .'
The marble bust of Clauss, benevolent distiller,
Guards his titanic vats, German epigonos
Who found Greece free and under a foreign king,
Frockcoats instead of turbans. Now in the heat
Missolonghi yawns and cannot close its mouth
And all its bad teeth show. The tired horizon
Remains a line of mud. In the plain around
The fruit trees, like his Souliots, wear white stockings,
The oleanders are pink and dry beside the river
Which weeps for Meleager. Crackle and hiss
On the hearths of Calydon and Kirkby Mallory.
Who had faced the brute, his life in the log—
But so far away—was burning away.

The heroism of Mesolonghi's resistance to three sieges in the
course of four years inspired a number of ballads. The following
short one was heard by Robert Pashley from a Roumeliote in Crete:

Would that on high I could ascend,
    And like a bird could fly,
To gaze on Messolonghi's walls
    In distant Rumeli.

To see with all the Moslem host
    And four Pashas its fight,
While balls like drops of rain descend,
    And bombs like hail alight.

To see there too the light tufeks
    Like sands on the sea shore;
They said that it surrendered had,
    And would contend no more:

They said that Messolonghi had
    Submitted to the foe,

> While still in war alone she seeks
>   Her bravery to show.
>   R. Pashley, *Travels in Crete*
>   (London, 1837), II, 134f.

A longer version of the same song given in G. F. Abbott's *Songs of Modern Greece* (Cambridge, 1900) celebrates the resistance of the city with Markos Botsaris as its leader:

> They all swore by Ahmed Mohammed to enter Meso-longhi and feast there on Christmas day, before sunrise. 'Allah! Allah!' they shouted and rushed forward. The Turks planted ladders to climb on the trenches, but the musket-shots and the sabre strokes made them fall as thick as frogs.

The town with its low defence wall finally fell to the Turks in April 1826. Ibrahim Pasha, who led the victorious army, boasted that his men collected 3,000 heads, and that ten barrels of salted human ears were sent to Constantinople for the Sultan's delectation.

Akri (Actium)

Actium, now Akri, in the Gulf of Preveza, was the site of a great battle of antiquity, that of 2 September 31 B.C., at which the fleet of Antony and Cleopatra was decisively defeated by Octavian, the future Emperor Augustus. Roman poets were encouraged to celebrate the event. Propertius' account, written many years later, is the most graphic:

> The scene: The Athamanian coast, the shore of Apollo,
>   a sheltering bay out of Ionian sea rumble;
>   Actium's sea, a relief to sailors,
>   a memorial to Julian craft.
> Here the fleets of the world assembled,
>   great bulks of pine, stock-still on the water.
> The bird of providence failed one side,
>   one fleet to be ruined by Trojan Augustus,
>   for the shame of a Roman lance in the hands of
>   a woman.
>   And under conquering insignia
>   sails tightened
>   in Jovian blessing,
> & Nereus bent the twin ranks in a sharp crescent,
>   & the painted water shimmered
>   In the radiation of arms.

    & Rome came back victorious
       with Apollo's help; and that woman
      was brought to ruin; the Ionian floated broken scepters.

Propertius, IV, 6;
translated by J. P. McCulloch

Shakespeare's Antony and his men see the conflict from the other viewpoint:

Scarus: The greater cantle of the world is lost
With very ignorance; we have kiss'd away
Kingdoms and provinces
Enobarbus: How appears the fight?
Scarus: On our side like the token'd pestilence,
Where death is sure. Yon ribald-rid nag of Egypt,
Whom leprosy o'ertake! i' the midst o' the fight,
When vantage like a pair of twins appear'd,
Both as the same, or rather ours the elder,
The brize upon her, like a cow in June,
Hoists sail, and flies.
Enobarbus: That I beheld:
Mine eyes did sicken at the sight, and could not
Endure a further view.
Scarus: She once being loof'd,
The noble ruin of her magic, Antony,
Claps on his sea-wing, and like a doting mallard,
Leaving the fight in height, flies after her:
I never saw an action of such shame;
Experience, manhood, honour, ne'er before
Did violate so itself.

William Shakespeare,
Antony and Cleopatra, III, viii

Arta

In many countries it was traditional to wall up a human sacrifice to ensure the solidity of a bridge. The following, one of the most famous of Greek songs, derives its theme from this practice. The same story is told of a bridge near Canea, of the "Lady's Bridge" over the river Ladon, of one over the Hellada near Thermopylae, and the bridge of Antimachia in Cos (J. C. Lawson, *Modern Greek Folklore and Ancient Greek Religion*, 262). The sacrifice of a Moslem or a Jew was regarded as desirable at the building of any new bridge in Zakynthos late in the last century (ibid., 276).

The Bridge of Arta

Forty-five builders and sixty apprentices
Were building the foundations to bridge the river at Arta.
They built all day, and every night their work
    crumbled away.
The builders and the apprentices began to weep and mourn
    their wasted work:
'Worthless is all our work and toil, a doom is on our labour:
We build all day, and every night our work crumbles away.'
A little bird flew by, it settled on the farther bank,
It did not sing like any bird, it sang not like a swallow,
It sang and spoke with human voice:
'Unless you make a man a ghost, your bridge will
    never stand:
But do not destroy an orphan, a stranger or a traveller:
Destroy instead the lovely wife of your own master-builder,
Who comes each morning late, and late again each
    evening comes.'
The master-builder heard this and he sickened unto death:
He sends a message to his wife by a bird, a nightingale:
Let her come slowly, slowly come, and bring him late
    his dinner:
Let her come slowly, slowly come, and cross the bridge
    of Arta.
But the bird misheard, and misdelivered what he asked,
    and said
'Oh come now quickly, quickly come, and bring him soon
    his dinner:
Oh come now quickly, quickly come, and cross the bridge
    of Arta.'
Now she appears and comes in sight upon the
    gleaming pathway:
The master builder sees her come, his heart breaks
    into fragments.
From far she greets them, and from near she speaks to them
    and says
'Joy, health to you, you builders and to you apprentices:
But why is the master builder so downcast, and why
    so silent?'
'His ring has fallen down below the first arch of the bridge,
And who will go, and who will go, and bring him out
    his ring?'
'Builder, do not lament, for I will fetch it up for you,

And I will go, and I will go, and bring you out your ring.'
She scarce was down, and had not reached the middle of
    the river—
'Pull up the chain, my love, pull up the chain and
    me together
I have turned over all the place, but not found anything.'
And the master-builder seized a rock, and hurled it down
    upon her.

'Alas our fate, our destiny, alas our great misfortune.
We were three sisters, three we were, with evil
    dooms predestined:
For one of us built the Danube bridge, and one of us
    the Euphrates,
And I, the youngest of the three, I built the bridge of Arta.
May this bridge shake like a poppy-head, so may it shake
    and tremble,
And as the leaves fall from the trees, so may the
    travellers tumble.'
'Woman, woman, leave off your words, and let your curse
    be altered;
For you have but one brother, and he may one day cross
    this bridge.'
And the woman left off her words, and let her curse be
    altered:
'If the high mountains tremble, let this bridge then tremble:
If the wild birds fall from the sky, let the traveller tumble;
For I have one brother at home, and he may cross
    this bridge.'

Greek folk song, in C. A. Trypanis, ed.,
Penguin Book of Greek Verse, no. 225; translated by RS

Pindus

The philhellene poet William Haygarth (see also the chapter on Athens, page 125), whose style in topographical poetry has been overshadowed by the greater genius of Byron, describes the Pindus range in his address to Nature:

O let me seek thy haunts upon the brow
Of Pindus, where thou dwell'st 'midst solitudes
Of stern sublimity: with slow, slow step,
Painfully press'd upon th' unyielding rock,
I scale its rugged steeps; the dang'rous path,

Now lost behind a broken mass of crag,
And now along the precipice's edge
Trac'd fearfully, eludes at length the eye,
Its course first shewn by a long line of flocks,
On whose white fleeces ev'ning's level beam
Glances. Wilder, and sterner to the view,
The prospect opens: here the torrent pours
Its waters, breaking into gems of foam
O'er the black rock, that midway in its stream
Rears its rough front; or round the shatter'd root
Of some vast tree, torn from its parent cliff,
Curling in silv'ry eddies: there the pine
Stretches his giant limbs, scorch'd by the fires
Of Heav'n, and stands to guard yon narrow pass,
An aged warrior, cover'd o'er with wounds.
More distant the brown woods around me rise,
Range over range, a sylvan theatre,
Their tops illumin'd by a flood of light,
The rest deep sunk in shade; whilst far above
The broad bare peaks shoot boldly to the clouds,
Flinging from their bleak bosoms the last hues
Of day; yellow and purple melting soft
Into the russet tints that sleep below.
　　Within the windings of yon wood, which glides
With easy curve along the mountain's side,
The Muses dwelt . . .

William Haygarth,
Greece: A Poem (London, 1814)

Here is Byron describing the same terrain:

Monastic Zitza! from thy shady brow,
Thou small, but favour'd spot of holy ground!
Where'er we gaze, around, above, below,
What rainbow tints, what magic charms are found!
Rock, river, forest, mountain, all abound,
And bluest skies that harmonise the whole:
Beneath, the distant torrent's rushing sound
Tells where the volumed cataract doth roll
Between those hanging rocks, that shock yet please the soul.

Amidst the grove that crowns yon tufted hill,
Which, were it not for many a mountain nigh
Rising in lofty ranks, and loftier still,

Might well itself be deem'd of dignity,
The convent's white walls glisten fair on high:
Here dwells the caloyer, nor rude is he,
Nor niggard of his cheer; the passer by
Is welcome still; nor heedless will he flee
From hence, if he delight kind Nature's sheen to see.

Here in the sultriest season let him rest,
Fresh is the green beneath those aged trees;
Here winds of gentlest wing will fan his breast,
From heaven itself he may inhale the breeze:
The plain is far beneath—oh! let him seize
Pure pleasure while he can; the scorching ray
Here pierceth not, impregnate with disease:
Then let his length the loitering pilgrim lay,
And gaze, untired, the morn, the noon, the eve away.

Dusky and huge, enlarging on the sight,
Nature's volcanic amphitheatre,
Chimaera's alps extend from left to right:
Beneath, a living valley seems to stir;
Flocks play, trees wave, streams flow, the mountain fir
Nodding above; behold black Acheron!
Once consecrated to the sepulchre.
Pluto! if this be hell I look upon,
Close shamed Elysium's gates, my shade shall seek for none.

No city's towers pollute the lovely view;
Unseen is Yanina, though not remote,
Veil'd by the screen of hills: here men are few,
Scanty the hamlet, rare the lonely cot:
But, peering down each precipice, the goat
Browseth; and, pensive o'er his scatter'd flock,
The little shepherd in his white capote
Doth lean his boyish form along the rock,
Or in his cave awaits the tempest's short-lived shock.

Oh! where, Dodona! is thine aged grove,
Prophetic fount, and oracle divine?
What valley echo'd the response of Jove?
What trace remaineth of the Thunderer's shrine?
All, all forgotten—and shall man repine
That his frail bonds to fleeting life are broke?
Cease, fool! the fate of gods may well be thine:

Wouldst thou survive the marble or the oak?
When nations, tongues, and worlds must sink beneath
    the stroke!

Lord Byron, Childe Harold's Pilgrimage, ii, 48–53

Since Byron wrote, the site of Dodona has been ascertained. In his time, almost nothing was known of the site of the Oracle of Zeus other than the allusions of Pausanias, and Achilles' address to Zeus in the *Iliad:*

> Great Dodonaeus, president of cold Dodona's tow'rs,
> Divine Pelasgicus, that dwell'est far hence; about
>   whose bow'rs
> Th' austere prophetic Selli dwell, that still sleep on
>   the ground,
> Go bare, and never cleanse their feet . . .

Homer, Iliad, 16, 234–36;
translated by George Chapman

Christopher Wordsworth wrote in his *Description of Greece* (London, 1882), "to ascertain the site of Dodona would seem now to require a response from the Oracle itself"; however, he went on to describe the considerations which led him to settle on the now-agreed site at Dramisus, a conclusion confirmed by the excavations of Constantine Carapanos in 1875 and subsequent years.

In 1827 David Urquhart (1805–77), from Braelangwell in Cromarty, set sail to take part in the War of Independence. In 1830 he was appointed British commissioner to accompany Prince Leopold to the newly independent Greece, but the Prince declined and Urquhart returned. In 1833 he returned to Constantinople to investigate trade openings, and obtained the confidence of the Turkish government, until he was removed from the Porte by Lord Palmerston. He continued, however, to promote the "pacification of the Levant" by all means in his power. His account of his adventures during the war makes a lively book, and his adventures and escapades were numerous. It was published in 1838 with the title *The Spirit of the East.* Here he describes his reception at a camp of Pallikari (Greek "heroes") in the Makron Oros, at the southern end of the Pindus range, above the Gulf of Arta:

> Arriving at Veli's bivouac, we found on a little knoll, shaded by an oak, and commanding a prospect of the Gulf and Plain of Arta, a large table, and an ample sofa on each side, formed of branches fixed in the ground, woven with boughs, thickly covered with oak-leaves; quite of a different character,

but quite as tasteful—more so it could not be—as the chamber over the sea in which we had been received in the morning. Whilst we were taking our coffee, the Palicars formed a large circle around, and shewed, by the conscious smile that followed our encomiums on their Arcadian taste, the part and interest they had taken in the preparations for our reception. They paid us a pretty compliment by the mouth of the Grammaticos; and, after standing about ten minutes, their chief said, 'The Hellenes may now retire'. Formerly it would have been the 'Palicars'; but their hopes were now warmer, their aspirations higher, and they disclaimed even the names that were associated with their previous history.

Our evening repast was positively sumptuous; five large fires had been put in requisition for it. A community of shepherds could not have boasted greater variety, or excellence of laitage, and here, in the wilderness, we had whiter and sweeter bread than I ever tasted in Paris or London. Young *zarcadia* (wild deer) and little brindled boars picked up the crumbs around, and disputed them with the pups of Macedonian greyhounds. When the evening set in, and the moon arose, the long Romaika was led out on the mountain's brow.

> Their leader sung, and bounded to his song,
> With choral voice and step, the martial throng.

For two long hours did the leaders dip and twirl, while the long tail ebbed and flowed, like a following wave, to the mellifluous air—

> Πως το τρίβουν, το πιπέρι,
> Οἱ διαβόλοι καλογέροι.

Yannina

Yannina, with its unusual situation beyond the mountains of Epirus on Lake Pambotis, was one of the strongholds of Turkish rule in Greece for many centuries before Ali Pasha established his virtually independent satrapy in the city, whose fortress he rebuilt in 1798–99. It had been the scene of one of the earlier, and best documented, insurrections against Turkish rule, led by Metropolitan Dionysios of Trikala in 1580. This rising was suppressed with extreme savagery by the Turks, who enlisted the aid of the Jews of Yannina to devise ingenious ways of putting the Christians to death; these made plentiful use of the cross, the hammer and nails, the spit, the grid-iron, and the flaying knife. (See A. Paradissis, *Fortresses and Castles of Greece, Athens,* 1974, II, 111ff.) This tradition of cruelty was continued by Ali Pasha, whose rule in Yannina became a byword for luxury. François Pouqueville, who was French vice-consul in Yannina in the early years of the nineteenth century, is remarkably flattering in his description of Ali. (Schooled in the French Revolution, he perhaps tolerated Ali's excesses, as well as finding the food better than that at Athens! Charles Cockerell, when he visited him, found him "a Frenchman of the worst type," a vulgar braggart.)

Though now forty-eight years of age, no traces of premature old age are discernible in his exterior. His countenance is open and dignified, indicating a strong mind; and his features always express very powerfully the passions by which he is agitated. Master, however, when he pleases, of the variations of his physiognomy, he can assume at will the most engaging smile, masking by it a sentiment very contrary to what it appears to express. Yet his anger cannot be restrained when he inflicts punishment; it is dreadfully manifested in the workings of his countenance, and by a convulsion of his frame, which unfolds the violence of his character. For the rest, he is courageous in the extreme. His stature is tall and athletic; and he cannot uncover his arms or his breast without showing honourable scars.

Ali governs the people subjected to him by the double means of terror and confidence. Formerly the shops were shut the moment he appeared in the streets, and he congratulated himself upon being feared; but he begins to discover that it is better to be loved, and he has thrown aside a part of the ostentation by which he was surrounded. Free from that excess of barbarous ferocity which sheds blood without a motive, the massacres with which he may be reproached have never been perpetrated without a conviction in his own mind that they were necessary to his interest or tranquillity: it must however be allowed that his suspicious character has often led to his considering himself as surrounded with imaginary dangers. He protects industry and commerce, and is anxious to attract the latter to the countries he governs: on these and many points he has enlarged views, which appear surprising in a man living in a state of so much supposed barbarism.

François Pouqueville, *Travels in the Morea, Albania and Other Parts of the Ottoman Empire* (London, 1813)

The luxury, and the cruelty, are more vividly expressed in the accounts of Thomas S. Hughes and of Lord Byron:

The next day was still dedicated to the satisfaction of our curiosity in viewing the city. We first proceeded to the suburbs at its northern extremity, for the purpose of visiting the beautiful kiosk or pavilion of Ali Pasha, situated in the midst of extensive gardens, where indeed a natural, more than artificial taste, predominates, and fine elms or beeches, mixed with the plane tree and the cypress form umbrageous shades impervious to the sun. These gardens are the vizir's favourite retirement, and in this pavilion he enjoys leisure and relaxation from the fatigues of business, without removing too far from the occupations of government and the engagements of his capital. There is also a small room in a different part of the garden where he frequently transacts business, administers justice, and pays his troops. But there are, I should suppose, not less than thirty of these little tenements in and about Ioannina, to which this chieftain is in the habit of retiring for the enjoyment of his pleasures or the transaction of his most important affairs: as he selects a different place almost every day, it is never known where he can be found until he is actually housed. This custom seems to originate more from caprice than any fear which a tyrant might be suspected to entertain: for no one can expose himself more openly than Ali. He seems to know no terror of this sort. He constantly rides through Ioannina on horseback attended by one single guard, and admits freely all persons into his presence armed or unarmed, whether he may be alone or surrounded by his attendants. His very confidence seems to be his protection, and the multitude fancy that he bears a charmed life.

At the entrance into the gardens of the kiosk are some quarters for Albanian troops: in the court a fine leopard is kept, which by constant association with man has become so tame that we saw it let out loose into the yard whilst we stood by: but the sight of persons in a strange dress seemed to revive its natural ferocity, and it became necessary for our safety to throw a large piece of meat before the animal. A long alley which in summer is overspread with vines, led us up to the entrance of the kiosk. It is an elegant building, profusely ornamented with carving and gilding in the best Turkish style, and its construction does credit to the architects of Ioannina. Its interior is divided into eight compartments, or deep recesses, diverging out of the great area, in the middle of which stands a curious jet d'eau. This consists of a small castle built of marble surmounted by cannon, and surrounded by regular lines which play upon each other in imitation of a bombardment: between the cannon, on the parapet, stand figures of parrots, lions, and other birds or beasts, who spout water also out of their mouths as if in mockery at what is going forward: the motion of the water gives voice to a small organ attached to a pillar in the apartment. The whole may be considered an apt measure of the national taste where the curious is preferred to the beautiful, and that which can astonish a vulgar mind to what might captivate a cultivated and refined one.

Thomas S. Hughes, *Travels in Sicily, Greece and Albania*
(London, 1820)

> In marble-paved pavilion, where a spring
> Of living water from the centre rose,
> Whose bubbling did a genial freshness fling,
> And soft voluptuous couches breathed repose
> Ali reclined, a man of war and woes:
> Yet in his lineaments ye cannot trace,
> While Gentleness her milder radiance throws
> Along that aged venerable face,
> The deeds that lurk beneath, and stain him
>   with disgrace.
>
> It is not that yon hoary lengthening beard
> Ill suits the passions which belong to youth;
> Love conquers age—so Hafiz hath averr'd,
> So sings the Teian, and he sings in sooth—
> But crimes that scorn the tender voice of ruth,
> Beseeming all men ill, but most the man
> In years, have marked him with a tiger's tooth;
> Blood follows blood, and, through their mortal span,
> In bloodier acts conclude those who with blood began.

Lord Byron, *Childe Harold's Pilgrimage*, II, 62–63

Ali's savage treatment of his opponents was famous; the administration of the Turkish brand of justice took similarly savage forms.

The following ballad alludes to the events of 11 January 1801, when a Greek lady named Phrosyne and seventeen others suffered the traditional punishment meted out by the Turks to adulterous women, and were sewn in sacks and drowned. Phrosyne had had a clandestine liaison with Mukhtar Pasha, from whom she had received a gold ring. When the liaison was over, and she fell into poverty, she attempted to sell the ring, which was recognized and led to her condemnation.

The story is also told in Henry Gally Knight's poem, *Phrosyne*. Byron describes how one day in 1801, when returning from Piraeus, he met a group of soldiers setting out to inflict a similar fate on a Greek woman; by a combination of threats and bribery, he secured the release of the unfortunate girl.

Hear what occurred at Yannina, at the lake of Yannina,
How they drowned the seventeen, with lady Phrosyne.
　　Ah, worthy Phrosyne!
　　Woe for your suffering!

No other threw off her rich dress, her fine
　　embroidered gown,
Phrosyne was the first, and she first went into the water.
　　Ah, worthy Phrosyne,
　　Famed throughout the world.

They didn't tell you, Phrosyne, to hide your finger-ring:
If Ali Pasha learns of it, the snake will swallow you.
　　Ah, worthy Phrosyne,
　　What evil shall befall!

'If you are Turks release me, I will give you a
　　thousand florins,
Drag me to Mukhtar Pasha, to speak two words with him.'
　　Ah, worthy Phrosyne,
　　What evil shall befall!

'Pasha, where are you, come to me, run forward now
　　and save me;
Persuade great Ali to relent, and give him what you will.'
　　Ah, Phrosyne, my partridge,
　　What you suffer, my lady!

Your florins and your weeping will not alter the Vizier,
And you and the other seventeen shall be the fishes' dinner.
　　Ah Phrosyne my partridge,
　　My bowels are wrenched for you.

Would that the stones were sugar, they would crumble in
　　the lake,
And make the bitter water sweet for lady Phrosyne.
　　Ah worthy Phrosyne,
　　Lying in the lake.

Blow north winds, blow Thracian winds, and make the
   waters churn,
That they may cast the women out with lady Phrosyne.
   Ah worthy Phrosyne,
   Lying in the lake.

Phrosyne, your house weeps for you, your children weep
   for you,
All Yannina is mourning you, and weeping for your beauty.
   Ah Phrosyne my partridge,
   My bowels are wrenched for you.

> Ballad, from N. G. Politis, ed., *Kleftika Demotika Tragoudia*;
> translated by RS

An excellent, if relentlessly blood-curdling, account of the life of
Ali Pasha is given in William Plomer's *The Diamond of Yannina*
(London, 1970).

River Acheron

Not far to the southwest of Yannina rises the Acheron, homony-
mous with the gloomy river of the underworld, and sufficiently
magnificent in its awesome setting to have been the very model
for the latter. It is presently joined by Cocytus (the river of wailing),
another underworld river, and flows into the sea south of Parga.
Just up river is the ancient Oracle of the Dead. Thomas S. Hughes
describes the river, whose grandeur moves him to unwonted verse:

> After riding half an hour and then turning to the left we
> were astonished by a view of the dark rocks of Suli and the
> defile of the Acheron: but no pen can do justice to this
> scenery! It seemed as if we were about to penetrate into Tar-
> tarus itself and the awful recesses of the Plutonian realms;
> ἵν' Ἄδης χωρὶς ᾤκισται θεῶν The magnificence of this scene
> is but imperfectly represented in the annexed plate; I was
> unable to take much more than the outline, and it required the
> talents of a professed artist to do justice to all its parts: if that
> friend who has kindly embellished this sketch had been pre-
> sent to take it originally, the reader would have gained a much
> truer impression of the mountains of the Acheron. This river
> flows in a fine curve through the plain after it has left the rocky
> channel, which during successive ages it has worn through this
> terrific chasm, amidst the crags of which its hoarse murmurs
> are distinctly heard. Proceeding a little further we came to

the ruins of a Greek monastery which had been destroyed during the Suliot wars: it stood on the very brink of the Acheron and within the precincts of an ancient temple: this was evident from a considerable number of columns, some of which lay scattered on the ground, whilst others, though broken, still rested upon their bases: it seemed as if the temple itself had been at some time or other repaired or enlarged; for though many of the pillars were of antique construction and the granite of which they were made was in a state of decomposition, others were marble, of smaller dimensions, and a more modern form. Whilst we were debating with ourselves whether these fragments were ever included in one of Pluto's Acherusian temples, or whether we might not be standing upon the site of that Pandosia which with the fatal Acheron Alexander king of Epirus thought he was commanded by the oracle to avoid, a party of Albanian peasants came up, of whom we inquired the name of the place where we stood, and heard with no little surprise that it was called Aidonati. This appeared to confirm our conjectures—for Aidoneus or Pluto, a king of the Molossi, was fabled to have carried off Proserpine, the beautiful daughter of Ceres, from Sicily to this very region, where Theseus and Pirithous were afterwards confined, when they attempted to deprive him of his prize.

Deeply impressed with the fatal effects of tyranny and the still more degrading vassalage to which superstition subjects her votaries, I took up my journal and threw together a few thoughts by way of poetical address to the Acheron, which was flowing near my feet: the reader will probably pardon its insertion, since I have not before obtruded any similar effusions upon his notice.

> The sun is set, and solemn silence reigns
> Above, around, on Acherusia's plains;
> Save where on Suliot hills the watch-dogs bay
> Some tawny robber prowling for his prey,
> Or distant Acheron from rock to rock
> Bounds with impetuous force and thundering shock.
> Hail Acheron! thou dark mysterious stream!
> Hail! tho' thy terrors like a frightful dream
> Be vanish'd: tho' the fearless eagle soar
> In circling flight around th' Aonian shore
> And scare with rapid lightnings of his eye
> The tender broods that in thy coverts lie:

Tho' thy transparent waves no longer glide.
Beneath the granite temple's lofty pride;
Nor the black victim with his reeking blood
Stain the bright surface of that crystal flood,
Which plunging headlong to Tartarean night
Sprang back in horror to the realms of light,
Still hail immortal stream! thy mystic name
Shines in the records of Hellenic fame:
And he whose soul the flame of genius fires,
Whom rapture loves, or solemn thought inspires,
On the green margin of thy waves reclin'd
May tune to meditation sweet his mind,
Or 'mid thy sounding rocks and roaring flood,
Dark Suli's crags and Kiaffa's night of wood,
From Fancy's treasure steal ideal bliss,
And call thy spirits from their dark abyss,
While to Imagination's mirror true
Dim shadows of past ages start to view;
Ages that toil'd to Glory's height sublime,
Then floated downward on the stream of time;
That noiseless stream which on its current bears
All human joys and grandeur, woes and cares;
Still rolling onward to a shoreless sea,
The boundless ocean of Eternity.

Thomas S. Hughes, *Travels in Sicily,*
Greece and Albania (London, 1820)

II: Thessaly

Where Eurus blows, and wintery suns arise,
Thessalia's boundary proud Ossa lies;
But when the god protracts the longer day,
Pelion's broad back receives the dawning ray.
Where through the Lion's fiery sign he flies,
Othrys his leafy groves for shades supplies.
On Pindus strikes the fady western light,
When glittering Vesper leads the starry night.
Northward, Olympus hides the lamps, that roll
Their paler fires around the frozen pole.
The middle space, a valley how depress'd,
Once a wide, lazy, standing lake possess'd;
While growing still the heapy waters stood,
Nor down through Tempe ran the rushing flood:

But when Alcides to the task apply'd,
And cleft a passage through the mountains wide;
Gushing at once the thund'rous torrent flow'd,
While Nereus groan'd beneath th' increasing load.

The gushing waters various soon divide,
And every river rules a separate tide;
The narrow Aeas runs a limpid flood,
Evenos blushes with the Centaur's blood;
That gently mingles with th' Ionian sea,
While this, through Calydonia, cuts his way.

Thick Achelous rolls his troubled waves,
And heavily the neighbour isles he laves;
While pure Amphrysus winds along the mead,
Where Phoebus once was wont his flocks to feed:
Oft on the banks he sat a shepherd swain,
And watch'd his charge upon the grassy plain.
Swift to the main his course Sperchios bends,
And, sounding, to the Malian gulph descends.
No breezy air near calm Anauros flies,
No dewy mists, nor fleecy clouds arise.
Here Phoenix, Melas, and Asopus run,
And strong Apidanus drives slow Enipeus on.
A thousand little brooks, unknown to fame,
Are mix'd, and lost in Peneus' nobler name:
Bold Titaresus scorns his rule, alone,
And, join'd to Peneus, still himself is known:
As o'er the land his haughty waters glide,
And roll, unmingling, a superior tide.
'Tis said, through secret channels winding forth,
Deep as from Styx he takes his hallow'd birth:
Thence, proud to be rever'd by gods on high,
He scorns to mingle with a mean ally.

Lucan, *Pharsalia*, VI, 333–80;
translated by Nicholas Rowe (London, 1718)

Ovid describes the celebrated Vale of Tempe:

There is a land in Thessaly enclosed on every syde
With woodie hills, that Timpe hight, through mid whereof
   doth glide
Penaeus gushing full of froth from foote of Pindus hye,

Which with his headlong falling downe doth cast up violently
A mistie streame lyke flakes of smoke, besprinckling all about
The toppes of trees on eyther side, and makes a roaring out
That may be heard a great way off. This is the fixed seate,
This is the house and dwelling place and chamber of
    the greate
And mightie Ryver: Here he sittes in Court of Peeble stone,
And ministers justice to the waves and to the Nymphes
    eche one,
That in the Brookes and waters dwell.

Ovid, *Metamorphoses*, 1, 568–76;
translated by Arthur Golding (London, 1567)

Above Tempe towers Olympus:

> Olympus, the reputed seat
> Eternal of the Gods, which never storms
> Disturb, rains drench, or snow invades, but calm
> The expanse and cloudless shines with purest day.

Homer, *Odyssey*, 6, 41–46;
translated by William Cowper (London, 1791)

Hardly a description to be taken at face value by mountaineers. The mountain, and its neighbor (anciently Ossa), take on a personality of their own in the following well-known Greek ballad:

Mount Olympus and Mount Kissavos

Olympus and Kissavos, the two mountains, were at strife,
Thereon Olympus turned and cried to Kissavos:
'Revile me not, O Kissavos, trampled by Turkish feet!
I am the old Olympus, in all the world renowned;
I have two and forty summits and two and sixty springs—
For each spring I have a banner, for every branch a Klepht;
Upon my highest summit an eagle is alit,
And in her talons she holds a hero's head.
"O head, what hast thou done to be entreated so?"—
"Feed on, O bird, upon my youth, and feast upon
    my manhood,
Thy wing will grow a cubit long, and thy talon to a span.
I was an Armatole in Louros and Xeromeros,
And twelve years through a Klepht on Khasia and Olympus:
I have killed sixty Agas, and I have burned their villages,
And for the rest, Turks and Albanians, that I have left
    laid low,

They are many in number, bird, and never have
    been counted;
And then to me my turn came too to perish in the fight.'"

Klephtic poem, from Fauriel's text;
translated by J. Rennell Rodd (cf. C. A. Trypanis, ed.,
Penguin Book of Greek Verse, no. 265)

WITCHES OF THESSALY

In ancient times Thessaly was famous as the home of all kinds of witchcraft. The healing or magical properties of its plants were widely believed in, and attributed to the effects of the poisons and drugs Medea had dropped there when she came back with Jason from Colchis. Lucius, the hero of Apuleius' *The Golden Asse*, was susceptible to the reputation of the area, and was himself in due course changed into an ass in error by his mistress Photis.

> As soone as night was passed, and the day began to spring, I fortuned to awake, and rose out of my bed as halfe amazed, and very desirous to know and see some marvellous and strange things, remembring with my selfe that I was in the middle part of all Thessaly, whereas by the common report of all the World, the Sorceries and Inchauntments are most used, I oftentimes repeated with my self the tale of my companion Aristomenus touching the manner of this City, and being mooved by great desire, I viewed the whole scituation thereof, neither was there any thing which I saw there, that I did beleeve to be the same which it was indeed, but every thing seemed unto me to be transformed and altered into other shapes, by the wicked power of Sorcerie and Inchantment, insomuch that I thought the stones which I found were indurate, and turned from men into that figure, and that the birds which I heard chirping, and the trees without the walls of the city, and the running waters, were changed from men into such kinde of likenesses. And further I thought the Statues, Images, and Walls could goe, and the Oxen and other brute beasts, could speake and tell strange newes, and that immediately I should see and heare some Oracles from the heavens, and from the gleed of the Sun.

Apuleius, *The Golden Asse*;
translated by William Adlington (London, 1566)

The witch Erictho, whom Lucan's Pompey consults to ascertain his fortunes in the war with Caesar, is a masterpiece of Grand Guignol that far outdoes Macbeth's evil trio.

New mischief she, new monsters durst explore,
And dealt in horrors never known before.
From towns and hospitable roofs she flies,
And every dwelling of mankind defies;
Through unfrequented deserts lonely roams,
Drives out the dead, and dwells within their tombs.
Spite of all laws, which heaven or nature know,
The rule of gods above, and man below;
Grateful to hell the living hag descends,
And sits in black assemblies of the fiends.
Dark matted elf-locks dangling on her brow,
Filthy, and foul, a loathsome burden grow:
Ghastly, and frightful-pale her face is seen,
Unknown to chearful day, and skies serene:
But when the stars are veil'd, when storms arise,
And the blue forky flame at midnight flies,
Then, forth from graves, she takes her wicked way,
And thwarts the glancing lightnings as they play.
Where-e'er she breathes, blue poisons round her spread,
The withering grass avows her fatal tread,
And drooping Ceres hangs her blasted head . . .
        Oft in the grave the living has she laid,
And bid reviving bodies leave the dead:
Oft at the funeral pile she seeks her prey,
And bears the smoking ashes warm away;
Snatches some burning bone, or flaming brand,
And tears the torch from the sad father's hand;
Seizes the shroud's loose fragments as they fly,
And picks the coal where clammy juices fry.
But when the dead in marble tombs are plac'd,
Where the moist carcase by degrees shall waste,
There, greedily on every part she flies,
Strips the dry nails, and digs the gory eyes.

Lucan, *Pharsalia* VI;
translated by Nicholas Rowe

A tenderer breed of witch is the one imagined by Thomas Love
Peacock in his romantic tale of Rhododaphne, who casts her spell
on the youth Anthemion to gain his love. A stranger warns him of
the trap that has ensnared him. (I recommend reading the complex denouement of the poem.)

    —'Oh youth, beware! that laurel-rose
    Around Larissa's evil walls

In tufts of rank luxuriance grows,
'Mid dreary valleys, by the falls
Of haunted streams; and magic knows
No herb or plant of deadlier might,
When impious footsteps wake by night
The echoes of those dismal dells,
What time the murky midnight dew
Trembles on many a leaf and blossom,
That draws from earth's polluted bosom
Mysterious virtue, to imbue
The chalice of unnatural spells.
Oft, those dreary rocks among,
The murmurs of unholy song,
Breathed by lips as fair as hers
By whose false hands that flower was given,
The solid earth's firm breast have riven,
And burst the silent sepulchres,
And called strange shapes of ghastly fear,
To hold, beneath the sickening moon,
Portentous parle, at night's deep noon,
With beauty skilled in mysteries drear.
Oh, youth! Larissa's maids are fair;
But the dæmons of the earth and air
Their spells obey, their councils share,
And wide o'er earth and ocean bear
Their mandates to the storms that tear
The rock-enrooted oak, and sweep
With whirlwind wings the labouring deep.
Their words of power can make the streams
Roll refluent on their mountain-springs,
Can torture sleep with direful dreams,
And on the shapes of earthly things,
Man, beast, bird, fish, with influence strange,
Breathe foul and fearful interchange,
And fix in marble bonds the form
Erewhile with natural being warm,
And give to senseless stones and stocks
Motion, and breath, and shape that mocks,
As far as nicest eye can scan,
The action and the life of man.
Beware! yet once again beware!
Ere round thy inexperienced mind,
With voice and semblance falsely fair,
A chain Thessalian magic bind,

Which never more, oh youth! believe,
Shall either earth or heaven unweave.'
T. L. Peacock, *Rhododaphne*
(London, 1818)

Meteora

Ta Meteora (Up-in-the-air) is a remarkable formation of rocks at
the edge of the mountains north of Trikala. Richard Monckton
Milnes, first Baron Houghton (1809–85), who was later the biographer of Keats, made a tour of Greece, "chiefly poetical," in 1832,
in the company of the more learned and less impressionistic
Christopher Wordsworth. His description of their first sight of
these towering rocks is vivid:

> The 'Rocks of Meteora' are, perhaps, the most marvellous
> combination of Nature and Art, of the strange humors of geol-
> ogy and humanity, that the world presents. My attention was
> excited, from some distance, by a group of naked cliffs of
> unequal heights standing out against the twilight sky, the high-
> est of which seemed pointing to the evening star, that rested
> glimmering a little way above. But on a close approach in full
> morning light, through a grove of white mulberry trees that
> cover a gentle ascent, the feeling of singularity became so
> intense, that pleasure could not keep itself silent, but burst
> forth in loud and repeated laughter. The rocks come on, clus-
> ter on cluster, splinter and mass, some light and slender
> enough to be confounded with the cypresses at their sides, oth-
> ers immense, solid, and cathedral: others again in huge globes
> or formless clumps, so that the general outline is as wildly
> irregular as well was ever drawn along paper by the half-
> unconscious hand of an absent man, who lets a pen trail up and
> down and on at random, while his thoughts are other where.
> But it is wild-witted manhood that, for purposes of self-
> defence, or pious seclusion, or both, has given fresh peculiarity
> to this prodigy of Nature. The dwelling-places here con-
> structed are of two kinds: small huts of reeds stand in artificial
> caves, of an oblong form, scoopt at a fearful highth in perpen-
> dicular cliffs of sand-stone or pudding-stone, and accessible
> only by fragile ladders, fraily attacht to one another. The
> spectator at first is almost incredulous of their reality; he sends
> his imagination away into distant history, and can find nothing
> to connect with the scene before him, except the record of the
> people of Edom, who dwelt 'in the clefts of the rock', and held

'the height of the hill', and made their 'nest, as high as the eagle'. But the excavations in the rocks of the city of Idumea (whatever may have been their use in times of danger) seem to have been generally applied to sepulchral objects; and, though perhaps more remarkable as works of human ingenuity, their appearance, at least in their present desolation, can hardly be more astonishing than this. The greater part, however, of the houses are of the common Eastern construction and planted on the tops of isolated rocks, not only covering the whole of the irregular surfaces, but stretching out broad verandahs over the unbroken precipice. Of this kind are the two principal monasteries, whose aërial positions are attainable by the simple and rapid mode of elevation in a net, a safe ascent of about four minutes and a half.

Richard Monckton Milnes, *Memorials of a Tour in Greece, Chiefly Poetical* (London, 1834)

The poet C. A. Trypanis evokes the present-day atmosphere of these improbable settlements, now easier of approach than in the days when a basket on a rope was the only access to some, and correspondingly reduced in population.

Meteora

These rocks rise tormented
Like the Byzantine soul to the sky.
Wounded obelisks, beast of a granite
Nightmare, towering cubes and tablets
Fit for the Ten Commandments to be carved upon,
They move disdainful away
From the ashen, pestilent plain.

Monasteries cling to their tops,
Deserted in a world that has forgotten
How to pray, suspended
Far from the warm flowers of spring
In the sad fight of man to trample
His flesh—the look
In the upturned eyes of ascetics
And saints on their pale, fading frescoes.

Who were the first, hunted by what enemies,
That turned to these haughty flanks,
Who shaped the hand and the foot
To fit such perilous rocks? And did they escape?
Did they not carry up the frowning face of the stone

The blind precipice, their last enemy,
The human blood? Or, lashed
By solitude, the winds and prayer,
Did the storm of the flesh die down,
And the soul when called, move untroubled
From the fringe of the sky where it had nestled
Into the luminous blue?

But far below the villages of Thessaly,
Bathed in the fever of the plain,
Cling to the earth, watching in awe the huge
Hewn steps that lead from their fields to the sky.

C. A. Trypanis, *The Pompeian Dog*
(London, 1964)

In the 1830s the bibliophile Robert Curzon (1810–73) made a tour of the Levant in search of ancient manuscripts and codices. He describes his travels and adventures in *Visits to the Monasteries in the Levant* (London, 1849). After some years' diplomatic service as private secretary to Sir Stratford Canning, ambassador to Turkey, he made a similar tour of Italy. His account of the Meteora is worth reading in its entirety, particularly the moment when he presents to the head man of a village on his way letters of authority (which he is unable to read) enjoining on his hosts protection against that very man! The latter nonetheless guarantees him the protection of his band of brigands, who henceforth accompany him on all his travels to defend his cause in such wrangles as the one described here:

THE GREAT MONASTERY OF THE METEORA

After looking over the books on the shelves, the librarian, an old grey-bearded monk, opened a great chest in which things belonging to the church were kept; and here I found ten or twelve manuscripts of the Gospels, all of the eleventh or twelfth century. They were upon vellum, and all, except one, were small quartos; but this one was a large quarto, and one of the most beautiful manuscripts of its kind I have met with anywhere. In many respects it resembled the Codex Ebnerianus in the Bodleian Library at Oxford. It was ornamented with miniatures of the same kind as those in that splendid volume, but they were more numerous and in a good style of art; it was, in fact, as richly ornamented as a Romish missal, and was in excellent preservation, except one miniature at the beginning, which had been partially smeared over by the wet finger of some ancient sloven. Another volume of the Gospels, in a very small, clear hand, bound in a kind of silver filagree of the same date as the book, also excited my admiration. Those who take an interest in literary antiquities of this class are aware of the great rarity of an ornamental binding in a Byzantine manuscript. This must doubtless have been the pocket volume of some royal personage. To my great joy the librarian allowed me to take these two books to the room of the agoumenos, who agreed to sell them to me for I forget how many pieces of gold, which I counted out to him immediately, and which he seemed to pocket with the sincerest satisfaction. Never was any one more welcome to his money, although I left myself but little to pay the expenses of my journey back to Corfu. Such books as these would be treasures in the finest national collection in Europe . . .

. . . Just as I was ready to start there arose a discussion among them as to the distribution of the money which I had paid for the two manuscripts. The agoumenos wanted to keep it all for himself, or at least for the expenses of the monastery; but the villain of a librarian swore he would have half. The agoumenos said he should not have a farthing, but as the librarian would not give way he offered him a part of the spoil; however, he did not offer him enough, and out of spite and revenge, or, as he protested, out of uprightness of principle, he told all the monks that the agoumenos had pocketed the money which he had received for their property, for that they all had a right to an equal share in these books, as in all the other things belonging to the community. The monks, even the most dunderheaded, were not slow in taking this view of the subject, and all broke out into a clamorous assertion of their rights, every man of them speaking at once. The price I had given was so large that every one of them would have received several pieces of gold each. But no, they said, it was not that, but for the principles of justice that they contended. They did not want the money, no more did the librarian, but they would not suffer their rules to be outraged or their rights to be trampled under foot.

After a while the agoumenos, calling my interpreter, said that as the monks would not agree to let him keep the money in the usual way for the use of the monastery, he could have nothing to do with it; and to my great sorrow I was therefore obliged to receive it back, and to give up the two beautiful manuscripts, which I had already looked upon as the chief ornaments of my library in England. The monks all looked sadly downcast at this unexpected termination of their noble defence of their principles, and my only consolation was to perceive that they were quite as much vexed as I was. In fact, we felt that we had gained a loss all round, and the old librarian, after walking up and down once or twice with his hands behind his back in gloomy silence, retreated to a hole where he lived, near the library, and I saw no more of him.

My bag was brought forward, and when the books were extracted from it, I sat down on a stone in the courtyard, and for the last time turned over the gilded leaves and admired the ancient and splendid illuminations of the larger manuscript, the monks standing round me as I looked at the blue cypress trees, and green and gold peacocks, and intricate arabesques, so characteristic of the best times of Byzantine art. Many of the pages bore a great resemblance to the painted windows of the earlier Norman Cathedrals of Europe. It was a superb old book: I laid it down upon the stone beside me and placed the little volume with its curious silver binding on the top of it, and it was with a sigh that I left them there with the sun shining on the curious silver ornaments . . .

When my servants arrived and informed them of our recent disappointment, 'What!' cried they, 'would they not let you take the books? Stop a bit, we will soon get them for you!' And away they ran to the series of ladders which hung down another part of the precipice: they would have been up in a minute, for they scrambled like cats; but by dint of running after them and shouting we at length got them to come back, and after some considerable expenditure of oaths and exclamations, kicking of horses, and loading of guns and saddlebags, we found ourselves slowly wending our way back towards the valley of the Peneus.

After all, what an interesting event it would have been, what a standard anecdote in bibliomaniac history, if I had let my friendly thieves have their own way, and we had stormed the monastery, broken open the secret door of the library, pitched the old librarian over the rocks, and marched off in triumph, with a gorgeous manuscript under each arm! Indeed I must say that under such aggravating circumstances it required a great exercise of forbearance not to do so, and in the good old times many a castle has been attacked and many a town besieged and pillaged for much slighter causes of offence than those which I had to complain of.

Robert Curzon, Visits to the Monasteries
in the Levant (London, 1849)

Thermopylae

To the southeast, on the Malian Gulf, lies Thermopylae, the scene of the heroic resistance in 480 B.C. by Leonidas and his Spartans to the Persian invasion, at which the Spartans were annihilated. Simonides composed both an epigram and a formal ode for the Spartan dead:

> Go tell the Spartans, thou who passest by,
> That here obedient to their laws we lie.

Simonides, epigram 22 Page;
translated by William Lisle Bowles
(1762–1830)

> Great are the fallen of Thermopylae,
> Nobly they ended, high their destination—
> Beneath an altar laid, no more a tomb,
> Where none with pity comes or lamentation,
>   But praise and memory—
>   A splendour of oblation
> No rust shall blot nor wreckful Time consume.
>
> The ground is holy: here the brave are resting,
> And here Greek Honour keeps her chosen shrine.
> Here too is one the worth of all attesting—
> Leonidas, of Sparta's royal line,
> Who left behind a gem-like heritage,
>   Of courage and renown,
>   A name that shall go down
>   From age to age.

Simonides, fragment 531 Page;
translated by T. F. Higham (1938)

The story has become a byword for heroism, and was the theme of a short poem by Constantine Cavafy. In 1955 a monument to Leonidas and his men was erected by the Greek government.

III: Mount Athos

Mount Athos, the Holy Mountain, has little classical past, though it is one of the chain of beacons that brought Clytemnestra the news of Troy's fall (see page 92), and Apollonius Rhodius describes the remarkable circumstance of its shadow at evening:

> But when the morn display'd her orient light,
> Tall Athos rose conspicuous to the sight;
> Which though from Lemnos far remov'd it lay,
> As far as ships can sail till noon of day,
> Yet the proud mountain's high-exalted head,
> A gloom umbrageous o'er Myrina spread.
>
> *Argonautica*, 1, 601–06;
> translated by Francis Fawkes (1780)

The same detail was noted by John Mandeville (though the actual distance is nearer to seventy kilometers); the rest of his description has less substance:

> And there is another hill that is cleped Athos that is so high that the shadow of him reacheth to Lemnos that is an isle, and it is seventy-six mile between. And above at the cop of that hill is the air so clear that men may find no wind there, and therefore may no beast live there, so is the air dry. And men say in these countries that philosophers sometime went upon these hills and held to their nose a sponge moisted with water for to have air, for the air above was so dry. And above in the dust and in the powder of those hills they wrote letters and figures with their fingers. And at the year's end they came again and found the same letters and figures the which they had written the year before without any default. And therefore it seemeth well that these hills pass the clouds and join to the pure air.
>
> Sir John Mandeville, *Travels*, chapter 3

Byron's description is characteristic:

> . . . With lowering port majestic Athos stands,
> Crowned with the verdure of eternal wood,
>   As yet unspoiled by sacrilegious hands,
> And throws his mighty shade o'er seas and distant lands.
>
> And deep embosom'd in his shady groves
>   Full many a convent rears its glittering spire,
> Mid scenes where Heavenly Contemplation loves

Edward Lear, *Mount Athos and the Monastery of Stavroniketes*. Yale Center for British Art, New Haven, Connecticut, Paul Mellon Collection (detail).

> To kindle in her soul her hallowed fire,
> Where air and sea with rocks and woods conspire
> To breathe a sweet religious calm around,
> Weaning the thought from every low desire,
> And the wild waves that break with murmuring sound
> Along the rocky shore proclaim it holy ground.
>
> *The Monk of Athos* (fragment)

Athos has attracted many travelers, not least in this century Robert Byron. Here are two earlier travelers, a botanist and a bibliophile:

> Sep. 25, 1794.—We coasted the western shore of Athos; steep rocks covered with shrubs, traversed by deep ravines, marked with the lively verdure of evergreen-trees offered the most romantic sites for the monasteries and monastic cells. Several of the latter excavated in the rock seemed to be in situations almost inaccessible; we could scarcely discover the little path that conducted the hermit to his cell. Nothing could be more picturesque than the situation of the monasteries we passed; they commanded in extensive view of the sea, and were surrounded by the finest sylvan scenery. The head of a vale or ravine laid into vineyards and olive grounds was the most general situation; the mountain itself broken grandly into ridges was ornamented with various foliage, through which

was seen the slaty substance of the rock. Having cast anchor I was impatient to land on Athos and examine its shores, which from their verdure promised me a considerable addition to my Flora. On landing, I found the rock almost blue with the autumnal Scilla, and in the shade under the cover of the trees was the Cyclamen; above on the hanging cliffs, the yellow Amaryllis all in flower. This was a cheerful sight to a botanist who had just left the sun-burnt plains of Lemnos, and arid rocks of Imbros. I climbed along the shore to the port of Daphne through trees and shrubs, consisting of Arbor Judas, Alaternus, Phillyrea, Arbutus, Evergreen and Kermes oak. At Daphne, the bay mixed with the wild-olive was spread over the rocks: a rivulet flowing down, watered the roots of some huge plane trees, around which the Smilax was entwined diffusing from its flowers a grateful odour.

Oct. 1.—A caloyer had brought from a distant vineyard a basket of grapes, and I took the opportunity of having him for a conductor to visit part of the mountain, which from its height, promised to gratify my botanical researches. I mounted his mule and pursued from the beach a rugged path-way winding up the rocks; ascending for an hour this rough road through evergreen shrubs, I came to a mixture of pines and chesnuts; the latter were now laden with ripe fruit, and the crew of our boat that lay in the port of Daphne were busily employed in collecting a stock for their voyage. The pine did not appear to me different from the silver fir; but I could discover no fruit upon it. A range of mountains cloathed with these pines encircled a beautiful plain; here the convent of Xeropotamo has four Kilia or farms, where their caloyers reside. They were now busy in making their wine, and the vineyards were richly laden with the empurpled fruit; my caloyer conducted me to his Kili; and spread before me a rustic table with grapes, figs, dried cherries, walnuts, and filberds. We drunk from a chrystalline rill that flowed along wooden pipes, through the pine grove from the mountain; the trunks of some of the pines which I observed in my walk had been pierced to draw their resin from them; and many grown old had their branches bearded with filamentous lichens.

John Sibthorp, in Walpole*

MONASTERY OF CARACALLA

I picked up a single loose leaf of very ancient uncial Greek characters, part of the Gospel of St Matthew, written in small square letters and of small quarto size. I searched in vain for the volume to which this leaf belonged.

As I had found it impossible to purchase any manuscripts at St Laura, I feared that the same would be the case in other monasteries; however, I made bold to ask for this single leaf as a thing of small value.

'Certainly!' said the agoumenos: 'what do you want it for?'

My servant suggested that, perhaps, it might be useful to cover some jam pots or vases of preserves which I had at home.

'Oh!' said the agoumenos, 'take some more;' and, without more ado, he seized upon an unfortunate thick quarto manuscript of the Acts and Epistles, and drawing out a knife cut out an inch thickness of leaves at the end before I could stop him. It proved to be the Apocalypse, which concluded the volume, but which is rarely found in early Greek manuscripts of the Acts: it was of the eleventh century. I ought, perhaps, to have slain the *tomecide* for his dreadful act of profanation, but his generosity reconciled me to his guilt, so I pocketed the Apocalypse, and asked him if he would sell me any of the other books, as he did not appear to set any particular value upon them.

'Malista, certainly,' he replied; 'how many will you have? They are of no use to me, and as I am in want of money to complete my buildings, I shall be very glad to turn them to some account.'

After a good deal of conversation, finding the agoumenos so accommodating, and so desirous to part with the contents of his dark and dusty closet, I arranged that I would leave him for the present, and after I had made the tour of the other monasteries, would return to Caracalla, and take up my abode there until I could hire a vessel, or make some other arrangements for my return to Constantinople. Satisfactory as this arrangement was, I nevertheless resolved to make sure of what I had already got; so I packed them up carefully in the great saddle-bags, to my extreme delight. The agoumenos kindly furnished me with fresh mules, and in the afternoon I proceeded to the monastery of Philotheo . . .

Robert Curzon, *Visits to the Monasteries in the Levant* (London, 1849)

IV: Vergina (Aegae)
and Alexander the Great

> I think it is in Macedon where Alexander is porn. I tell you, cap-
> tain,—If you look in the maps of the 'orld, I warrant you shall
> find, in the comparisons between Macedon and Monmouth,
> that the situations, look you, is both alike. There is a river in
> Macedon; and there is also moreover a river at Monmouth: it
> is called Wye, at Monmouth; but it is out of my prains what is
> the name of the other river; but 'tis all one, 'tis alike as my
> fingers is to my fingers, and there is salmons in both.
>
> Shakespeare, *King Henry V*, iv, vii

The royal family of Macedon, into which Alexander was born,
claimed Greek descent—in fact from Heracles—while the people
of Macedon counted among the Greeks as barbarians. The hellenic descent enabled the royal family to participate in the Pan-
hellenic Games, and one of Alexander's ancestors, Alexander I, the
son of Amyntas (king 494–54), had been celebrated by Pindar for
an athletic victory:

> Namesake of the blessed sons of Dardanus,
> Bold son of Amyntas, . . .
> one must hymn the noble in lovely songs:
> This alone touches a man to immortal honours,
> But a noble deed, kept silent, dies.
>
> Pindar, fragment 120; translated by RS

In 1977–78 the excavation of a royal tomb at Vergina occasioned
speculation that this might be the very tomb of Philip II, the father
of Alexander the Great, and the site Aegae. Most persuasive of the
evidence was the find of a pair of greaves of unequal size: Philip is
known to have been lame. But some archaeologists date the tomb
later; it seems however certain that here at Vergina was the capital
of Macedon, where Alexander was born.

Alexander the Great soon began to accumulate legends to sup-
plement the almost fantastic true history of his exploits. Arrian,
writing the most reliable biography, based his account on those of
Ptolemy and Aristobulus, contemporaries of Alexander; but already
in antiquity a fabulous account of his life had come to be attributed to Callisthenes, who was one of the companions of Alexander
in his expedition to Persia. This appears to be the fountainhead of
four major traditions of Alexander-legends: the Armenian, the Jewish, the Syriac, and a Bulgarian one which became the source of one
in demotic Greek. The Syriac version was translated into Latin by

Leo of Byzantium between 941 and 959, and this poem became the source of the dull epic of Walter of Châtillon, as well as of innumerable medieval romances.

Probably independently of these, Alexander became a folk hero of the Greek people, and many legends in the oral tradition have attached themselves to his name.

Even if we confine ourselves to the events of Alexander's years in Macedon, before his oriental adventures, the plethora of tales begins before his birth with the legend of his conception. Some of the more respectable legends held that his father was really the Egyptian god Ammon, the horned bull-god, who had visited his mother Olympias as she slept. The Greek poem by D. Zenos, printed at Venice in 1529, turns this legend into a conjuring trick by the court magician, ex-king Nektanebos of Egypt:

> By night there came to Olympias God Ammon in a dream:
> He came within the palace walls, he found her all alone.
> He saw her and embraced her; and Queen Olympias
> Gave him the humour he desired, and served him as
>   he would.
> He came upon her, and he laid her flat upon her bed,
> And prayed her to conceive for him, and bear him a
>   male child.
> Olympias woke with a start, and called for Nektanebos:
> 'A god has visited me,' she said, 'his dream image
>   came to me.
> I saw him here, the god himself, ask me to lie with him.'
> And Nektanebos said to her, 'How did he seem to you?'
> 'A goat with giant horns he was, two horns upon his head:
> And bid me come to bed with him, and make a child
>   with him.'
> And Nektanebos said to her, 'Tonight I'll bring him to you,
> To lie in your embrace, I'll bring him to your very arms.'
> And Nektanebos calmed her fears, and planned to bring
>   the god
> That very night into her bed, with all his magic powers.
> He found a pair of giant horns, a goatskin white as milk,
> He put the skin on, and he put the horns upon his head.
> And then the cunning wizard went again into the house,
> And made as if he were the god, and climbed into her bed,
> And spoke to her in gentle tones, that she should have
>   his child.
> 'The child shall be a male,' he said, to win her swift consent,

'And he shall have this kingdom, and shall rule the whole
    known world.'
And then he left her bed and made his way out of the house.
Olympias leapt out of bed, caught sight of Nektanebos,
And spoke of what she just had done to please the great
    god Ammon,
And asked that he should come each night, and visit her
    in bed.

D. Zenos, *Alexander*; translated by RS

A woodcut in the French Alexander Romance shows Nektanebos
consorting with Olympias in the form of a dragon.

Not surprisingly, his birth was attended by cosmic upheavals,
described at length in the fifteenth-century alliterative romance
which follows a Latin version of the Greek romance written about
1070 by Simon Seth, Keeper of the Imperial Wardrobe of Anti-
ochus in Constantinople:

Bot now is mervaile / to me of this wondire
Quen this man fro his modire wombe / on the molde felle
For alle the erd evyn over / sa eagerly schakis
That teldis templis and townis / tomble on hepis
The light lemand late / laschis fra the hevyn
Thonere thrastis ware thra / thristed the welkyn
Cloudis clenely to-clefe / clatirs unfaire
All blakeind aboute / and boris the sonne
Wild wedirs up werpe / and the wynd ryse
And all flames the flode / as it fire were
Nowe bright nowe blaa / nowe one blase efter
And than overqwelmys in a quirr / and qwater ever elike
Than slike a drekness ther drafe / and demyd the skewys
As blesenand as bale fire / and blake as the helle
That that was never bot as nyght / fra the none tyme
Till it to mydday was meten / one the morne efter
Gife this ware mervale to myn / yet emange othir
The rekils it unrudly / and raynes doune stanes
Fell fra the firmament / as a hand lyftynge
And some as hoge as thi hede / fra a hevyn falles
Sa ferd was Philip of that fare / that his flesch trymblid
For sere sygnes at he saye / as selly ware ellis
As wyde as alle the werd was thurghe / warnyng thai hadd
That houre that Olympadas / was of hire sonne lighter

*Alliterative Romance of Alexander**

A popular motif was Alexander's taming of the horse Bucephalus, graphically evoked in another English alliterative poem:

> Ther was a Prince full price / of powre y-holde,
> Keeper of Cappadoce / that Kyng Philip aught.
> A huge horse and a hy / hee had that tyme,
> The moste seemely in syght / that ever seg wyst.
> Hee bore a hedde as a bole / y-brested to-ryght,
> And had hard on his hedde / hornes y-grow,
> Menne were his meate / that hee moste looved;
> For as many as hee myght / murdre hee woolde.

Philip dreams a dream, which informs him:

> Who prickes on a playne feelde / the perelous beaste,
> Hee shall raigne as a ryng / ryall and noble,
> And bee Kyng of thy kith / Knyghtes too leade,
> When thou art doone and dedde / and thy daye endes.

In due course Alexander comes face to face with the beast:

> In a tyme betyd / as I tell after,
> . That many menne of Attenes / with myckle oother people,
> Did them forthe on a day / by the deepe cave,
> There the steede in stoode / strayned in bondes.
> They saw lygge in theyr looke / Legges and armes,
> Fayre handes and feete / freaten to the bonne,
> Of menne that myslych wer / murdred therin,
> By justes unjoyfull / jugged too death.
> When Alisaunder was ware / of the wylde beaste,
> That was of body so bolde / bremlych yshaped,
> Too hym hee helde forthe his hand; / the horss it awaytes.
> Hee layed the neck oute along / and lycked his handes,
> And sythe hee foldes his feete / and falles too the grounde,
> And abowed to the burn / on his best wyse.
> When Alisaunder so sawe / in his syght there,
> How the steede was styll / and no stryfe made . . .
> Soone hee leapes on-loft / and lete hym worthe,
> To fare as hym lyst faine / in feelde or towne.
> The steed strauht on his gate / and stired him under,
> And wrought no wod res / but his waye holdes.
>
> Anon, circa 1340, edited by W. W. Skeat*

This, like many other tales of his early life, appears first in the biography by Plutarch. Plutarch also recounts how Philip ensured his son's education by employing the philosopher Aristotle as his tutor:

> Looking upon the instruction and tuition of his youth to be of greater difficulty and importance than to be wholly trusted to the ordinary masters in music and poetry, and the common school subjects, and to require, as Sophocles says, 'The bridle and the rudder too', he sent for Aristotle, the most learned and most celebrated philosopher of his time, and rewarded him with a munificence proportionable to and becoming the care he took to instruct his son. For he repeopled his native city Stagira, which he had caused to be demolished a little before, and restored all the citizens, who were in exile or slavery, to their habitations. As a place for the pursuit of their studies and exercise, he assigned the temple of the Nymphs, near Mieza, where, to this very day, they show you Aristotle's stone seats, and the shady walks which he was wont to frequent.
>
> Plutarch, *Alexander*; translated by J. Dryden

One of the most celebrated events of his youth was the encounter with Diogenes, the Cynic philosopher, at that time living in his barrel at Corinth.

> King Alisaundre, that conquered realms,
> Came riding down, and gan himself delight
> This philisopher to seen and visite,
> Himself sequestered sole from all the press,
> And came alone to see Diogenes.
>
> Proffered to him great richesse and treasure,
> Bad him ask what thing that he would,
> That might him please or do to him succour;
> But of all that, he nothing ne told,
> But praised him full lowly, that he should
> Not draw from him that thing, again(st) all right,
> Which for to give lay not in his might.
>
> 'What thing is that?' quoth Alisaundre again,
> 'I have by conquest all earthly treasure won.'
> The philisopher said he spake in vain,
> 'Thou hast', quoth he, 'no lordship of the sun.
> Thy shadow lets his beames from my tun;
> And sith thou hast no power of his light,
> I pray thee friendly, forbear me not his sight.'
>
> John Lydgate, *Fall of Princes*
> 1, 6233–51 (modernized)

It was no doubt in memory of his ancestor's glory that Alexander, when he conquered Thebes in 355 B.C., spared the house of Pindar, an act of generosity omitted in the hostile account by Walter of Châtillon of the savage conquest. The events of Alexander's adult life—the conquest of Persia, his clemency to Darius and the firing of the palace of Persepolis (theme of Dryden's ode for St Cecilia's Day, *Alexander's Feast*), the exploration of India and meeting with the Brahmins, the forced march through the Gedrosian desert, his mourning for his general and lover Hephaestion—commemorated by a giant stone lion at Ecbatana (Hamadan), to which magical properties still attach—all reappear time and again through the tradition. At the same time, the extensive citing of Alexander as a moral example by Cicero and Seneca assured his stature as a subject of moralizing in the Middle Ages—a fate like that which Juvenal attributed to Hannibal.

> Go, climb the rugged Alps, ambitious fool,
> To please the boys, and be a theme at school.
>
> *Satire* x; translated by J. Dryden

In the folk tradition of Greece, Alexander became a worker of many wonders, and even found a place in the traditional repertoire of the Karagiozis shadow-puppet plays as a slayer of a great dragon. Here is a Cretan song on the same theme:

> Great Alexander killed the serpent, he slew it in the meadow,
> He did not let it escape.
> He sat and measured out its length, measured it with
>   his hand,
> It had two heads, its size was huge, its tails were likewise two,
> One above and one below . . .
>
> Kalonaros*; translated by RS

Alexander's popularity declined in the West with the Renaissance return to the classical age of Greece for its ideals.

> Alexander died, Alexander was buried, Alexander returneth into dust; the dust is earth; of earth we make loam: and why of that loam, whereto he was converted, might they not stop a beer-barrel?

> Imperial Caesar, dead, and turn'd to clay,
> Might stop a hole to keep the wind away:
> O, that that earth, which kept the world in awe,
> Should patch a wall to expel the winter's flaw!
>
> Shakespeare, *Hamlet*, v, i

But in Greece the story is different, as you will discover if you are lashed by a storm while at sea in the Aegean. A mermaid, Alexander's sister, will emerge from the waves, and cry out to you, "Where is Alexander the Great?" If you unwisely reply that he is dead, the storm will lash your ship until it sinks. But if you have been forewarned, you will reply to her by calling out "Alexander the Great lives and rules and keeps the world at peace!" The storm will then subside and you may sail tranquilly on to your destination.

11

The Aegean Islands

Think of Greece and you think of the islands of the Aegean, dusty blossoms in a scatter on the glittering sea. From the air, they seem alike except in pattern: The distinctions thus obscured are in reality marked, for each island has its own character, its own geology, its own history. Ovid's description of the mythical journey of King Minos through the Cyclades (which in Minoan times were probably subject to Crete) represents them in all their rich variety:

> King Minos was preparing war . . .
> And thereupon with flying fleete where passage did permit
> He went to visit all the Iles that in those seas do sit.
> Anon the Iles Astypaley and Anaphey both twaine
> The first constreynde for feare of war, the last in hope
>   of gaine,
> Tooke part with him. Low Myconey did also with him hold
> So did the chalkie Cymoley, and Syphney which of olde
> Was verie riche with veynes of golde, and Scyros full of bolde
> And valiant men, and Seryphey the smooth or rather fell,
> And Parey which for marblestone doth beare away the bell.
> And Sythney which a wicked wench callde Arne did betray
> For Mony: who upon receit thereof without delay
> Was turned to a birde which yet of golde is gripple[1] still,
> And is as blacke as any cole, both fethers, feete and bill.
> A Cadowe[2] is the name of hir. But yet Olyarey,
> And Didymey, and Andrey eke, and Tene, and Gyarey,
> And Pepareth where Olive trees most plenteously doe grow,
> In no wise would agree their helpe on Minos to bestow.
>
>   Ovid, *Metamorphoses*; translated by A. Golding, VII, 581–604

But the process of depopulation, which has periodically afflicted all the outlying areas of Greece since at least the end of the Byzantine Empire, seems to have been prefigured in the later classical era. Antipater of Thessalonica, writing at the turn of the

---

1. Tenacious, greedy.

2. Jackdaw. Ovid is among our main sources for this obscure myth.

era, laments the decline and ruin of once magnificent islands in a characteristic epigram:

> Deserted islands, broken sherds of land
> held in by the Aegean's belts of noise,
> you have copied Siphnos and the dry Cyclades—
> their wretched loss of an archaic glory.
> Or Delos, brilliant once, taught you her way,
> the first to meet the god of desolation.
>
> Antipater of Thessalonica, in *Anthologia*
> *Palatina*, 9,421; translated by Alistair Elliot in
> Peter Jay, ed., *The Greek Anthology*
> (London, 1973)

This did not stop Friedrich Hölderlin celebrating them, more than 1,700 years later, as a paradise of fruitfulness and glory. His image of the Greek islands is one of the most remarkable creations of a landscape of the mind. Even more than the poets' Arcadia, Hölderlin's Archipelago has a meaning to him which is quite dissociated from its reality.

THE ARCHIPELAGO

> Are the cranes returning to you, and the
>   mercantile vessels
> Making again for your shores? Do breezes longed for and
>   prayed for
> Blow for you round the quieter flood and, lured from
>   beneath it,
> Does the dolphin now warm his back in a new year's
>   gathering radiance?
> Is Ionia in flower? Is it the season? For always in springtime
> When the hearts of the living renew themselves, the first
>   love of
> Human kind, reawakened, stirs and the golden age
>   is remembered,
> You, old Sea-God, I visit and you I greet in your stillness.
>
> Even now you live on and, mighty as ever, untroubled
> Rest in the shade of your mountains; with arms ever youthful
> Still embrace your beautiful land, and still of your daughters,
>   O Father,
> Of your islands, the flowering, not one has been taken.
> Crete remains, and Salamis lies in a dark-green twilight
>   of laurels,

In a ring of blossoming beams even now at the hour
    of sunrise
Delos lifts her ecstatic head, and Tenos and Chios
Still have plenty of purple fruit, and the Cyprian liquor
Gushes from drunken hillsides while from Calauria the silver
Brooks cascade, as before, into the Father's old vastness.
Every one of them lives, those mothers of heroes, the islands,
Flowering year after year, and if at times the subterranean
Thunder, the flame of Night, let loose from the
    primal abysses,
Seized on one of the dear isles and, dying, she sank in
    your waters,
You, divine one, endured, for much already has risen,
Much gone down for you here above your
    deeper foundations.

        Friedrich Hölderlin; translated by Michael Hamburger

Possibly Byron's most famous lines are the poem, "The Isles of Greece," which he puts in the mouth of the poet in Haidee's entourage in *Don Juan,* and which epitomizes the laments of the philhellene poets, and the intentions of those foreign philhellenes of whom Byron was, if not the most effective in the end, certainly the most vocal. The poem is a concentration of an epoch:

THE ISLES OF GREECE

The isles of Greece, the isles of Greece!
    Where burning Sappho loved and sung,
Where grew the arts of war and peace,
    Where Delos rose, and Phoebus sprung,
Eternal summer gilds them yet,
But all, except their sun, is set.

The Scian and the Teian Muse,
    The hero's harp, the lover's lute
Have found the fame your shores refuse.
    Their place of birth alone is mute
To sounds which echo further west
Than your sires' 'Islands of the Blest'.

The mountains look on Marathon,
    And Marathon looks on the sea.
And musing there an hour alone,
    I dreamed that Greece might still be free,
For standing on the Persian's grave,
I could not deem myself a slave.

A king sate on the rocky brow
      Which looks o'er sea-born Salamis;
And ships by thousands lay below,
      And men in nations—all were his!
He counted them at break of day,
And when the sun set where were they?

And where are they? And where art thou,
      My country? On thy voiceless shore
The heroic lay is tuneless now,
      The heroic bosom beats no more!
And must thy lyre, so long divine,
Degenerate into hands like mine?

'Tis something in the dearth of fame,
      Though linked among a fettered race,
To feel at least a patriot's shame
      Even as I sing, suffuse my face.
For what is left the poet here?
For Greeks a blush, for Greece a tear.

Must we but weep o'er days more blest?
      Must we but blush? Our fathers bled.
Earth! Render back from out thy breast
      A remnant of our Spartan dead!
Of the three hundred grant but three,
To make a new Thermopylae!

What, silent still? And silent all?
      Ah no! The voices of the dead
Sound like a distant torrent's fall
      And answer, 'Let one living head,
But one arise—we come, we come!'
'Tis but the living who are dumb.

In vain—in vain—strike other chords.
      Fill high the cup with Samian wine!
Leave battles to the Turkish hordes,
      And shed the blood of Scio's vine!
Hark, rising to the ignoble call,
How answers each bold bacchanal!

You have the Pyrrhic dance as yet,
      Where is the Pyrrhic phalanx gone?
Of two such lessons, why forget
      The nobler and the manlier one?

You have the letters Cadmus gave;
Think ye he meant them for a slave?

Fill high the bowl with Samian wine!
    We will not think of themes like these.
It made Anacreon's song divine;
    He served, but served Polycrates,
A tyrant; but our masters then
Were still at least our countrymen.

The tyrant of the Chersonese
    Was freedom's best and bravest friend.
That tyrant was Miltiades.
    Oh that the present hour would lend
Another despot of the kind!
Such chains as his were sure to bind.

Fill high the bowl with Samian wine!
    On Suli's rock and Parga's shore,
Exists the remnant of a line
    Such as the Doric mothers bore.
And there perhaps some seed is sown,
The Heracleidan blood might own.

Trust not for freedom to the Franks;
    They have a king who buys and sells.
In native swords and native ranks
    The only hope of courage dwells,
But Turkish force and Latin fraud
Would break your shield, however broad.

Fill high the bowl with Samian wine!
    Our virgins dance beneath the shade.
I see their glorious black eyes shine,
    But gazing on each glowing maid,
My own the burning teardrop laves,
To think such breasts must suckle slaves.

Place me on Sunium's marbled steep,
    Where nothing, save the waves and I,
May hear our mutual murmurs sweep;
    There, swan-like, let me sing and die.
A land of slaves shall ne'er be mine—
Dash down yon cup of Samian wine!
                    Lord Byron, *Don Juan*, iii, 86ff.

Byron's view of the Greeks themselves remained quite unsentimental, as is evident from the cheerful irony of his description of Haidee's father:

> A fisherman he had been in his youth,
>   And still a sort of fisherman was he.
> But other speculations were, in sooth,
>   Added to his connexion with the sea,
> Perhaps not so respectable, in truth.
>   A little smuggling and some piracy
> Left him at last the sole of many masters
> Of an ill-gotten million of piastres.
>
> A fisher therefore was he, though of men,
>   Like Peter the Apostle, and he fished
> For wandering merchant vessels now and then
>   And sometimes caught as many as he wished.
> The cargoes he confiscated, and gain
>   He sought in the slave market too and dished
> Full many a morsel for that Turkish trade,
> By which no doubt a good deal may be made.
>
> He was a Greek, and on his isle had built
>   (One of the wild and smaller Cyclades)
> A very handsome house from out his guilt,
>   And there he lived exceedingly at ease.
> Heaven knows what cash he got or blood he spilt;
>   A sad old fellow was he, if you please.
> But this I know, it was a spacious building,
> Full of barbaric carving, paint, and gilding.
>
> Lord Byron, *Don Juan*, II, 125–27

Panagiotis Soutsos (1806–68), the pioneer of Romantic poetry in Greece, was the author of lyric poems as well as of several larger works, among which his masterpiece is *The Traveller*. His feeling for landscape—or in this case seascape—is thoroughly Romantic:

> Sweetest of sights, the Greek horizon appears.
> Sapphire and gold the rise and set of stars.
> The Aegean Sea, studded with snowy sails,
> Seems like a lake, where swans make rendezvous.
> The moon, still brighter than the northern sun,
> Runs through the cloudless air, and looking down
> On the water, smiles to see
> The nymphs in every valley of the sea.
>
> Panagiotis Soutsos; translated by RS

James Elroy Flecker (1884–1915), best known as the author of *The Golden Journey to Samarkand*, spent the mature years of his short life in diplomatic service in Beirut. His melodious "Hyali" celebrates an imaginary but typical Greek island:

Hyali

Island in blue of summer floating on,
 Little brave sister of the Sporades,
Hail and farewell! I pass, and thou art gone,
 So fast in fire the great boat beats the seas.

But slowly fade, soft Island! Ah to know
 Thy town and who the gossips of thy town,
What flowers flash in thy meadows, what winds blow
 Across thy mountain when the sun goes down.

There is thy market, where the fisher throws
 His gleaming fish that gasp in the death-bright dawn:
And there thy Prince's house, painted old rose,
 Beyond the olives, crowns its slope of lawn.

And is thy Prince so rich that he displays
 At festal board the flesh of sheep and kine?
Or dare he—summer days are long hot days—
 Load up with Asian snow his Coan wine?

Behind a rock, thy harbour, whence a noise
 Of tarry sponge-boats hammered lustily:
And from that little rock thy naked boys
 Like burning arrows shower upon the sea.

And there by the old Greek chapel—there beneath
 A thousand poppies that each sea-wind stirs
And cyclamen, as honied and white as death,
 Dwell deep in earth the elder islanders.

Thy name I know not, Island, but *his* name
 I know, and why so proud thy mountain stands,
And what thy happy secret, and Who came
 Drawing his painted galley up thy sands.

For my Gods—Trident Gods who deep and pale
 Swim in the Latmian Sound, have murmured thus:
'To such an island came with a pompous sail
 On his first voyage young Herodotus.'

Since then—tell me no tale how Romans built,
 Saracens plundered—or that bearded lords

Rowed by to fight for Venice, and here spilt
　　　Their blood across the bay that keeps their swords.

That old Greek day was all thy history:
　　　For that did Ocean poise thee as a flower.
Farewell: this boat attends not such as thee:
　　　Farewell: I was thy lover for an hour!

Farewell! But I who call upon thy caves
　　　Am far like thee,—like thee, unknown and poor,
And yet my words are music as thy waves,
　　　And like thy rocks shall down through time endure.

James Elroy Flecker

D. H. Lawrence's imagination was captured by the thought of that seafaring dawn in the Aegean when men first knew the Greeks.

THE GREEKS ARE COMING

Little islands out at sea, on the horizon
keep suddenly showing a whiteness, a flash and a furl, a hail
of something coming, ships a-sail from over the rim of
　　　the sea.

And every time, it is ships, it is ships,
it is ships of Cnossos coming, out of the morning end of
　　　the sea,
it is Aegean ships, and men with archaic pointed beards
coming out of the eastern end.

But it is far-off foam.
And an ocean liner, going east, like a small beetle walking
　　　the edge
is leaving a long thread of dark smoke
like a bad smell.

The islands are honored as a group by Odysseus Elytis in *Axion Esti*, in the great litany of the natural glories of Greece—its mountains, its winds, its flowers and fruits: its islands:

Praised be . . .

　　　The islands with all their minium and lampblack
the islands like the vertebra of some Zeus
　　　the islands with their boat yards so deserted
the islands with their drinkable blue volcanoes

Facing the meltemi with jib close-hauled
riding the southwester on a reach
    the full length of them covered with foam
with dark blue pebbles and heliotropes

Sifnos, Amorgos, Alonnisos
Thasos, Ithaka, Santorini
Kos, Ios, Sikinos . . .

Odysseus Eytis, Axion Esti;
translated by E. Keeley and George Savidis

Islands, like men, have their exits and their entrances. Some maintain a reputation, a fascination, through centuries: Others surface
briefly (as it were) and are lost to thought. They catch the imagination at different historical moments.

We will make an imaginary voyage, setting out from Athens
east and then northeast at first, and find what echoes still rever-
berate; then south via the Sporades to the Dodecanese and Crete.

Kea (Keos, Ceos)

The closest island to the Attic coast already in the open sea is Kea,
celebrated in antiquity as the home of the lyric poet Bacchylides.
"There are plenty of Muses," said Pindar, "on the island." In
medieval and Turkish times it was known as Zea; one of its sur-
viving Muses visited Tom Moore, the biographer of Byron, who,
though he never went to Greece, had done his homework.

There is a fount on Zea's isle,
Round which, in soft luxuriance, smile
All the sweet flowers, of every kind,
    On which the sun of Greece looks down,
        Pleas'd as a lover on the crown
His mistress for her brow hath twin'd,
When he beholds each flow'ret there,
Himself had wish'd her most to wear;
Here bloom'd the laurel-rose, whose wreath
    Hangs radiant round the Cypriot shrines,
And here those bramble-flowers, that breathe
    Their odour into Zante's wines:—
The splendid woodbine, that, at eve,
    To grace their floral diadems,

The lovely maids of Patmos weave:—
    And that fair plant, whose tangled stems
Shine like a Nereid's hair, when spread,
Dishevell'd, o'er her azure bed;—
All these bright children of the clime,
(Each at its own most genial time,
The summer, or the year's sweet prime,)
Like beautiful earth-stars, adorn
The valley, where that fount is born:
While round, to grace its cradle green,
Groups of Velani oaks are seen,
Tow'ring on every verdant height—
Tall, shadowy in the evening light,
Like Genii, set to watch the birth
Of some enchanted child of earth—
Fair oaks, that over Zea's vales,
    Stand with their leafy pride unfurl'd;
While Commerce, from her thousand sails,
    Scatters their fruit throughout the world!

        Thomas Moore, *Evenings in Greece*, I

The laurel rose is the oleander, most characteristic shrub of the Greek summer. The woodbine is identified by Moore in a note, where he acknowledges his use of the writings of the botanist John Sibthorp, as *Lonicera caprifolium*, a variety of honeysuckle which, it appears, is not found in Greece, though it closely resembles *Lonicera implexa*, which is. The Nereid's hair is *Cusenta europaea*, the large dodder, known to the ancients as "vetch-strangler," a trailing parasitic plant which forms a mesh of reddish stems over the host plant. The importance of the acorn to the Kean economy is expounded in Clarke's *Travels*, also cited by Moore.

When the botanist Tournefort visited Zea in 1701, he made few records of the plant life of the island, but turned his caustic eye on its human inhabitants.

    The burghers of Zia generally get together when they spin their silk; they sit upon the very edge of their terrass-roofs, and let fall the spindle into the street, and then draw it up again in winding the thread. We found the Greek bishop in this posture; he ask'd us who we were, at the same time giving us to understand that 'twas a sign we had not much to do, if we came thither only to hunt for plants and pieces of antiquity: to which we reply'd, we should be much more edified to find him reading St Chrysostom's or St Basil's sermons, than winding off bottoms of silk.

Joseph Pitton de Tournefort, *Voyage into the Levant;*
translated by John Ozell (1718)

Syros (Syra)

Syros caught the imagination of Herman Melville when he traveled through the Levant in 1856–57, and he described it both in his journal and in a poem:

> Some old men looked like Pericles reduced to a chiffonier—such a union of picturesque and poverty stricken.
>
> All round barren tawny hills, here and there terraced with stone.
>
> View of the islands—little hamlets, white, half way up mountains.—The azure of the sea, and ermine of the clouds, the Greek flag (blue and white) seems suggested by the azure of her sky and ermine of her clouds.
>
> The wharf, a kind of semicircle, coinciding with the amphitheatre of hills.—In December tables and chairs out of doors, coffee and water pipes.—Carpenters and blacksmiths working in the theatrical costumes.
>
> The crowds on the quays all with red caps, looking like flamingoes. Long tassells—laborers wear them, and carry great bundles of codfish on their heads.—Few seem to have anything to do. All lounge. Greek signs over a pieman's.

Herman Melville, *Journal of a Visit to Europe
and the Levant 1856-7*

> I saw it in its earlier day—
> Primitive, such an isled resort
> As hearthless Homer might have known
> Wandering about the Aegean here,
> Sheds ribbed with wreck-stuff faced the sea
> Where goods in transit shelter found;
> And here and there a shanty-shop
> Where fez-caps, swords, tobacco, shawls,
> Pistols, and orient finery, Eve's—
> (The spangles dimmed by hands profane)
> Like plunder on a pirate's deck
> Lay orderless in such loose way
> As to suggest things ravished or gone astray.

Above a tented inn with fluttering flag
A sunburnt board announced Greek wine
In self-same text Anacreon knew,
Dispensed by one named 'Pericles'.
Got up as for the opera's scene,
Armed strangers, various, lounged or lazed,
Lithe fellows tall, with gold-shot eyes,
Sunning themselves as leopards may.

Off-shore lay xebecs trim and light,
And some but dubious in repute.
But on the strand, for docks were none,
What busy bees! no testy fry;
Frolickers, picturesquely odd,
With bales and oil-jars lading boats,
Lighters that served an anchored craft,
Each in his tasselled Phrygian cap,
Blue Eastern drawers and braided vest;
And some with features cleanly cut
As Proserpine's upon the coin.
Such chatterers all! like children gay
Who make believe to work, but play.

I saw, and how help musing too.
Here traffic's immature as yet:
Forever this juvenile fun hold out
And these light hearts? Their garb, their glee,
Alike profuse in flowing measure,
Alike inapt for serious work,
Blab of grandfather Saturn's prime
When trade was not, nor toil, nor stress,
But life was leisure, merriment, peace,
And lucre none and love was righteousness.

Herman Melville,
Syra: A Transmitted Reminiscence

Mykonos

In 1628 Rev. Charles Robson, the chaplain at Aleppo, was traveling in the Greek islands. He performed some service to scholarship by bringing back some oriental manuscripts on his return to
England in 1630. His expectations of the Greek scene are condi-
tioned by his learning, which in fact reveals a considerable naïveté
in the following charming encounter:

At this Mycona we stayed three dayes by reason of the extremitie of weather: a barren iland of small extent some fifteene miles in compasse, wholly inhabited by poore Greekes, having but one, I cannot tell whether to call it, village or town of the same name with the iland, subject to the dominion and spoile of the Turkes. In all my life I never saw a place better peopled with woemen; their number exceeding the number of men five for one: the barrennesse of the ile is much helped with the industry of the people, forcing corne out of the rocky mountaines, scarce passable for men: yet they continue so poore by reason of the Turkes pillages, that unlesse they were merry Greekes indeed, any would wonder what delight they could take in living, living in continuall feare, in continuall and extreame necessitie. Here (as Travellers use to doe) the first thing I visited was one of their churches: where by chance I found their Septuagint, and an old man nothing differing in poverty or habit from the rest, there conning his lesson, I tooke the Bible and red in it; he stood amazed at it, and offring to kisse my hand spoke to me in the common Greeke, which is so degenerate from the true and ancient, that there is either none or little affinitie betwixt them. I answered in the learned, but I perceived he understood me as much as I did him, which was scarce a word. Then I thinking that though he understood not me he understood the Bible, I spoke my minde to him by pointing out sentences in the Bible, but he understood them as much as hee did me. I wondred at this ignorance, and Gods Justice: and relating this story to one of the merchants that had lived some time amongst them at Sio, hee told mee that none of their Colieroes (priests) but that read the Bible in the learned Greeke, their Leturgy being in the same, but scarce one of a hundred could understand it. I did not wonder at this, calling to minde the history of our Masse-mumbling priests in Queene Maries dayes. In all their churches fairer then their ordinary houses, scarce either fairer or larger then ours, they have painted, but no carved images.

Rev. Charles Robson, *News from Aleppo* (London, 1628)

Delos

Center of the Cyclades, Delos was sacred to the god Apollo, who was born there after his mother, Leto (the daughter of Coeus in Pindar's lines, below), had strayed over most of the Greek world looking for a place that would receive her to give birth. Delos was also the central sanctuary of the Delian League of the fifth century B.C., which became the Athenian Empire. It has never been inhabited, and it was indeed considered ill-omened to die there; it has accordingly preserved something of its numinous character. Pindar, Homer, and Callimachus all celebrated it in poetry:

> Hail, god-founded, all-desirable scion of the children of gleaming-haired Leto, unmoved marvel of the wide world, which mortals name Delos, but the blessed on Olympus call the far-resplendent star of the cyan earth.

> Formerly it was blown by all the winds over the billowed sea: but when the daughter of Coeus once trod thereon, racked in the pains of labour, then four mighty pillars, shod in adamant, sprung upright from the bottom of earth, and held the rock on their brows; and there she gave birth to her blessed son.

> Pindar, *Hymn* I; translated by RS

> And many a temple, all ways, men ordain
> To the bright Godhead; groves, made dark with trees,
> And never shorn, to hide the Deities,
> All high-lov'd prospects, all the steepest brows
> Of far-seen hills, and every flood that flows
> Forth to the sea, are dedicate to thee.
> But most of all thy mind's alacrity
> Is rais'd with Delos; since, to fill thy fane,
> There flocks so many an Ionian,
> With ample gowns that flow down to their feet,
> With all their children, and the reverend sweet
> Of all their pious wives. And these are they
> That (mindful of thee) even thy Deity
> Render more spritely with their champion fight,
> Dances, and songs, perform'd to glorious sight,
> Once having publish'd, and proclaim'd their strife.
> And these are acted with such exquisite life
> That one would say, 'Now, the Ionian strains
> Are turn'd Immortals, nor know what age means.'

> *Homeric Hymn to Apollo;*
> translated by George Chapman (London, 1616)

> Though to tempestuous seas and storms expos'd,
> Its firm foundations rooted in the deep,
> Unshaken stands the isle; round whose rough shores
> (More pervious to the cormorant than horse;

Where whilom lonely fishers made abode:)
Th'Icarian waves their white foam roaring dash;
Yet to old Ocean's and his Tethys' court
When move the islands, murmuring none beholds
Majestic Delos graceful lead the train
Claiming prime honour: Corsica demands
The second place: Euboea next appears,
Her follows sweet Sardinia, and the isle
Which happily received the queen of love,
When from the waves emerging; for reward,
Its shores her kind protection ever share.
These boast for their defence strong walls and towers,
But Delos her Apollo—and what tower
Impregnable as he? for towers and walls
Strymonian Boreas levels with the ground:
But ever unremov'd firm stands the God;
Thy guardian, happy Delos, thy defence.

> Callimachus, *Hymn to Delos*;
> translated by William Dodd (London, 1755)

Samos

Sailing due east, just before reaching the Ionian coast, our boat
reaches Samos, the home, in the sixth century B.C., of the tyrant
Polycrates, the patron of the lyric poets Ibycus and Anacreon,
whose good fortune was proverbial among his contemporaries.

All worldly riches his lusts did obey;
And when he found she was so favourable,
For a season, as she that list to play,
This blind goddess, unsure and ever unstable,
Set him so high up at Fame's table,
Of false intent, in his estate royal
When he sat high'st to make him have a fall.

·⌣·

And for t' attempt of goddes the power,
And of Fortune the variant doubleness,
He took a ring of gold full bright and clear,
Therein a ruby of excellent richnesse,
Seeking occasion of some new heaviness,
Which never aforne had know of no such thing,—
Into the sea anon he cast his ring,

Disespeired again it to recure,
For he deemed it was an impossible.
But right anon fishers of aventure,
Like a mervaile very incredible,
Among the waves hidous and horrible
Cast in their nettes, if it would avail,
Taking a fish, the ring in his entrail.

Which was presented at a solemnity
To Policrate with full great reverence,
When he sat crowned in his most dignity
At a feast of famous excellence.
The fish undone anon in his presence,
Mid th' entrails his carver found the ring
Of aventure, and took it to the king.

Which deemed of pride and high presumption,
That Neptunus, god of the salte sea,
Had of his ring made restitution,
And durste not offend his majesty.
Whereupon a fantasy caught he,
Nother heavenly gods nor Fortune blind of sight
Were both unhardy t' attempt his might.

John Lydgate, *Fall of Princes*,
IV, 995–1036 (modernized)

His fall was as wretched as his previous fortune had been glorious. Deceived by the Persian satrap, who invited him to accept his assistance in the attempt to win control of the Aegean sea, he was murdered in a way Herodotus forbears to specify, and his body nailed to a cross and exposed to rot, thus fulfilling the prophetic dream of his daughter who saw her father "washed by Zeus and anointed by the Sun."

Sir Henry Blount set off in 1634 on a voyage to the Levant, his avowed intention to increase his knowledge of men and their manners. His account of Samos is typical in the samples of lore he transmits:

> Samos is the only place in the world, under whose rocks grow spunges: the people from their infancy, are bred up with dry biscuit, and other extenuating diet, to make them extreme lean; then taking a spunge wet in oil they hold it, part in their mouths and part without, so they go under water, where at first they cannot stay long; but after practice, some of the leanest

stay above an hour and a half, even till all the oil of the spunge be corrupted; and by the law of the island, none of that trade is suffered to marry, until he have stayed half an hour under water: thus they gather spunges from the bottom of the rocks, more than an hundred fathom deep; which with many stories of these islands was told me by certain Greeks in our galleon.

H. Blount, A Voyage into the Levant (London, 1636)

Samos is not, and never was, the only place where sponges grow; but sponge fishing is still an important occupation in several of the islands, and in summer the divers will often go as far as the Libyan coast to dive.

Chios

Turning north our boat reaches Homer's "rocky Chios," which has a strong claim to be the birthplace of Homer, though it vies for that distinction with seven other cities.

> Some, Homer, say Colophon was your nurse,
> Some lovely Smyrna, and some say Chios.
> Some, Ios, some cry out for lucky Salamis,
> Some say Thessaly, home of the Lapithae.
> Others call for other places: but if Apollo
> Gives me reliable prophecy,
> I say your home is heaven, and your mother
> No mortal, but the Muse Calliope.

Anthologia Planudea, 4, 296;
translated by RS

The legend that the blind Homer came from Chios derives from the address to the maids of Delos in the Homeric Hymn to Apollo:

> And you, O Delian virgins, do me grace,
> When any stranger of our earthy race,
> Whose restless life affliction hath in chace,
> Shall hither come and question you, who is,
> To your chaste ears, of choicest faculties
> In sacred poesy, and with most right
> Is author of your absolut'st delight,
> Ye shall yourselves do all the right ye can
> To answer for our name:—'The sightless man

Of stony Chios. All whose poems shall
In all last ages stand for capital.'

Homeric Hymn to Apollo;
translated by George Chapman
(London, 1616)

The island was allowed certain privileges under Turkish rule, and,
as a result, was unusually prosperous and populous by comparison
with much of the rest of Greece in the seventeenth century. Few
travelers fail to note the celebrated beauty of its women.

> [Chios] is not inferior to the best island in the archipel-
> ago; though it is not so large as Negro Ponte, it is much the
> richer, and the inhabitants enjoy greater privileges than any
> Greeke in the Grand Signiors dominions; and more liberty
> cannot be in any part, than what they injoy. In the summer
> time every evening the marine is full with all sorts of people
> with musick, singing, and dancing, and none offer to molest
> them. At their festivals, they are very open in their worship
> . . . The inhabitants are most Greeks, of which many are of
> the Church of Rome.

Bernard Randolph, *The Present State of the Islands
in the Archipelago* (London, 1687)

> The women of the citty Sio, are the most beautiful dames,
> (or rather angelicall creatures) of all the Greekes, upon the face
> of the earth, and greatly given to Venery.

> If Venus' foe saw Sio's fair-fac'd dames,
> His stomacke cold, would burne, in lust-spred flames.

> They are for the most part exceeding proude, and sump-
> tuous in apparell, and commonly go (even artificers wives) in
> gownes of satin and taffety; yea, in cloth of silver and gold, and
> are adorned with precious stones, and gemmes, and jewels
> about their neckes, and handes, with rings, chaines, &
> bracelets. Their husbands are their pandors, and when they see
> any stranger arrive, they will presently demaund of him if he
> would have a mistresse: and so they make whoores of their
> owne wives, and are contented for a little gaine, to weare
> hornes: such are the base minds of ignominious cuckolds. If a
> straunger be desirous to stay all night with any of them, their
> price is a chicken[3] of gold, nine shillings English, out of which

---

3. Sequin, zechino.

this companion receiveth his supper, and for his paines, a belly full of sinfull content.

William Lithgow, *Totall Discourse of the Rare and Painefull Peregrinations* (London, 1632)

Three days after our imbarkment (as quicke a passage as ever was heard of) we arrived at Sio, famous Iland called formerly Chios, which signifieth white, of Chione a nymph,

> —Who rich in beautie
> A thousand suiters pleasd—
> Ovid, *Metam.* 9

and therefore so named. Others say of the snow, that sometimes covers those mountaines. Sixe score and five miles it containeth in circuite, extending from south unto north: the north and west quarters extraordinarily hilly. In the middest of the island is the mountain Arvis [now Amista] producing the best Greeke wines, so praised by the ancient:

> Pleasant with plenteous Bacchus, when we feast
> By th' fire, if cold: in shades, if heate molest:
> I bolles will with Arvisian Nectar fill.
> Verg., *Ecl.* 5

But the Lentiske tree, which is wel-nigh onely proper to Sio, doth give it the greatest renowne and endowment. These grow at the south end of the iland, and on the leisurely ascending hills that neighbour the shore. In hight not much exceeding a man, leaved like a service, and bearing a red berry, but changing into black as it ripeneth. Of this tree, thus writeth an old poet:

> The lentiske ever greene, and ever great
> With gratefull fruite, three different sorts doth beare,
> Three harvests yeelds, is thrice drest in one yeare:
> Cic., *De divin.*

And that with no lesse diligence then vines; otherwise they will afford but a little Masticke: which yearly yeelds to the inhabitants eighteene thousand sultanies. In the beginning of August lanch they the rine, from whence the masticke distilleth until the end of September, at which time they gather it. None is suffered to come amongst them during the interim, it being death but to have a pound of new mastick found in their houses. The wood thereof is excellent for tooth-picks, so commended of old:

> Lentiske excels: if tooth-picks of the lentiske
> Be wanting, of a quill then make a tooth-picke.
>
> Mart., 14.22

By reason of these trees they have the best hony of the world, which intermingled with water, is not much inferiour in rellish to the costly shurbets of Constantinople: the iland produceth corne and oile in indifferent plenty. Some silke they make, and some cottons here grow, but short in worth to those of Smyrna. It hath also quarries of excellent marble: and a certaine greene earth, like the rust of brasse, which the Turks call Terra Chia: but not that so reputed of by the ancient Physicions. The coast, especially towards the south, is set with small watch-towers, which with smoke by day and fire by night, do given knowledge unto one another (and so to the upland) of suspected enemies. The environing sea being free from concealed rocks, and consequently from perill . . .

Their orchards are here enriched with excellent fruits: amongst the rest, with oranges, lemons, citrions, pomegranates, and figs, so much esteemed by the Romans for their tartnesse:

> The Chian figs, which Setia to me sent,
> Taste like old wine: they wine and salt present.
>
> Mart., 13.23

Upon the fig-trees they hang a kind of unsavourie fig: out of whose corruption certain small wormes are ingendered, which by biting the other (as they say) procure them to ripen. Partridges are here an ordinary food: whereof they have an incredible number, greater than ours, and differing in hiew: the beake and feete red, the plume ash-colour. Many of them are kept tame: these feeding abroad all day, at night upon a call returne unto their severall owners.

Sir George Sandys, *A Relation of a Journey begun 1610* (London, 1615)

One of the bloodiest episodes of the War of Independence was the massacre of Chios (March 1822), portrayed in a series of grisly

Eugène Delacroix, Massacre at Chios. Musée du Louvre, Paris. (Photo: Giraudon/Art Resource, New York).

paintings by Eugène Delacroix. Alfred de Vigny evokes the enthusiastic beginning of the Greek insurrection, as well as its suppresion, in his cantata-like poem, *Helena:*

Hear, hear that solitary bell
Ringing from the peak of desolate Scio.
Its clangour, full of sombre ecstasy,
Brings armed men from the mountains to the port:
The winds have risen now for vengeance,
And the night is excited with their knowledge.
Greek scarlet covers their brows
Like the innocent purple which adorns
The heads of choirboys
When mass is said at our altars.

This sign is fixed to the warriors' foreheads.
Who will dare to flee or stay in hiding?
Lighted tapers gleam and smoke in their hands;
The air is aflame as from a distant fire:
The sable of the sea shows its gilded flanks,
And high on the mountains the cedars flash.
The crowds are on the shore, their eager hope
Casts glances on the tumbling waves in vain,
When, with a friendly whistle from the dark,
A rebel ship emerges from the shadows.
A bloody standard slaps around its pole.
An astonishing number of armed warriors
Pours on to its three gangways: the cannon
Which flashes from its porthole repeats its thunder.
Cries greet it, cries are returned:
The hymn of slaughtered Rigas echoes round:
The impatient tocsin's rebellious note
Sounds liberty from the roof of the chapel.
Assembling, excitement, arming and being armed;
At the sound the eagle leaves its rock in terror.

Alfred de Vigny, Helena I; translated by RS

As many as forty thousand were sold into slavery; sack upon sack of human fragments were proudly sent to the Sultan, and the mastic trees and other crops of the island were entirely destroyed in an orgy of ruin from which the island has never recovered. The American poet, George Hill, described the appearance of the island a few years after the massacre:

SCIO

Pass we the peak, by summer suns imbrowned;
   The dewy glen, where, wooed by bubbling rill,
Unheeded Beauty strews her flowers around;
   The chapel perched, like snow-flake, on the hill—
And lo! a spot as of enchanted ground.
O God! it is a heart-sore sight, to see
   The fairest work by human hands defaced.
Look on this garden of the bird and bee!
   Where Love, 'twould seem, his paradise had placed.
   Yet here the Moslem, dull, as in a waste,
Like tiger, from the relics of his prey
   Unroused, by no avenging weapon chased,

Heeds not the spring-flower's bloom, nor blithe bird's lay;
The ground is red with blood whereon he kneels to pray.

The Ruins of Athens (Boston, 1839)

Psara

Psara lies just to the northwest of Chios and has earned a place in history through the destruction of its city by the Turks on 21 June 1824—an event lamented in a lapidary epigram by Dionysios Solomos. (It also stirred Gérard de Nerval to a wordy poem in irregular meter, severely sub-Byronic in its sentiments and expression.)

> On the island's blackened stone
> Glory paces all alone,
> Thinking on the shining dead,
> Wears a garland on her head
> Of the little that is found
> Green upon the wasted ground.

D. Solomos;
translated by J. N. Mavrogordato

Lesbos

The home of Sappho, born probably at Eresos, and of Alcaeus, as well as of the legendary Arion, of Terpander, and of the scientist Theophrastus, who succeeded Aristotle as head of the Academy. The pleasant holy grove described by Sappho in an address to Aphrodite was perhaps in the neighborhood of Eresos:

> Come to me from Crete, to this holy temple, where is your pleasant grove of apple trees, and altars fragrant with frankincense; there cold water babbles among apple branches, all the place is shaded with roses, sleep comes down from the trembling leaves. There is a meadow for horses, blossoming with spring flowers, and gentle breezes blow . . .

Sappho, fragment 2; translated by RS

Sir George Sandys is ready, as always, to air his learning on the topic of the Lesbian poets.

> A number of celebrated wits have in their birth made this countrey happy; as Pittacus, one of the seven sages, Sappho, and Alcaeus:

Sad Sapphon Aeolian strings
Of harder hearted virgins sings.
Alceus in a higher key
On golden lire, of ills at sea,
In flight sustain'd: and wars sterne ire,
Th' attentive ghosts do both admire:
Worthy of sacred silence—

Hor., C. 2.13

succeeding Orpheus in the excellency of lyricall poesie.
Whereupon the fable is grounded, that when Orpheus was
cut in pieces by the Ciconian women, the river

Hebrus had head and harpe. Whilst borne along,
The harpe sounds something sadly: the dead tongue
Sighs out sad ditties: the banks sympathize
That bound the river, in their sad replies.
Now borne to sea, from countries streame they drive,
And at Methymnian Lesbos shore arrive.

Ovid, Met. 11

It is said also that the nightingales of this countrey sing more
sweetly than elsewhere.

Sir George Sandys, A Relation of a Journey begun 1610
(London, 1615)

The women of Lesbos seem to have had in antiquity the reputation for beauty that in our era attaches to those of Chios. One of the
star attractions of Agamemnon's promised conciliatory gifts to
Achilles makes this clear.

Sev'n Lesbian ladies he shall have, that were the most select,
And in their needles rarely skill'd, whom, when he took
the two
Of famous Lesbos, I did choose; who won the chief renown
For beauty from their whole fair sex . . .

Homer, Iliad, ix, 129f.;
translated by George Chapman (London, 1611)

An ancient commentator adds:

On Lesbos, a Beauty Contest is held for women in the
Sanctuary of Hera; it is called the Kallisteia.

Alcaeus also mentions this contest, "Where Lesbian girls go to and fro with trailing robes, being judged for beauty, while the marvellous sound of the loud cries of women echoes round them every year" (fragment 130 Page).

Lemnos

A now extinct volcano was the center of a cult of Hephaestus in antiquity, and probably also the origin of the legendary Lemnian earth, described by many travelers from the west.

> On the side hills, on the contrary side of the valley, directly over against the middle point betwixt this hill and Παναγιὰ κοτζινὰτζ, is the place where they dig the *terra sigillata*. At the foot of a hard rock of grey hard freestone enclining to marble is a little clear spring of most excellent water, which, falling down a little lower, looseth its water in a kind of milky bogge; on the East side of this spring, within a foot or my hand's breadth of it, they every year take out the earth on the 6th of August, about three houres after the sun. Several papas, as well as others, would fain have persuaded me that, at the time of our Saviour's transfiguration, this place was sanctifyed to have this virtuous earth, and that it is never to be found soft and unctuous, but always perfect rock, unlesse only that day, which they keep holy in remembrance of the Metamorphosis, and at that time when the priest hath said his liturgy; but I believe they take it onely that day, and set the greater price upon it by its Scarcenesse. Either it was the Venetian, or perhaps Turkish policy for the Grand Signor to engrosse it all to himselfe, unless some little, which the Greekes steal; and they prefer no poor Greek to take any for his own occasions, for they count it an infallible cure of all agues taken in the beginning of the fit with water, and drank so two or three times. Their women drink it to hasten childbirth, and to stop the fluxes that are extraordinary; and they count it an excellent counter-poyson, and have got a story that no vessel made of it will hold poison, but immediately splinter in a thousand pieces.

> Dr John Covel,* *Diary* (1669–77)

Lemnos was the place of exile of the hero Philoctetes, the stench of whose suppurating foot made his company insupportable to the other heroes besieging Troy. Yet Troy could not be captured, according to Fate, without the use of his bow.

When Philoctetes in the Lemnian isle
Like a Form sculptured on a monument
Lay couched; on him or his dread bow unbent
Some wild bird oft might settle and beguile
The rigid features of a transient smile,
Disperse the tear, or to the sigh give vent,
Slackening the pains of ruthless banishment
From his loved home, and from heroic toil.
And trust that spiritual creatures round us move,
Griefs to allay which Reason cannot heal;
Yea, veriest reptiles have sufficed to prove
To fettered wretchedness, that no Bastille
Is deep enough to exclude the light of love,
Though man for brother man has ceased to feel.

William Wordsworth

Finally released from his lonely torment to return with his bow to
Troy, he accompanied Odysseus and Neoptolemus on the voyage
to Troy. His farewell to the island, in Sophocles' play, evokes a
scene of wintry desolation, the terror of an uninhabited rock even
in the mildest of seas:

PHILOCTETES:

Come, then, I leave this isle,
And speak my parting words;
Farewell, o roof, long time
My one true guard and friend;
And ye, O nymphs that sport
In waters and in fields;
Strong roar of waves that break
On jutting promontory,
Where oft my head was wet,
(Though hid in far recess),
With blasts of stormy south;
And oft the mount that bears
The name of Hermes gave
Its hollow, loud lament,
Echoing my stormy woe;
And now, ye streams and fount,
Lykian, where haunt the wolves,
We leave you, leave you now,
Who ne'er had dreamt of this.

Farewell, O Lemnos, girt by waters round,
With fair breeze send me on . . .

Sophocles, *Philoctetes*, 1452−65;
translated by E. H. Plumtre

Thasos

. . . which, like a donkey's back
Stands crowned with savage woodland . . .
A land not lovely, not desirable,
Not loved—not like that by the river Siris.

Archilochus, fragment 21–2 West;
translated by RS

The explorer, Cyriac of Ancona, indulged in one of his rare flights of verse while searching for antiquities on Thasos in 1944. He envisages the island of Lesbos commending him to the attention of the Prince of Mytilene, Francesco Gattilusio, who did indeed assist him in his excavations and searching, as did many of the local governors of the archipelago.

What fate, what destiny or whirl of stars,
What ancient order, or new senate's word,
What rule of governor, or alarms of wars,
What general's triumph, or civil overlord,

What siren song or what Apolline choir,
What human or divine consistory
Of instruments all making harmony,
What nymphs of Thasos, or great Orpheus' lyre

Could take from me my master, and beguile
Francesco to desert our shores, which claim
His lasting honour to our lovely isle?

But if the duty of a father's name
Draws you to Thasos, as to a second child,
I hope to have a share in your fair fame—

And, hoping for the same,

On Thasos wanders faithful Cyriac,
Seeking your glory in its every rock.

Cyriac of Ancona, *Journeys**

Samothrace

The mysterious cult of the Kabeiroi made this island famous in classical times. These chthonian deities were also worshiped on Lemnos, at Thebes, and elsewhere. The earliest traces of the sanctuary are of the eighth century B.C., but the cult became popular in Hellenistic and Roman times, when the gods were assimilated to the Kouretes and Korybantes, and sometimes to the Dioscuri, Castor and Pollux. The Kouretes are celebrated in one of the Orphic hymns, attributed to the god Orpheus who sailed on the Argo, but in fact composed in the Roman period:

> Brass-beating Salians, ministers of Mars,
> Who wear his arms the instruments of wars;
> Whose blessed frames, heav'n, earth, and sea compose,
> And from whose breath all animals arose:
> Who dwell in Samothracia's sacred ground,
> Defending mortals through the sea profound.
> Deathless Curetes, by your pow'r alone,
> The greatest mystic rites to men at first were shown.
> Who shake old Ocean thund'ring to the sky,
> And stubborn oaks with branches waving high.
> 'Tis yours in glittering arms the earth to beat,
> With lightly leaping, rapid, sounding feet;
> Then ev'ry beast the noise terrific flies,
> And the loud tumult wanders through the skies.

>   ٠ﾗ

> Great Jove's assessors; whose immortal breath
> Sustains the soul, and wafts her back from death;
> Aerial-form'd, who in Olympus shine
> The heavenly Twins all-lucid and divine:
> Blowing, serene, from whom abundance springs,
> Nurses of seasons, fruit-producing kings.

> *Orphic hymn*, 38;
> translated by Thomas Taylor

Apparently genuine Orphic doctrine is preserved in a remarkable series of inscribed gold sheets found in Lower Italy, near Rome, and in Crete. These, too, probably stem from the Hellenistic period. Robert Graves has made an imaginative cento of their doctrine, and attached it to the dark rituals of Samothrace:

Instructions to the Orphic Adept

So soon as ever your mazed spirit descends
From daylight into darkness, Man, remember
What you have suffered here in Samothrace,
What you have suffered.

After your passage through Hell's seven floods,
Whose fumes of sulphur will have parched your throat,
The Halls of Judgement shall loom up before you,
A miracle of jasper and of onyx.
To the left hand there bubbles a black spring
Overshadowed with a great white cypress.
Avoid this spring, which is Forgetfulness;
Though all the common rout rush down to drink,
Avoid this spring.

To the right hand there lies a secret pool
Alive with speckled trout and fish of gold;
A hazel overshadows it. Ophion,
Primaeval serpent straggling in the branches,
Darts out his tongue. This holy pool is fed
By dripping water; guardians stand before it.
Run to this pool, the pool of Memory,
Run to this pool.

Then will the guardians scrutinize you, saying:
'Who are you, who? What have you to remember?
Do you not fear Ophion's flickering tongue?
Go rather to the spring beneath the cypress,
Flee from this pool.'

Then you shall answer: 'I am parched with thirst.
Give me to drink. I am a child of earth,
But of Sky also, come from Samothrace.
Witness the glint of amber on my brow.
Out of the Pure I come, as you may see.
I also am of your thrice-blessed kin,
Child of the three-fold Queen of Samothrace;
Have made full quittance for my deeds of blood,
Have been by her invested in sea-purple,
And like a kid have fallen into milk.
Give me to drink, now I am parched with thirst,
Give me to drink!'

But they will ask you yet: 'What of your feet?'
You shall reply: 'My feet have borne me here

Out of the weary wheel, the circling years,
To that still, spokeless wheel:—Persephone.
Give me to drink!'

Then they will welcome you with fruit and flowers,
And lead you toward the ancient dripping hazel,
Crying: 'Brother of our immortal blood,
Drink and remember glorious Samothrace!'
Then you shall drink.

You shall drink deep of that refreshing draught,
To become lords of the uninitiated
Twittering ghosts, Hell's countless populace—
To become heroes, knights upon swift horses,
Pronouncing oracles from tall white tombs
By the nymphs tended. They with honey water
Shall pour libations to your serpent shapes,
That you may drink.

Robert Graves

Antiparos

A second voyage out from Athens will carry us southeast, to Paros and Antiparos; the celebrated grotto of the latter was an essential call for sightseers in the seventeenth and eighteenth centuries. Charles Swan describes his impressions in his journal:

> Everywhere hang huge masses of one shape or other; those from the roof are principally pointed, with a drop of clear water appended. On the lower part arise pillars, rounded at the top like a pine-apple, and fretted in a similar manner. In some places the stalactite has partitioned off a portion of the cavern, making cells, whose roofs become ornamented with a broad and sloping stalagmite, something of the pattern of a fish's fin. We fired a couple of ship's blue lights from one of the higher parts of the cavern. The effect was uncommonly fine. They showed the whole place to perfection, and gave a magnificent tinge to the opaque bodies of the pendent stalactites. I brought off several specimens.

> In this cavern, AD 1673, according to M. Tournefort, the Marquis de Nointel, French Ambassador to the Porte, had the folly or the vanity to continue 'the three Christian holidays'. He caused high mass to be celebrated upon a piece of stalactite, which still retains the name of the altar. 'Men were posted from space to space, in every precipice from the altar to

the opening of the cavern, who gave the signal with their handkerchiefs, when the body of our Lord was lifted up; at this signal fire was put to twenty four drakes, and to several patereroes that were at the entrance of the cavern: the trumpets, hautbois, fifes and violins, made the consecration yet more magnificent.'

Charles Swan, *Voyage to the Eastern Mediterranean*
(London, 1826)

Naxos

Naxos is traditionlly identified with Dia, where Theseus landed with Ariadne after she had helped him to overcome the Cretan Minotaur.

> And streight he having winde,
> With Minos daughter sailed away to Dia: where (unkinde
> And cruell creature that he was) he left hir post alone
> Upon the shore. Thus desolate and making dolefull mone
> God Bacchus did both comfort hir and take hir to his bed.
> And with an everlasting starre the more hir fame to spred,
> He tooke the chaplet from hir head, and up to heaven
>   it threw,
> The chaplet thirled through the aire: and as it gliding flew,
> The precious stones were turnd to starres which blased cleare
>   and bright,
> And tooke their place (continuing like a chaplet still to sight)
> Amid between the Kneeler Downe and him that gripes
>   the Snake.

Ovid, *Metamorphoses*, VIII, 174—82;
translated by Arthur Golding (1567)

The episode caught the imagination of Catullus (poem 64), and is the occasion for one of Ovid's *Letters of Heroines*, as well as the theme of an insipid poem by Leigh Hunt.

Melos

Melos is famous in history as the scene of the "Melian Dialogue," reported or elaborated by Thucydides, where representatives of Melos and Athens put forward, with uncommon honesty, the arguments for and against the subjugation of the island by Athens, a textbook analysis by Thucydides of power politics. (Athens, of course, had its way.)

    Bartolommeo Zamberti, who probably came from Venice,

composed a description of the Aegean islands in a series of sonnets, illustrated by sketch maps of the islands, which he published in 1485. No island is omitted: Some get several sonnets. Here is his repertory of notable facts about Melos:

The goddess Cybele was worshipped once
(Whom Aristotle calls the Western Wind)
In this fine island, noble and contented
As any I have found in the Aegean.

Above the port there is a level plain,
A broken tower, and two miles away
A castle; then, towards north east again
Another, strong and quite impregnable.

Below these are the bath and river bank
Where Melian ladies go to wash their clothes.
The earth is black in places, elsewhere white.

Here did Menestheus suffer his last pangs.
Molybdenum is plentiful in the rocks,
Abundant too are women, corn and honey.

Bartolommeo Zamberti degli Sonnetti
(?1485); translated by RS

Bernard Randolph likewise proffers some curious lore:

It has a very faire harbour, large, and secure against all winds. Here privateers do usually come to make up their fleets, and it is most commonly their rendezvous, at their first coming into the Archipelago . . . Here are several hot places for men to sweat, at the side of hills, which in some places are so hot as to rost an egg, if put between the hollow of some stones. All the whole island is esteemed to have fire under it, which is thought to consume the stones, which are very like to honeycombs, being all hollow.

Bernard Randolph, *Present State of the Islands in the Archipelago* (London, 1687)

In 1820 Melos came into the public eye through the discovery, or rather removal, of the statue of Aphrodite, known as the Venus de Milo, now in the Louvre. The first visitor to leave a description of the statue was the Frenchman Dumont D'Urville, an officer on the *Chevrette*, commanded by one Captain Matterer. The ship was making a voyage to the Black Sea where D'Urville was to carry out hydrographic studies. (He later became an admiral and a famous explorer.) When he saw the statue, its left arm was still intact, and the hand held an apple, surely that presented to her by the Shepherd Paris in the divine beauty contest on Mt. Ida. It had been found by a peasant called Yorgo when one of his sheep tumbled into a crevasse. The Armenian priest hastened to acquire it, with a view to presenting it to the dragoman, Prince Nikolaki Morusi, whose favor he wished to regain. But the French authorities, in the flood tide of Napoleon's acquisition of antiquities, had other ideas. The consul at Smyrna, Brest, was arranging to have it dispatched to the ambassador to the Porte, the Marquis de Rivière, and D'Urville had already left to inform Rivière of the find, when another French ship, the *Estafette*, arrived with the Count de Marcellus aboard. (He was then twenty-five.) His own disingenuous account of the purchase of the statue is exposed by the testimony of Captain Matterer:

> After our departure for Constantinople, several days elapsed, and the priest had time to buy his charming Venus Victrix, which he did, buying it from the Armenian for 2000 piastres or twelve hundred francs. When M. de Marcellus arrived at Melos, this statue was wrapped up, and had been brought down from the Castro, and was on the shore ready to be loaded on to a merchantman sailing to Constantinople to return it to the pasha who had paid for it.
>
> I cannot resist remarking here that if by a miracle this beautiful Venus had been able to transform herself in a flash into a living Venus, she would have groaned and wept hot tears to see herself dragged over the beach, jolted and rolled by men furious with anger; for she must have fallen into the sea, for the following reason.
>
> M. de Marcellus was on the gangway of the *Estafette*, ready to disembark, when he saw a great crowd of men on the shore, and was afraid that there would be a fight, since the Armenian priest had a rather high standing among the Greeks of his religion: so he said to M. Robert, 'We must arm ourselves with rifles and swords, and take twenty sailors similarly armed', which he did on the spot.
>
> They got into the boat, and reached land where there was an uproar around the case containing the Venus de Milo, and the Greeks appeared determined not to let the statue be removed; but at a signal from the captain of the *Estafette*, who cried out, 'Here, men, take that box and put it in my boat', the battle began. Sticks and swords rained blows, many of

them on the head and back of the poor Armenian priest, and on those of the Greeks who uttered cries of despair and commended themselves to God. The consul was there, armed with a sword and a thick staff, which he plied very vigorously; an ear was cut, blood flowed, and during the battle, some of the sailors got hold of the case which was being knocked from side to side in the mêlée, got it on to their boat and took it to the *Estafette*, which at once set sail for Constantinople.

Deposition of Capt. Matterer; quoted in Aicard*;

translated by RS

It was evidently during this fracas that the left arm was broken and mislaid. The Parisian establishment, naturally, were happy with Marcellus's acquisition and did not ask too many questions. His deed won outspoken praise from the secretary of the Académie des Beaux Arts, Quatremère de Quincy, and D'Urville was made a Knight of St Louis for his part in the discovery. The statue has been the pride of the Louvre ever since.

In May 1848, the already dying Heinrich Heine visited the statue, and dated his final decline from that moment:

> It was in May 1848, on the day on which I went out for the last time, that I took leave of the lovely idols to which I had prayed in the season of my happiness. With great difficulty I dragged myself to the Louvre, and I almost collapsed as I entered the grand hall where the blessed Goddess of Beauty, Our beloved Lady of Milo, stands on her pedestal. I lay a long time at her feet, and wept so profusely, that even a stone must have pitied me. The goddess did in fact cast me a sympathetic downward glance, but one so comfortless that she appeared to be saying 'Don't you see, I have no arms and therefore I cannot help you?'

Heinrich Heine, *Romanzero: Nachwort*;

translated by RS

S. F. A. Coles published a book of poems, *Cities of Troy*, in 1939. Most of them celebrate scenes of Greece and Asia Minor. One of the most vivid is "Melos in April":

> Poppies on the hillside:
> Poppies against the blue
> Of the tender sea;
> Olive trees, red poppies, green corn—
> Doves . . . Nature's ecstasy!

The silence of high noontide,
Arc of white marble seats,
Cycladic tower—
O poppies everywhere
Incarnadine the hour . . .

Here is rest for the weary,
Here is peace for the sad,
And health for the ill—
Where the Dionysian poppies
Riot down the hill!

Santorini

This volcanic crater is unlike any other Greek island. It has become famous in recent years owing to S. Marinatos's excavations of the Minoan palace outside the modern town. Its destruction in the volcanic eruption that ended Minoan civilization may have given rise to the legend of Atlantis. At all events, Santorini is full of ghosts, and not only those of the delicate Minoans overwhelmed in the cataclysm of 1500 B.C. The proverb runs "Vampires to Santorini," meaning the same as "Coals to Newcastle" or "Owls to Athens."

> Many Hydraens have assured me that there used to be a great number of Vampires in Hydra, and that their present freedom from them is to be attributed solely to the exertions of their bishop, who has laid them all in Santorene, where, on the desert isle, they now exist in great numbers, and wander about, rolling stones down the slopes towards the sea, 'as may be heard by anyone who passes near, in a kaik, during the night'.
>
> Robert Pashley, *Travels in Crete*
> (London, 1837), II, 261–62

Other supernatural monsters are also prevalent in Santorini. Christopher Kininmonth describes the giant Kallikanzaros or goblin of Messaria, who stands on Christmas Day astride the two churches of the town, ready to jump on latecomers to the service, and the Mesanikhtis or midnight-fellow, who will follow you home if you are out late and make the night loud, unless he is thwarted by your hanging out your coat. (*The Children of Thetis*, London, 1949, 57f.)

Before the exodus of vampires from Santorini, J. P. de

Tournefort witnessed the exorcism of a vampire in Mykonos, which he describes at length in his travels.

Perhaps the best of Santorinian vampire stories is that told by Père François Richard, one of the community of Jesuits established on Santorini in 1613, on the orders of Pope Paul V:

> Shortly before I arrived at Stampalia (Astypalaia), five bodies had been burned on this account (i.e. suspicion of being vampires), three of them those of married men, the fourth that of a Greek monk, and the fifth that of a young girl. The same had been done on the island of Nio (Ios), where the wife of one of the deceased had come to confession to me, and assured me that she had seen the body of her husband undamaged after fifty days' burial, even though its grave had been changed, and all the usual ceremonies had been performed on it; but when it was recognised that he was beginning again to torment the world, even to the extent of killing four or five persons, he was exhumed a second time, and burned in public. It is no more than two years since two other bodies were burned, for the same reason, on the island of Siphanto (Siphnos); and scarcely a year passes without another rumour of one of these false revenants.
>
> What caused the greatest astonishment on Sant-Erini, was the great familiarity which one of these *vrykolakes* exhibited towards his living wife. His name was Alexander, and while he was alive he had lived at the castle of Pyrgo, and was a shoemaker by trade. After his death he appeared to his wife as if he were still alive: he came to work in his house, he repaired his children's shoes, he drew water at the cistern, and often he could be seen in the valleys cutting wood for the support of his family; but after he had passed some time in this way, the people remaining horrified by it, his corpse was exhumed and burnt, and with the smoke of the burning the forces of the demon were dissipated.
>
> F. Richard, *Relation de ce qui est passé à St-Erini*
> (Paris, 1657); translated by RS

Several modern poets have written about the island: Seferis, Trypanis, and, here, Elytis, the most mystical or surreal of the three:

ODE TO SANTORINI

You came out of the thunder's belly
Shuddering in the penitential clouds
Bitter stone, tested, defiant

Carl Rottmann, *Santorini*. Staatliche Graphische Sammlung, Munich.

You summoned the sun to be your first witness
To confront with you the impetuous radiance
To open out with a crusading echo in the sea

Sea-woken, defiant,
You thrust up a breast of rock
Scored with the south wind's inspiration
For pain to engrave its guts there
For hope to engrave its guts there
With fire, lava, smoke
With words that concert the infinite
You gave birth to the voice of day
You raised,
To the green and rose porticos of vision,
The bells struck by the exalted intellect
Praising the birds in the mid-August light.

Close to the wave's thud, to the foam's lament,
Among the eucharists of sleep
When night wandered through the wilderness of stars
Searching for the testimony of dawn
You experienced the joy of birth

You were the first to leap forth into the world,
Porphyrogenite, sea-begotten,

You sent to the far horizons
Blessings nurtured in the sea's vigils
To caress the hair of daylight's waking hour.

Queen of the heartbeats, and wings of the Aegean,
With words that convert the infinite
With fire, lava, smoke,
You discovered the great lines of your destiny.

Now justice stands revealed before you
Black mountains sail in the brightness
Longings dig their craters
In the heart's tormented land
And from hope's struggle a new earth is made ready
So that on a morning full of iridiscence
The race that vivifies dreams
The race that sings in the sun's embrace
May stride forth with eagles and banners.

O daughter of the highest wrath
Sea-begotten, naked,
Open the glorious gates of man
So that health may sweeten the land
The senses may flower in a thousand colours
Their wings spread wide
So that freedom may blow from all directions.

In the wind's proclamation flash out
The new, the eternal beauty
When the three-hour-old sun rises up
Entirely blue to play the harmonium of creation.

Odysseus Elytis;
translated by E. Keeley and P. Sherrard

Patmos

Bearing northeast again we leave the Cyclades for the Dodecanese,
the northernmost of which is Patmos. The island scarcely appears
in history until it emerges with a fanfare of angelic trumpets as the
place where St. John the Divine, exiled by the Emperor Domitian,
is said to have received his Revelation . . .

> I John, who also am your brother, and companion in
> tribulation, and in the kingdom and patience of Jesus Christ,
> was in the isle that is called Patmos, for the word of God, and

for the testimony of Jesus Christ. I was in the spirit on the Lord's day, and heard behind me a great voice, as of a trumpet, saying, I am Alpha and Omega, the first and the last: and, What thou seest, write in a book, and send it unto the seven churches which are in Asia; unto Ephesus, and unto Smyrna, and unto Pergamos, and unto Thyatira, and unto Sardis, and unto Philadelphia, and unto Laodicea. And I turned to see the voice that spake with me. And being turned, I saw seven golden candlesticks; and in the midst of the candlesticks one like unto the Son of man, clothed with a garment down to the foot, and girt about the paps with a golden girdle. His head and his hairs were white like wool, as white as snow; and his eyes were as a flame of fire; and his feet like unto fine brass, as if they burned in a furnace; and his voice as the sound of many waters. And he had in his right hand seven stars: and out of his mouth went a sharp two-edged sword and his coun- tenance was as the sun shineth in his strength. And when I saw him, I fell at his feet as if dead.

St. John the Divine, Revelation i, 9–17

Not surprisingly, legends clustered thickly around the island there- after. A monastery was founded in 1088. Bernard Randolph reports of the Cave of the Apocalypse:

Also here is a mountain where is a deep cave, in which they say Cynops the magician lived in the time of St John; this cave they believe to be haunted; and to try it, a man was let down by a cord to see what was in the cave, but he was pull'd up almost dead.

Present State of the Islands of the Archipelago
(London, 1687)

The beauty of the view from the summit of the island is unparal- leled; until recently one could survey from the roof of the monastery a panorama that includes not only the inshore islands and Icaria, Samos, Leros, and Kalymnos, but Mt. Mycale on the Turkish coast, and, on a clear day, Naxos and Paros, all emerging like brown hills from a silver haze and rippled carpet of blue.

The idea of Patmos inspired Friedrich Hölderlin—who never visited Greece—to a dithyrambic celebration of the island, made by its own saint a pathway between men and gods, that constant theme of Hölderlin's poetry:

Patmos

The God is near, and
                       difficult to grasp.
But danger fortifies the rescuing power.
In sombre places dwell the eagles; the Alps' sons
Go fearless forth upon the roads of the abyss
Across lightly constructed bridges. And since all round
    there press
The peaks of time, and those so close
In love, are worn out on the separate heights,
Then give us the innocent waters,
O give us wings, that with the truest thought
We may fly yonder and return to this same place.

I spoke thus. And then rose
A guardian spirit, carried me away
More swiftly and still further than I dreamed,
Far from my house and home.
And as I passed, the light of dawn
Glowed on the shady woods and longed-for streams
Of my own land. I knew the earth no more.
And soon, with mysterious freshness shining
And rapidly growing beneath the footsteps of the sun,
In golden haze there blossomed forth
In a thousand peaks, a thousand glittering spires,

Asia, before my eyes. I blindly sought
For some familiar image,
A stranger to those wide streets where there descends
From Tmolus to the sea the Pactolus adorned with gold,
And the Taurus rises with the Messogis,
And the flowering garden like a peaceful fire,
But in the light on high, the silver snow
And sign of immortal life, on the unscaled wall
The age-old ivy grows, and on living pillars
Of cedar and of laurel
Stand the solemn palaces the Gods have built.

And all around the Asiatic gates,
Calling out here and there from the sea's uncertain plain,
There murmur the unshadowed roads:
But the pilot knows the islands.
When I heard
That Patmos was among the nearest isles,
I longed to disembark

And to approach its gloomy caves.
For it is not like Cyprus rich with springs
Or any of the other islands, it is not
In proud display that Patmos stands
But like a poor house full of hospitality,
And when from a wrecked ship, or weeping
For his lost land or for an absent friend
A stranger comes, she listens with good will;
And all her children, and the voices of the hot groves,
And the place where the sand falls, and where the fields
    are cracked,
And all the sounds
Hear him, and all resounds again
With love for the man's plaint.
Thus it was one day that she took in care
The belov'd of God, the seer
Who in his happy youth had gone
With the All-Highest's Son, inseparable from Him . . .

          Friedrich Hölderlin; translated by David Gascoyne

Kos (Cos)

Kos has a proud place in the history of mankind as the birthplace
of Hippocrates, the source of medical theory and practice. The verdant landscape and tranquil climate of the island made it an appro-
priate site for a sanctuary of Asclepius incorporating rooms for the
sick. Perhaps due to the mildness of the climate, too, is the
longevity of the remarkable plane tree in Kos town which is alleged
to be the very one under which Hippocrates taught.

The island was the home, too, of poets: Philetas the elegist and
Theocritus, whose most complex poem includes a description of
the Koan countryside of a type rare in classical literature:

Then to the left he turn'd, through flow'ry meads,
The winding path-way that to Pyxa leads;
While with my friends I took the right-hand road
Where Phrasidamus makes his sweet abode;
Who courteous bad us on soft beds recline
Of lentisck, and young branches of the vine;
Poplars and elms above, their foliage spread,
Lent a cool shade, and wav'd the breezy head;
Below, a stream, from the Nymphs' sacred cave,
In free meanders led its murmuring wave:
In the warm sun-beams; verdant shrubs among,

Shrill grasshoppers renew'd their plaintive song:
At distance far, conceal'd in shades, alone,
Sweet Philomela pour'd her tuneful moan:
The lark, the goldfinch warbled lays of love,
And sweetly pensive coo'd the turtle dove:
While honey-bees, for ever on the wing,
Humm'd round the flowers, or sipt the silver spring.
The rich, ripe season gratified the sense
With summer's sweets, and autumn's redolence.
Apples and pears lay strew'd in heaps around,
And the plum's loaded branches kiss'd the ground.
Wine flow'd abundant from capacious tuns,
Matur'd divinely by four summers' suns.

Theocritus, *Idyll*, vii, 130–47;
translated by Francis Fawkes (1767)

Rhodes

Rhodes boasts the distinction of being the sunniest place in Greece.
The point was not lost on the ancient inhabitants, among whom the
legend ran that it was created as a special gift to the god Helios,
the Sun, who had been absent at the original allocation of honors at
the birth of the world. The story is incomparably told by Pindar:

Ancient stories tell us
that when Zeus and the gods
were allotting the world,
Rhodes was not yet visible on the ocean surface—
it lay hidden,
an island in the briny depths.

And Helios was absent—no one assigned him a portion,
he was left without a place,
even he, the sacred god.
Then at his complaint
Zeus would have cast the lots
a second time,

but Helios forbade it,
saying he had seen
within the gray depths, growing
from the sea's floor, an island
that would be
rich in nurture for men and kindly to
their flocks.

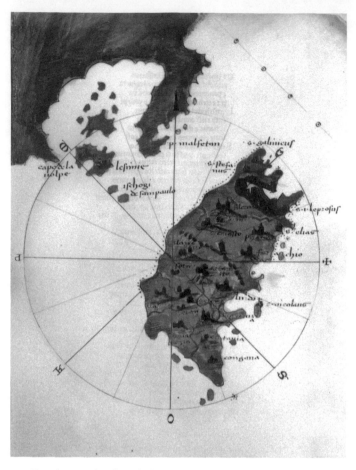

Bartolommeo Zamberti degli Sonnetti, *Map of Rhodes*. The National Maritime Museum, London.

He told Lachesis, garlanded in gold, to raise her hands
        and swear never to break
            the gods' great oath,
                but nod assent with Zeus
                    that once Rhodes
                        had broken through
                                    to bright air
                    it would be his prize.

He spoke, and what he said
     came, in truth,
to fulfillment:
               the sea's glittering furrows put forth
the island,
               and now the father, source of piercing light
and master of fire-breathing horses
has her for his own.

Pindar, *Olympian*, 7, 54–73;
translated by Frank J. Nisetich

This magnificent ode, celebrating the victory in boxing at the Olympic Games of one Diagoras, achieved the rare distinction of being inscribed–all ninety-five lines of the modern edition—in letters of gold on a block in the temple of Athena at Lindos.

Rhodes figures sporadically in classical history, and one of its most famous sons, Apollonius the poet, achieved his renown elsewhere in Alexandria, where he spent his working life. Rhodes was the site of one of the seven wonders of the world—the Colossus, a gigantic statue of the Sun God standing at the entrance to the harbor. It was erected to commemorate the raising of the siege of Rhodes by Demetrius Poliorcetes in 304 B.C. An anonymous contemporary poet described the massive statue:

To you, great Sun, the men of Dorian Rhodes
     Extended this bronze image up to heaven:
They crowned with it their island, when they quelled
     The storm and surge of war: its light leapt far
Not only on the blossom of the sea,
     But to the mainland, beacon of liberty.
The dominion of the sons of Heracles
     Is equal on land and on sea.

Anthologia Palatina, 6, 171;
translated by RS

Some wishful thinking in the last couplet!

The statue stood only about sixty years. In 653 the Saracen corsairs collected the fragments that still littered the shore, and sold them to Jewish merchants who melted them down. That eighth-century slumber of the shattered god seems an image of the slumber of Rhodes.

One of Zamberti's livelier "sonnets" gives a brisk résumé of the chief features of fifteenth-century Rhodes:

South west from Greece extends the sloping isle,
Shaped like a shield, a smooth plain to the north
Rising to a boss in the east: it glories in
The many castles which enrich its worth:

First Lindos, most impregnable of all
soars up from the port guarded by its reef;
Vasilika and others are in ruins,
But Aganea still provides the chief

Centre, with palaces, and peasants' huts;
Then Mount Silerno and its castle, where
Our gifts are welcomed by the inhabitants;
And then Rhodes Town itself, a jewel, rare.

The hospice of St John provides a lodging
—Its governor, Grand Master of the Order—
Its gardens are so lovely, you would think

Them fit for paradise or heaven itself.
Here was the mariner's art discovered first,
According to the local chronicles,

And here they did a famous statue raise,
Colossus, sculptured wonder of its days.

Bartolommeo Zamberti degli Sonnetti
(?1485); translated by RS

The Milanese pilgrim, Pietro Casola, visited Rhodes in 1494, only a few years after the conclusion of the siege by the Turks.

It has always been very strong, and proved it a few years ago when it offered such a strenuous resistance to the Grand Turk in the year 1480. Many traces of the siege remain which stupefy the beholder; it is an incredible thing to anyone who has not seen it. And, hearing the account, as I heard it, from those who were there during that war, one can more readily say and believe that it was a miracle than due to the power of man. For while the Rhodians believed they were going to the death, they gained the victory over the thousands of Turks who were besieging the city of Rhodes. I think the signs will remain until the day of the last Judgment. One cannot go about Rhodes without finding stones, and terrible ones, which were fired from the mortars. Some of them are so enormous that it seems incredible that they were fired from the cannon. It is also an incredible thing that so many having been fired as have left their traces—that is, the stones I mentioned, which are of every size—the city still exists; and yet there it is, and it does not ever appear to have been besieged.

P. Casola, Pilgrimage; translated by M. M. Newett

The remarkable resilience of the Greek people under war was equally noticeable in Crete at the end of the Second World War, when everything was rapidly restored to its former prosperity or better (Dilys Powell, *The Villa Ariadne*). Nevertheless, much hard work was needed to re-create Rhodes, as this song makes clear. (In recent years the same song has been sung, instead, of Cyprus.)

> The cities are rejoicing, the towns are light at heart,
> But Rhodes the victim of harsh fate is standing in its ruins.
> Three years besieged by sea and land, it withstood
>   its attackers,
> Its gates are sealed with spiders' webs, its keys rust in
>   the locks.
> Send for the master builder now, the best among
>   the builders:
> 'Come, master-builder, builder come, and bring your aid
>   to Rhodes.'

Papagregorakis,* "Song" (1520); translated by RS

The drama of the long siege made Rhodes a suitable subject for English poets too, and Davenant's drama, *The Siege of Rhodes* (1656), builds on the story of these years.

Rhodes returned to slumberous quietude and tranquil beauty under Ottoman rule, inspiring the pen of Claude-Etienne Savary (1750–88), a doctor who began his career as physician to the Count of Provence before leaving for an extended tour of the East in 1779, which lasted two years, including fifteen months on Crete. His travels appeared on his death in 1788, not only in French but in a German translation and two English ones.

> The isle of Rhodes is now in full view, and presents a range of hills resembling an amphitheatre, and terminated by a lofty mountain. We are going as near the wind as possible, and with a crowd of sail, to gain the harbour. But we shall not reach it before night. Already the sun is setting behind the mountains, which hide him from us, while his radiant beams still streak the clouds with gold and purple! How vivid are their colours! Some of them concentering thousands of his rays, again reflect them, and resemble globes of fire floating through the air. Others, the lower parts of which are entirely

dark, assume the appearance of dusky mountains of various forms, and emit, from their luminous points, the flash of the ruby, or the fire of the topaz; some opening in the centre, and edged with the brightest and liveliest colours, exhibit the azure of the sky set in gold. Others diversified with sattiny stripes, are slightly bounded with a yellowish border. How admirable, how magnificent, is this scene! What a sublime idea does it give of Him who said, *Let there be light, and there was light!* Night has thrown her dark veil over this glorious picture, yet the eye remains still fixed on the heavens, and the soul still feels deeply penetrated with sentiments of admiration and gratitude. How great are the works of the Creator! and how feeble the conceptions of man!

C.-E. Savary, Letters on Greece (Dublin, 1788)

Lady Hester Stanhope's experience of Rhodes was less relaxing.

Rhodes, December 1811

My dear—,

I write one line by a ship which came in here for a few days, just to tell you we are all safe and well. Starving thirty hours on a bare rock, even without fresh water, being half-naked and drenched with wet, having traversed an almost trackless country, over dreadful rocks and mountains, partly on foot and partly on a mule for eight hours, laid me up at a village for a few days: but I have since crossed the island on an ass, going for six hours a day, which proves I am pretty well now at least.

The Consul here is a dear old fellow of seventy five, who thinks he cannot do too much for us; but the bey pretends to be so poor, that he cannot give us more than £30, which will neither clothe nor feed eleven people for long; so we must send an express to Smyrna to get what we want. My locket, and the valuable snuff box Lord Sligo gave me, are all I have saved;—all the travelling equipage for Syria, &c, all gone;—the servants naked and unarmed: but the great loss of all is the medicine chest, which saved the lives of so many travellers in Greece. How to repair it, I know not. I expected more medicine out by Mr Liston; but whether he has forwarded it, or kept it, I know not: if you could assist me in this once more, I should thank you much. I may be able to get a little at Smyrna, but I am told all the medicine shops were burnt by the late fire . . .

Remember me most kindly to Mr Taylor: tell him I make conquests of Turks everywhere. Here they are ten times more strict than in Constantinople; yet a Turk has lent me a house and bath in the middle of an orange-grove, where I go to-morrow. The houses on the outsides of the walls where Franks live are only fit for poultry.

Lady Hester Stanhope

Lamartine was as enthusiastic about Rhodes as Savary had been.

Rhodes springs up like a verdant nosegay from the bosom of the waves; the light and graceful minarets of its white mosques rear themselves above its forests of palms, carobs, sycamores, planes, and fig-trees; they attract from a distance the mariner's eye to those delicious retreats of the Turkish cemeteries, where are to be seen, every evening, Mussulmans stretched out on the turf that covers the tomb of their friends, and quietly smoking and chatting, like sentries waiting till they are relieved, like indolent men that love to lie down in bed, and make an essay of sleep before the hour of their last repose . . .

Heaven seems to have formed this island as an advanced post on Asia: a European power that should be mistress of it, would hold at the same time the key of the Archipelago, of Greece, Smyrna, the Dardanelles, and of the Egyptian and Syrian seas. I know not in the world either a finer military maritime position, or a lovelier sky, or a more smiling and fertile land. The Turks have impressed upon them that character of inaction and indolence which they carry everywhere! Everything here is in a state of inertia, and in what may be called misery; but this people, who create nothing, who renew nothing, never break nor destroy anything either—they at least allow nature to act freely around them—they respect trees even in the very middle of the streets, and of the houses which they inhabit; water and shade, the lulling murmur and voluptuous coolness, are their first, their only wants. Thus, as soon as you approach a land possessed by Mohammedans, whether in Europe or in Asia, you recognise from afar the rich and sombre verdure which covers it, the trees for shade, the spouting fountains for lulling to repose, the silence, and the mosques with their light minarets rising at every step from the bosom of a religious soil—it is all that is necessary to this people. They leave this soft and philosophic apathy only to mount their desert coursers, the first servants of man, and fearlessly to rush upon death for their prophet and their God. The dogma of fatalism has made them the bravest people on the earth, and although existence may be to them both light and pleasant, that promised by the Koran as the reward of a life given up for its sake is the more prized, from their requiring but one weak effort to throw themselves from this to the celestial world, which they see before them redolent in beauty, repose, and love! It is the religion of heroes! but this religion grows faint in the faith of the Mussulman, and heroism is extinguished with the faith which is its principle, so that as the people shall believe less either in a dogma or an idea, they will die less willingly and less nobly. It is as in Europe; why die, if life avails more than death, if there is no immortal gain from the sacrifice to duty? Thus war will diminish and be abolished in Europe, until some faith shall reanimate and move the heart of man more highly than the base instinct of life.

August 27.—We set sail from Rhodes for Cyprus on a splendid afternoon. I have my eyes turned upon Rhodes, which sinks at last into the sea. I regret this beautiful island as an apparition one wishes to recall; I could have settled there, if it were less separated from the moving world in which destiny and duty compel us to live! What delicious retreats on the sides of the high mountains, and on the declivities, shaded by all the trees of Asia! I was shown a magnificent house belonging to the former pacha, surrounded by three extensive and abundant gardens, bathed by numerous fountains, and adorned with ravishing kiosks. They asked 16,000 piastres for the purchase; that is to say, 4000 francs (£165)—happiness at a cheap rate!

Alphonse de Lamartine, *Travels in the East*;
translated by TWR (Edinburgh, 1850)

Thackeray (1846) found here as elsewhere scope for his dyspeptic expostulations on the depravity of foreigners and the distance between reality and the expectations aroused by a classical education (cf. his remarks on Athens). He had to admit, however, despite this "appearance of decay and ruin," the splendor of "the chivalrous relics."

The chivalrous relics at Rhodes are very superb. I know of no buildings, whose stately and picturesque aspect seems to correspond better with one's notions of their proud founders. The towers and gates are warlike and strong, but beautiful and aristocratic: you see that they must have been high-bred gentlemen who built them. The edifices appear in almost as perfect a condition as when they were in the occupation of the noble knights of St John; and they have this advantage over modern fortifications, that they are a thousand times more picturesque. Ancient war condescended to ornament itself, and built fine carved castles and vaulted gates: whereas, to judge from Gibraltar and Malta, nothing can be less romantic than the modern military architecture; which sternly regards the fighting, without in the least heeding the war-paint. Some of the huge artillery, with which the place was defended, still lies in the bastions; and the touch-holes of the guns are preserved by being covered with rusty old corslets, worn by defenders of the fort three hundred years ago. The Turks, who battered down chivalry, seem to be waiting their turn of destruction now. In walking through Rhodes one is strangely affected by witnessing the signs of this double decay. For instance, in the streets of the knights, you see noble houses, surmounted by noble escutcheons of superb knights, who lived there, and prayed, and quarrelled, and murdered the Turks; and were the most gallant pirates of the inland seas; and made vows of chastity, and robbed and ravished; and, professing humility, would admit none but nobility into their order; and died recommending themselves to sweet St John, and calmly hoping for heaven in consideration of all the heathen they had slain. When this superb fraternity was obliged to yield to courage as great as theirs, faith as sincere, and to robbers even more dexterous and audacious than the noblest knight who ever sang a canticle to the Virgin, these halls were filled by magnificent Pashas and Agas, who lived here in the intervals of war, and, having conquered its best champions, despised Christendom and chivalry pretty much as an Englishman despises a Frenchman. Now the famous house is let to a shabby merchant, who has his little beggarly shop in the bazaar; to a small officer, who ekes out his wretched pension by swindling, and who gets his pay in bad coin. Mahometanism pays in pewter now, in place of silver and gold. The powerless old sword frightens nobody now—the steel is turned to pewter too, somehow, and will no longer shear a Christian head off any shoulders. In the Crusades my wicked sympathies have always been with the Turks. They seem to me the best Christians of the two; more humane, less brutally presumptuous about their own merits, and more generous in esteeming their neighbours. As far as I can get at the authentic story, Saladin is a pearl of refinement compared to the brutal beef-eating Richard—about whom Sir Walter Scott has led all the world astray.

W. M. Thackeray, *Notes of a Journey from Cornhill to Grand Cairo* (London, 1846)

Always at the fringe of Greece, subject at various times not only to the Romans and Venetians, but also of course to the Turks, and, from 1912 until the German occupation, to the Italians, the island betrays its oriental leanings by its mosques and minarets. Its Greekness differs as much from that of the Morea, say, as does that of Zakynthos. Of recent writing about Rhodes, the best is Lawrence Durrell's *Reflections on a Marine Venus*.

12

Crete

Thomas Abel Brimage Spratt, *View of Palaikastro, Crete*. From Thomas Abel Brimage Spratt, *Travels and Researches in Crete* (1865) (detail).

Next, Candy, Cradle of reputed Jove,
With nectar-dropping vines is over-spread:
Whence eastward sacred to the nymph of love,
Cyprus erects her myrtle-crowned head.
    Well twixt these two hath Neptune put some space,
    Whose fruits once met in one, marre any place.

The arch-sea rowling from th' unruly north,
Doth seeme to threaten Candyes overthrow;
But that the troops of Cyclades stand forth
To break the fiercenesse of his furious blow,

Like Xerxes fearefull army, Asia's wonder,
Cutting in broken streames his strength asunder.

Richard Zouche, *The Dove;*
or, Passages of Cosmography (London, 1613)

In middle of the sable sea there lies
An isle call'd Crete, a ravisher of eyes,
Fruitful, and mann'd with many an infinite store;
Where ninety cities crown the famous shore,
Mix'd with all-languag'd men. There Greeks survive,
There the great-minded Eteocretans live,
There the Dorensians never out of war,
The Cydons there, and there the singular
Pelasgian people.

Homer, *Odyssey*, XIX, 172ff.;
translated by George Chapman
(London, 1615)

The largest of the Greek islands, Crete is a world in itself, differing in important aspects of history, character, and culture from
other parts of Greece. Lying in an isolated position in the Mediterranean, between Greece and Egypt, it has no doubt provided many
sailors with material for hair-raising tales of storm, shipwreck, and
escape. Menelaus, blown off course on his return from Troy to
Sparta, describes to his hosts in Egypt the wreck of his companions off Crete.

Soon as Malaea's misty tops arise,
Sudden the Thunderer blackens all the skies,
And the winds whistle, and the surges roll
Mountains on mountains, and obscure the pole.
The tempest scatters, and divides our fleet;
Part, the storm urges on the coast of Crete,
Where winding round the rich Cydonian plain,
The streams of Jardan issue to the main.
There stands a rock, high, eminent and steep,
Whose shaggy brow o'erhangs the shady deep,
And views Gortyna on the western side;
On this rough Auster drove the impetuous tide:
With broken force the billows roll'd away,
And heav'd the fleet into the neighbouring bay.
Thus sav'd from death, they gain'd the Phaestan shores,
With shatter'd vessels and disabled oars:

But five tall barks the winds and waters toss'd,
Far from their fellows, on the Aegyptian coast.

Homer, *Odyssey*, iii, 286–300;
translated by Alexander Pope

A different hazard faced the Argonauts as they returned from the
quest for the Golden Fleece, in the form of Talus, the bronze giant,
the guardian of Crete.

The evening star now lifts, as day-light fades,
His golden circlet in the deepening shades;
Stretch'd at his ease the weary labourer shares
A sweet forgetfulness of human cares:
At once in silence sleep the sinking gales,
The mast they drop, and furl the flagging sails;
All night, all day, they ply their bending oars
Towards Carpathus, and reach the rocky shores;
Thence Crete they view, emerging from the main,
The queen of isles; but Crete they view in vain.
There Talus mountains hurls with all their woods;
Whole seas roll back, and tossing swell in floods.
Amaz'd the towering monster they survey,
And trembling view the interdicted bay.
His birth he drew from giants sprung from oak,
Or the hard entrails of the stubborn rock:
Fierce guard of Crete! who thrice each year explores
The trembling isle, and strides from shores to shores,
A form of living brass! one part beneath
Alone he bears, a part to let in death,
Where o'er the ankle swells the turgid vein,
Soft to the stroke, and sensible of pain.

Apollonius of Rhodes, *Argonautica*, iv, 1629–48;
translated by William Broome (1780)

Needless to say, the witch Medea successfully fashions a poison
which is duly shot at his vulnerable point, enabling their safe passage past the expiring giant.

William Falconer, the author of *The Shipwreck*, a poem in
three books, finds time, as his ship skims past on a calm sea, to recall
the legends and history of Crete:

The powerful sails, with steady breezes swelled,
Swift and more swift the yielding bark impelled:
Across her stem the parting waters run,

As clouds, by tempests wafted, pass the sun.
Impatient thus she darts along the shore,
Till Ida's mount, and Jove's, are seen no more;
And, while aloof from Retimo she steers,
Malaea's foreland full in front appears.
Wide o'er yon isthmus stands the cypress grove,
That once inclosed the hallowed fane of Jove;
Here too, memorial of his name! is found
A tomb in marble ruins on the ground:
This gloomy tyrant, whose despotic sway
Compelled the trembling nations to obey,
Through Greece for murder, rape, and incest known,
The Muses raised to high Olympus' throne;
For oft, alas! their venal strains adorn
The prince, whom blushing virtue holds in scorn:
Still Rome and Greece record his endless fame,
And hence yon mountain yet retains his name.

William Falconer, The Shipwreck, II
(London 1762)

Robert Pashley in 1837 records that only a few shattered stones remain of the famous tomb of Zeus:

> I found, as a guide up the mountain, a shepherd, who had become acquainted with the tomb of Zeus in tending his flock. A good hour was spent in reaching the summit, towards the extremity of which I observed foundations of the massive walls of a building the length of which was about eighty feet. Within this space is an aperture in the ground, which may perhaps once have led into a moderate-sized cave; but, whatever may have been its former size, it is now so filled up, that a man cannot stand in it, and its diameter is not above eight or ten feet. These then are the only remains of that object of deep religious veneration, the supposed tomb of 'the Father of gods and men', with its celebrated inscription,

> > All which devouring Time, in his so mighty waste,
> > Demolishing those walls, hath utterly defac'd:
> > So that the earth doth feel the ruinous heaps of stones,
> > That with their burd'nous weight now press his
> > sacred bones.

Travels in Crete, I, 213;
the quotation is from Drayton's Polyolbion, song XVI

Many writers provide us with information on the island at different stages of its history. One of the earliest modern records is probably that by Matthew Paris (d. 1259); he describes a voyage through Greece in the fifth chapter (in verse) of "The Jerusalem Expedition" (printed in *Purchas his Pilgrimes*, London, 1625):

Then sailet we forthe on our right hand,
And come to the Ile of Candy Land.
A cite ther was not ferr us fra,
That men callen Cananea:
And fifty mile that cite fro,
Is another that hight Retimo.
And from thennez milez fifty,
Is the chef cite of alle Candy.
And Candy the cite men calles,
A faire toun, and stron of valles.
There groeth alle the Malvesy,
That men have in all Christianty:
Or in any place in hethenese,
And at Modyn alle the Romeney I wis.
Another cite is in that Ile,
From that cef citte a C. mile,
On our lift hand as we did go,
Setea men calle it so.
That Ile bocthe large and longe,
viij. C. mile alle Umbegange.
iiij. good citeez hit hath full ryve,
And castellez xx. and fife:
Except Thorpez, and Hamelettez,
And housez that in the wynez ben settez
iiij. M. men there may be raiset,
Well horset, and well harnesset
Of hovelerez, and of albesterez
ij. C. M. ate alle yerez.

Matthew Paris*

Sir Richard Guylforde provides a curious telegraphic farrago of information in the account of his own pilgrimage:

In Candia sine Creta was musyke firste founde and also Tourneys and exercyse of armes on horsbacke / There was lawe firste put in wrytynge / Armour was first ther devysed and founde and so was ye makyng of Remys and rowynge in boots / In Candy be ye caves called Labor Intus there growe grete wynes / and specially malvesy and Muskadell / they speke all Greke / except the Venycyans that be Lordes and governours there / . . .

Sir Richard Guylforde, *Pylgrymage* (London, 1511)

More curious lore is given in the detailed account of the natural history of Crete by Pierre Belon (1589) and in the *Cosmography* of Peter Heylin (1677):

> Among notable plants there grows a sage which produces edible fruits, which the natives pick, and bring in sacks to the nearby towns for sale (*Salvia pomifera*). In early May they are found sticking to the leaves, about the size of galls, covered in wool, sweet and of pleasant flavour. At the same time they pick the flowers of spiny capers *(Capparis spinosa)* and bring them to market, not pickled, but graded and slightly salted. Mandragora, male and female, and two types of paeony, commonly called Psiphedile by the Greeks, grow in all the moist valleys and have a white flower (probably both *Paeonia clusii*) . . . Helichrysum flowers at the end of June, very frequent in the mountains, where scarcely another plant is to be seen. It makes a pleasant couch for hares, and the common people call it Lagochimithia (hares' beds) . . . The white flowered oleander is not found anywhere in the island, except in the valleys of Mt Ida near the village of Kameraki . . . There is a kind of thorn *(Scolymus,* Spanish oyster plant) in Crete which all call, in the local dialect, Askolimbros; the ancient Romans called it by the Greek name Glycyrrhizon, to be distinguished from Glycyrrhiza (liquorice). It grows wild everywhere, with a yellow flower and much sap. Root and leaves are eaten before the stem shoots up. When we were at Ravenna we saw these for sale, and at Ancona, where they were picked by young women and were called Riusi. I have seen them being collected near Rome too, where they are called Spinaborda.
>
> [Dioscorides says it 'is good for such as have the arme pits and the rest of ye body of a rank smell': see Huxley, A. J., and Taylor, W., *Flowers of Greece and the Aegean*, London, 1977, p. 137.]

Pierre Belon, *Plurimarum singularium et memorabilium rerum in Graeciae conspectarum . . . Observationes* (Antwerp, 1589); translated by RS

> Things most observable at the present are these that follow, 1. That it breeds no serpents, nor venomous worm, or ravenous or hurtfull creature; so that their sheep graze very

securely without any shepheard. 2. If a woman bite a man any thing hard, he will hardly be cured of it; which if true, then the last part of the privilege foregoing (of breeding no hurt-full creature) must needs be false. 3. They have an herb called Alimos, which if one chew in his mouth, he shall feel no hunger for that day, if Quade may be believed who speaks it. 4. Here is (besides many other medicinal herbs) that called Dictamnum, or Dictamnos (Dittany), of especial virtue against poison, either by way of prevention, or present cure; peculiar only to this island: it affordeth great store of Laudanum, a juice or gum forced with incredible labour out of a certain tree Cisto, of which the mountains yield abundance; good to cause sleep, if moderately and carefully taken, but if not very well prepared and taken with moderation, it brings the last sleep upon a man, out of which not to be awakened, till the sound of the last Trumpet raise him.

Peter Heylin, *Cosmography* (London, 1677)

The seventeenth century, and the later days of Venetian rule in Crete, saw a remarkable florescence of indigenous poetry, of which the main works were the tragedies, *The Sacrifice of Abraham* and *Erophile*, and a comedy, *Gyparis*, by G. Chortatsis, and the *Erotokritos*, a huge epic poem ascribed to Vintzentzos Kornaros. This latter poem has become one of the national poems of Greece as well as Crete, and its influence on the practice of modern writers such as Seferis has been profound. It is usually criticized for its longueurs by outsiders, but taken at their own pace, passages like the description of the young Charidemos and his life in the mountains with his bride can be very effective (*Erotokritos*, II, 610ff.; translated by RS). The young prince rides in to compete in a tournament:

> They saw a cloud of dust rising up to the sky, and a knight accompanied by many others. Black was his horse, black his armour, and black his lance. Black was all the attire of that knight. He was brave, and an expert in all matters of weaponry, and he had been born and brought up in the island of Crete. His home was the famous and beautiful city of Gortyn. The reason for his black garb, and the black garb of his attendants, was first Love, and last Death, who takes away all our joys.

The poet describes the idyllic life of the young knight and his bride on the slopes of Mt. Ida:

> Often they strolled, and every time with merriment, sometimes in the mountain forests, and sometimes by the

shore. For many years they dwelt on Ida, they loved that place and longed for it. There were meadows, mountains, forests and valleys, gardens, flowers, plants, fountains and springs, trees in mourning and trees in fruit, moist pastures full of flocks in plenty. And of all those who lived there, they found one shepherdess outstanding in beauty, whose master sent her to mind the flocks. She often encountered the young man when he went hunting with his bow: whatever beast he saw, it did not escape him: ibex, deer and hare he brought home, and all Crete knew no greater hunter than him.

Of course Charidemos unwittingly adds the shepherdess's heart to his list of trophies, and his lady becomes wild with jealousy, and eventually hides in a thicket to spy on him. A rustle in a thicket means but one thing to a huntsman:

> He saw the branches shake, the little bushes move, he took it for a deer or ibex: he shot his arrow at once—oh what a wicked thing, what a crime is there!

And hence the knight always wore black, and traveled from tournament to tournament to hang the prizes on her tomb.

One can scarcely put a date on the poems of the cycle of Digenis Akritas, "the twice-born Borderer," a hero of Byzantine days who is celebrated in formal written poetry and in the oral tradition which is particularly strong in Crete. One of the most memorable of these songs is his encounter with Charos, in modern Greece no longer the ferryman of the dead but the spirit of death itself. Charos's inexorable power is movingly expressed in a poem known throughout Greece:

> Why are the mountains dark, and why so woe-begone?
> Is the wind at war there, or does the rain storm
>   scourge them?
> It is not the wind at war there, it is not the rain that scourges,
> It is only Charos passing across them with the dead;
> He drives the youths before him, the old folks drags behind,
> And he bears the tender little ones in a line at his saddle-bow.
> The old men beg a grace, the young kneel to implore him,
> 'Good Charos, halt in the village, or halt by some
>   cool fountain,
> That the old men may drink water, the young men throw
>   the stones,

And that the little children may go and gather flowers.'
'In never a village will I halt, nor yet by a cool fountain,
The mothers would come for water, and recognize
    their children,
The married folk would know each other, and I should never
    part them.'

In C. A. Trypanis, ed.,
Penguin Book of Greek Verse, no. 264;
translated by Rennell Rodd

The hero Digenis Akritas, who is as big as a mountain, wrestles with Charos on the marble threshing floor, for no other ground can stand the force of their struggle.

Digenis is wrestling for his soul, earth trembles at
    his struggle.
The heaven thunders, lightnings flash, the upper world
    is shaking,
The world below has opened up, it cracks to its foundations,
The paving stones are shuddering: how shall they cover him?
How shall they cover the hero up, the eagle of the earth?
His house could not contain him, even the caves were found
    too small,
He stepped over the mountain slopes, he jumped across
    their peaks,
He played bowls with the mountain crags, he crushed the
    foothills flat,
He seized the young birds in their nests, the adults on
    the wing,
The deer and the wild mountain goats he captured on
    the run.
Charos is envious of the man, he watches from afar:
He has taken hold of Digenis' heart, he has entrapped
    his soul.

Jeannaraki*; translated by RS

The material condition of the Cretans under Venetian rule was not luxurious, but few Cretans welcomed the attack of the Turks, who gradually seized the whole island in a war lasting twenty-five years and culminating in the siege of Candia (modern Herakleion), which continued from 1648 to 1669. The Venetians had held it for 464 years. Bernard Randolph gives a vivid sketch of the Greeks' attempts to foil their Turkish besiegers:

Another invention they had to fish up the Turks, when they attempted to undermine their walls. They had hookes made in the forme of a boats grapling, the points sharp, fastn'd to a rope and four or five foot of chain at the end; these hooks they often cast over the walls, amongst the Turks, and seldom failed to bring up a Turke, some fastned by the clothes, others by the body. I have heard some of the officers say, they have taken several in a night. For when the hook was fastned, they gave them not time to unhook themselves but had them soon over the walls, and many a Turk have the common soldiers eaten.

Bernard Randolph, *Present State of the Islands in the Archipelago* (London, 1687)

Turkish domination was no more welcome to the Cretans than to other parts of Greece. There were no less than ten major revolts between 1770 and 1897. The first of these, the Revolt of Daskaloyannis, became the theme of several songs, of which the best known is the thousand-line version dictated by Barba-Pantzelios, an illiterate cheesemaker, to an amanuensis in 1786. Daskaloyannis, Teacher-John, was a comparatively well-educated man who led a revolt of Sfakia, in southwest Crete, relying on promised fellow-Orthodox Russian aid. This support not materializing, the revolt collapsed and John was flayed alive. A shorter version of the song, from the collection of Jeannaraki, represents Daskaloyannis as a rash adventurer, left to his fate by his wiser friends whom he nonetheless tries to protect. In Pantzelios's song, Daskaloyannis is a hero who, having given himself up, dies in silence. Here is a rough translation of the shorter song:

Whoever has a brain within his head, and can reason and understand, let him sit and listen to the tale of Yannis, of the teacher. Each Christmas he went up to the chapel and said to the Protopapas: I shall bring Moscow in. And when the Pasha heard of his threats and his boasting, he sent news to Castro and to Rethymno—Come and take arms against these banners of rebellion, and let us put to the fire these poor pockets of resistance.

They made their preparations, and marched against Sfakia, and set a watch over the rest of Crete. The rebels had no time to organise their troops, and it was only a short time before they were destroyed. They captured Anopolis and John the Teacher, and there was no one left to help his former

leader. After the Turks had captured him, he had no hope of
safety, for all his supporters had abandoned him. Aradhaina
had deserted him, and so had Ai Yanni, Sgouromallia fled from
his cause with swift feet.

—John, teacher from Sfakia, was it you who wished to make
Crete Greek?

They saddled up his horse for him to ride; his wife
inquired where his journey would take him.

—Lady, I go into exile, this is my news to you, and good news
I think it, that I shall never return.

'So keep the gates locked and the keys hidden, and the windows and doors firmly fastened.'

As many as are the stars in heaven, so much he took in
coin, and when he came to the steps of the Pasha's house, he
turned his eyes back to his home:

'Ah, where are you, my friends and my kinsmen, that you send
me to the Pasha to give up my life?'

They handed him over to the torturers; afterwards they
flayed him, right up to his eyes and his nose: bitterly, bitterly
he screamed at the tortures they inflicted.

When they had done their worst with him, the mercy of
death came on him.

Jeannaraki*; translated by RS

Many such exploits are celebrated in songs, many of them of little artistic merit. Another such is the story of Hadji Michali, a
chieftain of the Morea who led an expedition to Crete in support
of the Sfakiots in 1861. A version of the song was collected and
translated by Pashley; another is to be found in Jeannaraki's collection. In Pantzelios's song, the poet ends with a long lament for
the old Sfakia, which throws a vivid light on the life of eighteenth-
century Crete.

Mourn bitterly, and shed black tears
For they have given away Sfakia, the citadel of freedom,
Whose ships were famous, and her sailors heavy with praise,
Renowned even in Constantinople and in Venice.
They did not fear the ocean, they showed no respect
for storms,
They conquered even the roots of the sea.
Now they gaze at their ships, rotten and full of holes,
Sleeping, dry ruins, on the sandy beach.
Men, women and children plunged in mourning
Since this great suffering and this pale grief.

No more are the ladies to be seen with their long braids,
Their woven gold and embroidered garments,
Nor the plump maidens in their festal dress—
Alas for their golden ornaments, alas for their rich stuffs.
You will not see the young men silver in their armour,
Tall and slim-waisted, shapely as violins,
Dancing the maypole dance and capping songs,
Prinking and prancing, among such desolation;
Nor old men with white hair sitting at the tables
Eating and drinking and singing loudly,
Singing songs of the home and songs of war
Until the tables echo one to another.
The party-musicians have all gone, all the lovers of fun,
The place and its men are unrecognisable.
Where are the men of Sfakia, the brave and worthy men,
Renowned throughout the world, heavy with honour?

There follows a long litany of the towns of Sfakia whose flower
is gone.

Where are your houses and your chambers?
All are in ruins, and who will rebuild them,
When the owners have vanished to east and west?
They had not the heart to resist the Turks,
And others have gone into Hades for ever,
And those who remain wander around like strangers
And have no appetite to settle as before.

Barba-Pantzelios,* 901–26, 960–66;

translated by RS

Only ten years after the revolt, Claude-Etienne Savary was struck
by the evident antiquity of the customs of the Sfakiots. Clearly not
everything had been destroyed in the suppression of the revolt;
the isolated communities of the White Mountains have preserved
many ancient traditions and items of lore.

> Of all the Cretans, the Sphachiots alone have retained the
> Pyrrhic dance; this they perform, clad in their ancient dress,
> that is to say, a short robe bound with a girdle, breeches and
> buskins; a quiver, filled with arrows, is fastened over their
> shoulder, a bent bow hangs on their arm, and by their side they
> have a long sword. Thus accoutred, they begin the dance,
> which has three measures. The first marks the step, and they
> change feet in dancing like the Germans; the movements of
> the second are more lively, and resemble the dance of the

inhabitants of Lower Brittany; during the third measure, they leap backwards and forwards, first on one foot, and then on the other, with great agility. The dancers, who answer them, imitate the same steps, and sing and dance with them to the same time. In the course of this dance, they perform various evolutions; sometimes forming a circle, at others, dividing, and ranging themselves in two lines, and seeming to menace each other with their weapons. Afterward they separate into couples, and appear as if defying their antagonists to the combat; but, in all their movements, their ear is true to the music, and they never vary from the measure.

C.-E. Savary, Letters on Greece (Dublin, 1788)

Sfakia is a great repository of fairy tales and other lore of the supernatural, and the following is one of the items recounted by Pashley:

> Two men went, on a fine moonlight night, up the lofty mountains, intending to hunt the agrímia. They heard a great tumult, and at first supposed it to be caused by people coming to obtain snow, to take into the city: but, as they drew nearer, they heard the sound of musical instruments and varied sports. The men soon discovered that these were not mortals, but an assemblage of demoniacal beings: all of whom were clothed in varied garments, and rode on horses, some of which were white, and others of different colours. It appeared that there were 'both men and women, on foot and on horseback, a multitude of people: and the men were white as doves, and the women beautiful as the sunbeams': it was also evident that they were carrying something like a bier. The mountaineers determined to shoot at the aerial host, as they passed on singing,
>
> > We go, we go, to fetch the lady-bride
> > From the steep rock, a solitary nymph.
>
> As soon as the shot was fired, those who were last in the procession exclaimed. 'They've murdered our bridegroom—they've murdered our bridegroom': and, as they made this exclamation, they wept, and shrieked, and fled.

Travels in Crete (London, 1837)

Not all travelers enjoyed the peculiarities of Cretan landscape and customs. The dour Joseph Pitton de Tournefort, the botanist, visited Greece in 1700. All in all, Crete does not seem to have pleased him. He has not a good word to say about Mt. Ida.

We ascended it with much difficulty, on the third of July. This mighty mountain, which covers almost the middle of the island, has nothing of note but its name, so resonant in ancient history. This celebrated Mt Ida exhibits nothing but a huge overgrown, ugly, sharp-rais'd, bald-pated eminence; not the least shadow of a landskip, no delightful grotto, no bubbling spring, nor purling rivulet to be seen: there is indeed one poor sorry well with a bucket, to keep the sheep and horses from perishing with thirst. All the cattel bred on it, are a few scrubby horses, some sheep and starveling goats, which are forc'd to brouze on the very Tragacantha; a shrub so prickly, that the Greeks call it Goat-thorn. Begging Dionysius Periegetes' pardon, as likewise his commentator's, the Archbishop of Thessalonica; the praises they bestowed on this mountain, seem to be strain'd, or at least are now past their season. They who have advanc'd, that the upper parts of Mt Ida were quite bald, and that plants could not live there for snow and ice, came much nearer the truth. Theophrastus talks of a sort of vine growing here, and Pliny has done no more than translated the description of it. We look'd about to see if we could find any such vine, but to no purpose; and yet it can't be doubted but those authors meant Mt Ida of Crete: for on that of Phrygia there's neither snow nor ice to be seen. On whatever side we turned our eyes, from one heighth to another, we saw nothing but bottomless quagmires, and deep abysses fill'd with snow ever since the reign of King Jupiter, the first of the name.

Tournefort also suffered from the habitual obstructiveness of the Turks toward any enterprise of curiosity, however innocent.

At our return to Retimo, we were told, that this was the harvest time for Ladanum (a drug used by the apothecaries and perfumers) and if we had a mind to see it, we might go to Melidoni, a pretty village lying to the sea, twenty-two miles from Retimo: we lay there the 22nd of July at a Papas, to whom we were recommended by Dr Patelaro. This Papas promised to shew us all the curiosities of the country, and, especially, an inscription as you go into a cavern near that town. The next day we were mortify'd at the proceeding of a Turk, who was gathering the tythe in those parts, and whom we were afraid to invite to supper, because we had nothing to eat but a pig. This Turk understanding our design, came to the Papas, and forbid him shewing us to that cavern, saying we were spies, and that we made remarks on everything; that he had been informed the very trees and plants did not escape us; and that he could not let us proceed in this manner, or suffer us to go and consult those old marbles fill'd with prophecies relating to the Grand Signior . . .

So there is no seeing the inscription; however, Tournefort and his companions contrive to see the ladanum harvest despite everything, and he describes the harvest of the plant, *Cistus ladanifera cretica*, with its purple flowers:

> Seven or eight country-fellows in their shirts and drawers were brushing the plants with their whips; the straps whereof, by rubbing against the leaves of this shrub, lick'd up a sort of odoriferous glue sticking on the leaves: 'tis part of the nutritious juice of the plant, which sweats through the texture of those leaves like a fatty dew, in shining drops, as clear as turpentine.

> When the whips are sufficiently laden with this grease, they take a knife and scrape it down off the straps, and make it up into a mass or cakes of different size: this is what comes to us under the name of ladanum or labdanum. A man that's diligent will gather three pounds two ounces per day, and more, which they sell for a crown on the spot.
>
> Joseph Pitton de Tournefort, *Voyage into the Levant*;
> translated by J. Ozell (London, 1718)

In 1867 Crete followed the example of the rest of Greece forty-six years before, and rose against the Turkish Empire, to whose sphere the great powers had shortsightedly assigned it on the conclusion of the War of Independence. The revolt was bloodily suppressed, but it inspired Swinburne to a lengthy poem celebrating it:

From ODE ON THE INSURRECTION IN CANDIA
(JANUARY 1867)

As the soul on the lips of the dead
　　Stands poising her wings for flight,
　　　　A bird scarce quit of her prison,
　　　　　　But fair without form or flesh,
So stands over each man's head
　　A splendour of imminent light,
　　　　A glory of fame re-arisen,
　　　　　　Of day re-arisen afresh
　　　　　　　　From the hells of night.

In the hundred cities of Crete
    Such glory was not of old,
        Though her name was great upon earth
          And her face was fair on the sea.
The words of her lips were sweet,
    Her days were woven with gold,
        Her fruits came timely to birth;
          So fair she was, being free,
            Who is bought and sold.

So fair, who is fairer now
    With her children dead at her side,
        Unsceptred, unconsecrated,
          Unapparelled, unhelped, unpitied,
With blood for gold on her brow,
    Where the towery tresses divide;
        The goodly, the golden-gated,
          Many-crowned, many-named, many-citied.
          Made like as a bride.

And these are the bridegroom's gifts;
    Anguish that straitens the breath,
        Shame, and the weeping of mothers,
          And the suckling dead at the breast,
White breast that a long sob lifts;
    And the dumb dead mouth, which saith,
        'How long, and how long, my brothers?'
          And wrath which endures not rest,
          And the pains of death.

                        A. C. Swinburne

After the rising of 1896, Crete was "semi-liberated," and Prince George of Greece became High Commissioner. From that time, the Greek and Turkish populations coexisted in reasonable tranquility until 1920, when Smyrna was awarded to Greece for a trial period, resulting in the forced exchange of populations between Greece and Asia Minor in 1923. Pandelis Prevelakis's *Tale of a Town*, a work of classic charm first published in 1938, offers a picture of Rethemnos in his youth, an upper-class idyll very different from the image of Crete presented in its earlier literature:

> The decline of the old, substantial, upper-class town can be read in Tsar Street as clearly as an open book. The good old folk who once had dealings with Chios, Smyrna, Constantinople and Trieste today sit idly before their shop-fronts with

a duster in their hands or some other accessory of the sedentary life and meditate on the past. The drapery stores which in other days groaned under piles of cloth, Greek and Turkish velvets and satins—what velvets, what gold-patterned silks, what spidery-fine muslins!—have now made their adjustments after so many years of unemployment and carry cheaper goods—sateens, dimities, drills and every sort of country cloth. The gunsmiths with their heavy rifles and their shooting gear have declined too and have found themselves driven to fall in with the times. It is a shame to see their windows with the firearms and hunting-knives still in them, and, heaping up around them day by day and gradually smothering them, the requisites of the new *jeunesse dorée*, things like starch for shirt-fronts, scented soap, pocket mirrors and the like.

P. Prevelakis, *The Tale of a Town*, 15f.;
translated by K. R. Johnstone

But the life of the mountains changed little for all the luxury goods of the towns. And it was the mountain-folk, the shepherds of the villages, who provided the indomitable resistance to German occupation in the Second World War. A number of Englishmen also played their parts in the resistance, and parts of that story are told in Dilys Powell's *The Villa Ariadne*, Stanley Moss's *Ill Met by Moonlight*, and the remarkable book by George Psychoundakis, *The Cretan Runner*. Songs of defiance were current from the earliest days of the occupation:

Hitler, boast not that you have trodden Crete down,
Have found it weaponless, its children orphaned:
They fight you in foreign lands, in Albania . . .

I. I. Papagregorakis*; translated by RS

George Psychoundakis, the poet, sang of the disasters of the war in the fifteen-syllable *politikos* line, as poets had done for generations. This is his account of the destruction of the village of Yerakari:

The earliest beam from Ida's peak a-wakened Yerakari,
Highest in Crete, on Kedros peak, chief of the high Amari.
Nature endowed with teeming gifts the valleys of the county,
But on your leafy vales and hills, she scattered all her bounty:
So many trees to shade your lanes and flowers to star
     your mountains,

Whose stony breast ran bright with streams and flashed with
    crystal fountains.
Beneath your trees quiet waters flowed; above their
    branches woven
White houses lay like doves asleep along the sill of heaven.
When happy Spring awoke the woods and fields and
    glades, unfolding
Your flowers in Mount Kedros' lap, your rocks and
    pastures holding
In spells of scented breezes bound, she hung the twigs
    with berries
And summer bowed your vines and trees with clustering
    grapes and cherries.
While girls with baskets sent their laughter running through
    the meadows;
Under the cherry-branches, then, deep in the leafy shadows,
The Cretan lyre struck up beside the brook, the green
    woods ringing
With Cretan rhyming couplets and with village
    voices singing;
And each day dawned a holiday, the kindly sun's advancing
Marked by the clink of glasses while the forest shook
    with dancing!
True Paradise it seemed! When August beat on our
    Cretan mountains,
Ah, then we came from far and near to lie by your
    cool fountains!
Cool blew the breeze of summer there. What trick of
    Nature's scheming
Gathered such store of grace and blessing there, and heap'd
    such teeming
Abundance of all goodly things? How often have
    your bowers
And shades and songs and wines and fruits and waterfalls
    and flowers
Strewn blessings on our warriors, and hope and consolation?
Who sought thy refuge from the fight for our enslavèd
    nation?
Who fought through all those bitter years under the
    tyrants galling
And dwelt in lonely mountain tops, where rain and snow
    were falling;

When black despair hung in the air, when tyranny
    was master,
When blood was shed 'neath the tyrant's tread and Death
    reign'd and disaster?
You were the secret shelter for each Greek and English rival
Of tyranny, who grasped a gun for liberty's survival!
But when the Dark Hour came at last, the storm clouds
    broke asunder
Barbarian tempests flung their fire, high mountains crashed
    with thunder.
And now you lie there, cold and dead, ruined and black
    with burning,
Empty and silent in the hills and dark with fire
    and mourning.
Where are your *pallikaria* now, your chosen
    warriors sleeping,
Who fell that evil day and filled Amari's vales with weeping?
Where are your idle afternoons, your mornings bright
    with sunlight?
Your founts, your belfries in the dusk, your churches pale
    with moonlight?
Where are your dove-white houses now, your soft winds and
    your waters,
Your happy throngs in summer time, your golden sons
    and daughters?
One fiery moment burnt them all, when roofs and walls
    were riven,
And whirled them flaming to the sky and through the gates
    of Heaven.

> George Psychoundakis, *The Cretan Runner* (1955);
> translated by Patrick Leigh Fermor

The spirit of Crete, in the end, is that of the mountains, as this song
quoted by Michael Llewellyn-Smith makes clear:

Fie on the young men down in the plains
Who taste the good things of the world, the choicest foods,
And are base to look at like the creeping lizard.
Joy to the young men up in the hills,
Who eat the snow and the dew-fresh air
And are fine to look at like the orange tree.

> M. Llewellyn-Smith, *The Great Island*
> (London, 1965), 117

Knossos and the "Labyrinth"

The story of the labyrinth constructed by Daedalus to house the Minotaur, the hideous offspring of Queen Pasiphae and her beloved bull, goes back to the earliest days of Greek legend. Homer describes the picture on the shield of Achilles of:

> a dancing place
> All full of turnings, that was like the admirable maze
> For fair-hair'd Ariadne made, by cunning Daedalus
> *Iliad* XVIII, 590–92;
> translated by George Chapman (London, 1616)

Sophocles referred to its "tangled windings" (Pearson, *Fragments of Sophocles*, i, 110f.), and the story of the Minotaur is implied by Bacchylides in his poem on Theseus. Homer tells us the maze was "in broad Knossos," and the excavation by Sir Arthur Evans of the Minoan palace there, with its dark and sinister corridors, and its storehouses in the deep earth, seemed to provide a site for the fabled maze.

But travelers before Evans identified a most curious site, many miles away in the hills above dusty Gortyn, as the ancient labyrinth. Pierre Belon was sceptical of this identification and it is not made explicit in the description by Bernard Randolph, who explored it in the late seventeenth century, but the account of Savary which follows makes plain that he was sure he was treading the very cage-ground of the Minotaur. Here is Randolph:

> From Bonifacia to the Labarinth is about ten miles, or three hours riding W^d, most a plain. Several men have several opinions about this building (if I may call it so). But one Signior Venetando, who was born in a neighbouring village, gives this account, that a certain king of this island, had so great a hatred for all women, that he order'd this place for his court, and at last lived so private that he would not suffer any to come to him but such as ruled in his stead. He would seldome come out but to worship at a temple dedicated to Jupiter, which stood close by it. In this labarinth he ended his days, and had a famous tombe built for him, the ruins of which they shew you. The Labarinth is above two miles about, being so covered on the top with earth, as it seems to be all of firm land; we entred it with two torches, and candles in lanthornes, having a line to direct us out again. The way is plain under foot, and archt over head, some arches being about ten foot high, some more, some less, with several windings . . . There are abundance of batts, which hang

in clusters, and some are larger than ordinary . . . We had
almost ended our line, being about a hundred pikes, which is
above eighty yards, and then returned out, being a good hour in
the Labarinth. The damps are very great; against rain it is
always dropping, but very dry with Northerly winds. At the end
is a lake, and they tell you, that some have attempted to go to it,
and have been drawn into it. Our curiosity did not invite us to
see it, for were it not true, as in probability 'tis not, the noi-
som smells are enough to stifle one.

Bernard Randolph, *Present State of the Islands
in the Archipelago* (London, 1687)

And here is Savary, who wrote in 1779, but his account was first
published in 1788:

> We walked with precaution in the doublings of this vast
> labyrinth, amid the eternal darkness that reigns throughout
> it, and which our torches could hardly dispel. Thus situated,
> the imagination raises up phantoms; it figures to itself
> precipices under the feet of the curious, monsters placed as
> centinels, and, in a word, a thousand chimeras which can have
> no existence.
>
> The precaution we had taken of proceeding with the
> thread of Ariadne, and of fastening it at different distances
> lest it should break, allowed us to advance farther than Belon,
> Tournefort, and Pocock, were able to do for want of such
> assistance. We observed, in several parts of the middle avenue,
> the cyphers 1700 written with a black pencil, by the hand of
> the celebrated French botanist. An extraordinary circumstance
> which he remarks, and which we admired no less than he had
> done, is the property possessed by the rock of presenting the
> names engraven on it in relief. We saw several of them,
> wherein this sort of sculpture had arisen to the thickness of
> two lines (the sixth part of an inch). The substance of this relief
> is whiter than the stone.
>
> After straying for a long time in the frightful cavern of the
> Minotaur . . . we remained three hours in the Labyrinth, with-
> out being able to flatter ourselves with having seen everything.

Letters on Greece (Dublin, 1788)

The legend of the Labyrinth could hardly die with such topographical support, though if Savary had really read Belon, he carefully
ignored the comments of the latter, and it remained for J. B. S. Morritt in 1795 to puncture the legend with a dash of common sense.

Gortyna is at a village about twenty-five miles distant, at the foot of Ida, separated from the plain of Candia, and of Cnossus, by a chain of hills chiefly barren, stony, and uninteresting, though some of the dells on the western side are more deserving of notice, and have pretty and picturesque aspects. Gortyna is in the largest and finest plain of the island, opening at one end to the southern sea; it is rather fertile than picturesque, but now is thinly inhabited and ill cultivated. There is little to see here: old, prostrate columns, ornamented fragments, well-known inscriptions, and a stripped theatre as usual. The little river Lethe, which crosses it, still, as of old, overgrown with plane trees, and the shade famous for the amours of Jupiter and Europa, we looked at with more interest, as it applied more to our fancy than our eyes, and I have often experienced how much a pretty story, consecrated by anciently received opinon, gives consequence to scenes in themselves indifferent. Who did not look with pleasure at Shakespeare's mulberry, but the parson who cut it down? So the story of this little brook, with its reputation for oblivion, made us not pass it by, though it is a good deal less remarkable than the Greta. We don't want to forget or be forgotten, so I think did not take any draughts of it.

A mile beyond is what is called the Labyrinth. It is in a mountain, a large subterraneous range of passages, unequal in breadth and height, many crossing into one another, most ending at large, irregular chambers hewn out in the rock, and sometimes meeting or branching off from opener parts of the cave, which it is true make the road difficult to find, though not so difficult as has been represented. You ask me what I think of this; to say the truth, neither more nor less than a large stone quarry . . .

J. B. S. Morritt, *Letters* (London, 1794–96)

The site of the supposed labyrinth, Gortyn, had naturally been taken for the seat of government of King Minos, the legendary just king of Crete. In 1415 the Italian traveler, Cristoforo Buondelmonti, visited Gortyn, and has left us a detailed description of the ruins as they stood at the time. He makes no mention of the remarkable inscription of the Law Code of Gortyn, now the most prominent feature of the site.

To the side of the mountain I found the largest city and metropolis in the whole island, Gortyn, where the famous, very just king Minos gave judgment. Alas, what shall I say, or what shall I talk about, upon seeing such a situation? Let all Cretans lament such destruction, and let their wives, with their hair hanging loose, never tire of rending their garments! There was a mountain standing separate from the others, further north and close to the water, and round it were walls, where an undamaged gate was still to be seen. The Palace of Minos can be seen, its decaying windows wide open, and from there a water conduit descended from the high mountain and then sprinkled the whole city, which is about as big as our Florence, though Gortyn is fuller, and has no walls. In about the middle, between the east and the south there now stands a temple, its walls made of brick. Near the river, towards the north on the side where the temple was, is the church of Titus, the disciple of the apostle Paul, who was descended from Minos. Opposite this you will see a bridge of amazing size, which reaches to the square near this church; and to the east you will see two marble busts of the apostles, of an astonishing size. In the same church lies the body of archbishop Titus, and because the whole of this church now lies on the ground, all mixed up, it cannot be found. In the city, alongside the river, there now stand five windmills. I counted the marble columns and stones, upright or lying on the ground, and there were fourteen hundred of them; and there were also endless numbers of marble sheets and tombs.

Cristoforo Buondelmonti, Descriptio Insulae Cretae (1417); translated by RS

The prosaic reality was still romantic enough, and the report of a party of tourists lost in it in the 1950s provided the impetus for Lawrence Durrell's novel *The Dark Labyrinth*.

The real Knossos remained buried until the excavations of Evans brought to light a lost world, the Minoan civilization that perished about 1500 B.C. but is preserved for us in the luminous and exquisite frescoes that grace the palace here and on Thera. C. A. Trypanis evokes the atmosphere of that vanished world in his poem:

CNOSSUS

Minoan ships are sleeping in the trees,
The tight-hipped men, frieze over stucco frieze,
With blue-scaled fish that swallow and exude
An ochre sea, bulls in steep solitude.

At the King's festival—red petals blown
Across a wide court's emptiness,

How silent the libations of distress,
And soft the brush of wrinkled feet on stone . . .

All round, the climbing waste of broom,
The flower-cups swollen with the royal gold,
The buried jars that niggardly hold
Their hollow gloom.

King Minos' justice! feather-tilted scales
To weigh the thistledown that swirling sails
Out through the night, where neither tears nor gold
Can bribe the brooding gods when all is told.

C. A. Trypanis

13

Beyond Greece:
Istanbul, the Troad, and Izmir

In antiquity the Ionian seaboard was constantly disputed territory between the Greeks who dwelt there and the Persian Great King and his satraps who ruled it. The great Greek cities of the Ionian coast are an essential part of Greek history in the classical and Roman periods. With the decline of the ancient world, however, they lost their Greco-Roman character, apart from a few enclaves such as Constantinople and Smyrna. For this reason I have not included a survey of all the formerly Greek sites of the Turkish coast, but have concentrated on three special cases: Istanbul, for centuries the capital of the Greek-speaking world; the Troad, site of the war that stands at the fountainhead of classical literature, and a beacon for the learned and imaginative through many centuries; and Smyrna, the great cosmopolitan, but distinctively Greek, merchant city.

Istanbul

For centuries after the Greek city of Byzantion had become Constantinople, it was known among Greeks simply as the City (i Polis, stin Poli) from which its modern name derives. Paul the Silentiary, one of the circle of court poets around Agathias in the reign of the emperor Justinian (A.D. 527–65), describes the church of Hagia Sophia which Justinian built, in a long poem that lingers on every detail. Here is an extract:

> The roof is made of golden-plated tiles
> From which a sparkling blaze of gold sends beams
> No more supportable to human eyes
> Than Phaethon at his noon-day halt in spring,
> When every crag is bleached gold. Yes, my king,
> When he had brought the whole world to agree,
> And gathered wealth from Rome, and native wealth,
> Thought no stone honour worthy of the temple
> Of great, immortal God, in whom proud Rome
> Had placed her hopes entirely. Silver too
> He did not stint to pour forth. Sunium's crag

And Mount Pangaeum bled their silver veins
And treasured heaps of mighty kings were broached.
Where, in the east, the great perimeter
Enclosed the shrine of bloodless sacrifice,
No ivory, no bronze or carved stone stood,
But all the aisle was lined with brightest silver.
Not only on the sanctuary walls,
Where the initiate is enthroned, but even
The columns were entirely cased in silver,
Shining with leaping light, a dozen strong.

Paul the Silentiary,*
"Description of Hagia Sophia"; translated by RS

One of the fullest descriptions of Byzantine Constantinople is that of the Sephardic Jew, Benjamin of Tudela, who traveled through Greece in the 1160s:

> It hangs over two arms of the sea, one of which arises from the Russian Sea, and the other from the sea of Sepharad (Spain). Here merchants of every sort assemble together, from Babylon, from all Mesopotamia, Media, Persia, from all the Kingdom of Egypt, Canaan, Russia, Hungary, Pesiinki, Buria, Lombardy, and finally from the land of the Sephardim. This causes a perpetual hurry of people, who traffick in this place from all parts of the world by land and sea, insomuch that in this respect it exceeds other cities, except the great city of Bagdad, the metropolis of the Ishmaelites; here also is the high place of Sophia, and the Pope of the Javanites; because they are not obedient to the religion of the Roman Pope. The altars equal in number the days of the year. The immense wealth which is brought hither, from each region, citadel, and fortified place, as a yearly tribute, exceeds all conception, and outvies in riches all the high places in the world. In the middle of the high place of Sophia are found an innumerable quantity of gold and silver pillars, together with chandeliers, etc of the like metal. There is likewise a place where the emperor is accustomed to regale himself, near the wall of his palace, called the hippodrome; where he exhibits a great shew annually on the birthday of Jesus the Nazarene. At such times there are shewn in the presence of the king and queen, all sorts of people in the world, in their own likenesses, by different kinds of enchantment. They are likewise accustomed to bring out at these times, lions, bears, leopards, wild asses, and birds, which fight together for the amusement of the spectators. Nor

is any public shew to be found that can equal it. The Emperor Emanuel has likewise built a great palace near the sea for his residence, besides that built by his ancestors, and named it Bilchernas, which he has ornamented with pillars, and wrought over with the purest gold and silver, on which are represented, in sculpture, the wars of his ancestors, together with his own. In the same place he has erected a throne, composed of gold and gems, over which hangs a crown of gold, by a chain of the same metal, of equal dimensions with the seat below it. There are jewels in it, of such value as cannot easily be estimated; the lustre of it is so great as to make any other light altogether unnecessary in the night time. There are likewise many other curiosities, very difficult to be reckoned up.

Benjamin of Tudela, *Travels 1160–1173*;
translated by Rev. B. Gerrans (London, 1783)

Two hundred years later the Arab traveler, Ibn Battutah, was in a still-Christian Constantinople.

Account of the Great Church. I can describe only its exterior; as for its interior I did not see it. It is called in their language *Ayā Ṣūfiyā*, and the story goes that it was an erection of Āṣaf the son of Barakhyā´, who was the son of the maternal aunt of Solomon (on whom be peace). It is one of the greatest churches of the Greeks; around it is a wall which encircles it so that it looks like a city [in itself]. Its gates are thirteen in number, and it has a sacred enclosure, which is about a mile long and closed by a great gate. No one is prevented from entering the enclosure, and in fact I went into it with the king's father, who will be mentioned later; it is like an audience-hall, paved with marble and traversed by a water-channel which issues from the church. This [flows between] two walls about a cubit high, constructed in marble inlaid with pieces of different colours and cut with the most skilful art, and trees are planted in rows on both sides of the channel. From the gate of the church to the gate of this hall there is a lofty pergola made of wood, covered with grape-vines and at the foot with jasmine and scented herbs. Outside the gate of this hall is a large wooden pavilion containing platforms, on which the guardians of this gate sit, and to the right of the pavilions are benches and booths, mostly of wood, in which sit their qāḍīs and the recorders of their bureaux. In the middle of the booths is a wooden pavilion, to which one ascends by a flight of wooden steps; in this pavilion is a great chair swathed in woollen cloth on which their qāḍī sits. We shall speak of him later. To the left of the pavilion which is at the gate of this hall is the bazaar of the druggists. The canal that we have described divides into two branches, one of which passes through the bazaar of the druggists and the other through the bazaar where the judges and the scribes sit.

Travels; translated by H. A. R. Gibb (Cambridge, 1958–)

Constantinople fell for the last time, to the Turks, in 1453. The word among Greeks is still that the Mass in Hagia Sophia, interrupted five centuries ago when the priests faded into the walls and were covered in a layer of whitewash, will one day be completed. The melancholy event is the theme of several traditional songs:

The Last Mass in Hagia Sophia

God rings the bells, earth rings the bells, the sky itself
    is ringing,
The Holy Wisdom, the great church, is ringing out
    the message,
Four hundred sounding boards sound out, and two and
    sixty bells,
For every bell there is a priest, for every priest a deacon.
To the left the emperor is singing, to the right the patriarch,
And all the columns tremble with the thunder of the chant.
And as the emperor began the hymn to the Cherubim,
A voice came down to them from the sky, from the
    archangel's mouth:
Cease the Cherubic hymn, and let the sacred objects bow;
Priests, take the holy things away, extinguish all the candles;
God's Will has made our city now into a Turkish city.
But send a message to the West, and let them send
    three ships:
The first to take the cross, the second to remove the Gospel,
The third, the finest shall rescue for us our holy altar,
Lest it fall to those dogs, and they defile it and dishonour it.
The Holy Virgin was distressed, the very icons wept.
Be calm, beloved Lady, be calm and do not weep for them:
Though years, though centuries shall pass, they shall be
    yours again.

Greek folk song, in C. A. Trypanis,
ed., *Penguin Book of Greek Verse*, no. 254;
translated by RS

Hermann Corrodi, *The Bridge of Galata at Twilight.* Courtesy Gallery
J. Soustiel, Paris.

Lady Mary Wortley Montagu (1689–1762) was in Constantinople
with her husband Edward from 1716 when he was appointed
Ambassador to the Porte, and, besides her lively letters describing
her travels, she composed a long verse description of contemporary
Constantinople:

> Here from my Window I at once survey
> The crouded City, and Resounding Sea,
> In Distant views see Asian Mountains rise
> And lose their Snowy Summits in the Skies.
> Above those Mountains high Olympus tow'rs
> (The Parliamental seat of heavenly Pow'rs).
> New to the sight, my ravish'd Eyes admire
> Each gilded Crescent and each antique Spire,
> The Marble Mosques beneath whose ample Domes
> Fierce Warlike Sultans sleep in peacefull Tombs.
> Those lofty Structures, once the Christian boast,
> Their Names, their Glorys, and their Beautys lost,
> Those Altars bright with Gold, with Sculpture grac'd,
> By Barbarous Zeal of Savage Foes defac'd:
> Sophia alone her Ancient Sound retains
> Thô unbeleiving Vows her shrine prophanes.
> Where Holy Saints have dy'd, in Sacred Cells
> Where Monarchs pray'd, the Frantic Derviche dwells.
> How art thou falln, Imperial City, low!
> Where are thy Hopes of Roman Glory now?
> Where are thy Palaces by Prelates rais'd;
> Where preistly Pomp in Purple Lustre blaz'd?

Where Grecian Artists all their Skill display'd
Before the Happy Sciences decay'd,
So vast, that youthfull Kings might there reside,
So splendid, to content a Patriarch's pride,
Convents where Emperours profess'd of Old,
The Labour'd Pillars that their Triumphs told
(Vain Monuments of Men that once were great!)
Sunk undistinguish'd in one common Fate!
　　　One Little Spot the small Fenar contains,
Of Greek Nobillity, the poor remains,
Where other Helens show like powerfull Charms
As once engag'd the Warring World in Arms,
Those Names which Royal Auncestry can boast
In mean Mechanic arts obscurely lost,
Those Eyes a second Homer might inspire,
Fix'd at the loom, destroy their useless Fire.
　　　Greiv'd at a view which strikes upon my Mind
The short-liv'd Vanity of Humankind,
In Gaudy Objects I indulge my Sight
And turn where Eastern Pomp gives Gay Delight.
See; the vast Train in Various Habits drest,
By the bright Scimetar and sable vest,
The Vizier proud, distinguish'd o're the rest.
Six slaves in gay Attire his Bridle hold,
His Bridle rich with Gems, his stirrups Gold,
His snowy Steed adorn'd with Lavish Pride,
Whole troops of Soldiers mounted by his Side,
These toss the Plumy Crest, Arabian Coursers guide.
With awfull Duty, all decline their Eyes,
No Bellowing Shouts of noisie crouds arise,
Silence, in solemn state the March attends
Till at the Dread Divan the slow Procession ends.

Lady Mary Wortley Montagu

Thereafter Istanbul was a Turkish city; but Yeats made Byzantium a symbol of his own poetic aims and celebrated it in two poems, the earlier of which (1927) is a journey of a kind:

SAILING TO BYZANTIUM

That is no country for old men. The young
In one another's arms, birds in the trees
—Those dying generations—at their song,
The salmon-falls, the mackerel-crowded seas,
Fish, flesh, or fowl, commend all summer long

Whatever is begotten, born, and dies.
Caught in that sensual music all neglect
Monuments of unageing intellect.

An aged man is but a paltry thing,
A tattered coat upon a stick, unless
Soul clap its hands and sing, and louder sing
For every tatter in its mortal dress,
Nor is there singing school but studying
Monuments of its own magnificence;
And therefore I have sailed the seas and come
To the holy city of Byzantium.

O sages standing in God's holy fire
As in the gold mosaic of a wall,
Come from the holy fire, perne in a gyre,
And be the singing-masters of my soul.
Consume my heart away; sick with desire
And fastened to a dying animal
It knows not what it is; and gather me
Into the artifice of eternity.

Once out of nature I shall never take
My bodily form from any natural thing,
But such a form as Grecian goldsmiths make
Of hammered gold and gold enamelling
To keep a drowsy Emperor awake;
Or set upon a golden bough to sing
To lords and ladies of Byzantium
Of what is past, or passing, or to come.

W. B. Yeats

Sestos and Abydos

Facing each other across the Dardanelles stood the two towns of
Abydos and Sestos, homes respectively of Hero and Leander,
whose love was the theme of a Greek poem by Musaeus (fifth to
sixth century A.D.), translated by George Chapman, who also completed Christopher Marlowe's poem on the same theme:

> Two townes there were that with one sea were wald;
> Built neere, and opposite: this, Sestus cald;
> Abydus that: then Love his bow bent high,
> And at both cities, let one arrow fly.
> That two (a virgin and a youth) inflam'd:

The youth was sweetly grac'd Leander nam'd;
The virgin, Hero. Sestus, she renownes,
Abydus hee, in birth: of both which townes
Both were the beauty-circled stars; and both,
Grac'd with like lookes, as with one love and troth.
    If that way lye thy course, seeke for my sake,
A tower, that Sestian Hero once did make
Her watch-tower: and a torch stood holding there,
By which, Leander his sea-course did steere.
Seeke likewise, of Abydus ancient towers,
The roaring sea lamenting to these houres,
Leander's love, and death.

Musaeus, *Hero and Leander;*
translated by George Chapman

Byron's more successful emulation of Leander (though he only tried it once, and in summer) is legendary. He himself made a joke of it:

WRITTEN AFTER SWIMMING
FROM SESTOS TO ABYDOS

If, in the month of dark December,
    Leander, who was nightly wont
(What maid will not the tale remember?)
    To cross thy stream, broad Hellespont!

If, when the wintry tempest roar'd,
    He sped to Hero, nothing loth,
And thus of old thy current pour'd,
    Fair Venus! how I pity both!

For me, degenerate modern wretch,
    Though in the genial month of May,
My dripping limbs I faintly stretch,
    And think I've done a feat today.

But since he cross'd the rapid tide,
    According to the doubtful story,
To woo,—and—Lord knows what beside,
    And swam for Love, as I for Glory;

'Twere hard to say who fared the best:
    Sad mortals! thus the Gods still plague you!
He lost his labour, I my jest:
    For he was drown'd, and I've the ague.

Lord Byron, 9 May 1810

Troy

In Troy there lies the scene. From isles of Greece
The princes orgulous, their high blood chaf'd,
Have to the port of Athens sent their ships,
Fraught with the ministers and instruments
Of cruel war: Sixty and nine that wore
Their crownets regal, from the Athenian bay
Put forth toward Phrygia: and their vow is made
To ransack Troy, within whose strong immures
The ravish'd Helen, Menelaus' queen,
With wanton Paris sleeps,—and that's the quarrel.
To Tenedos they come;
And the deep-drawing barks do there disgorge
Their warlike fraughtage: Now on Dardan plains
The fresh and yet unbruised Greeks do pitch
Their brave pavilions: Priam's six-gated city,
Dardan, and Tymbria, Ilias, Chetas, Trojan,
And Antenorides, with massy staples,
And corresponsive and fulfilling bolts,
Sperr up the sons of Troy.

William Shakespeare,
Troilus and Cressida, Prologue

Not surprisingly, the plain of Troy was a cynosure for most classi-
cally educated Westerners, remembering Achilles' pursuit of Hector round its walls, and anxious to identify each spot mentioned
by Homer:

As Hector sees, unusual terrors rise,
Struck by some god, he fears, recedes, and flies.
He leaves the gates, he leaves the wall behind:
Achilles follows like the winged wind.

Now circling round the walls their course maintain,
Where the high watch-tower overlooks the plain;
Now where the fig-trees spread their umbrage broad,
(A wider compass,) smoke along the road.
Next by Scamander's double source they bound,
Where two famed fountains burst the parted ground;
This hot through scorching clefts is seen to rise,
With exhalations steaming to the skies;
That the green banks in summer's heat o'erflows,
Like crystal clear, and cold as winter snows:

Each gushing fount a marble cistern fills,
Whose polish'd bed receives the falling rills;
Where Trojan dames (ere yet alarm'd by Greece)
Wash'd their fair garments in the days of peace.

Homer, *Iliad*, 22, 136–56;
translated by Alexander Pope

But Troy's slumber was long: Ovid, Agathias, and Edmund Spenser
are representative of those who mourned its disappearance.

So see wee all things chaungeable. One nation
    gathereth strength:
Another wexeth weake: and bothe doo make exchaunge
    at length.
So Troy which once was great and strong as well in
    welth as men,
And able ten yeeres space to spare such store of
    blood as then.
Now beeing bace hath nothing left of all her welth to showe,
Save ruines of the auncient woorkes which grasse
    dooth overgrowe,
And tumbes wherin theyr auncetours lye buryed on a rowe.

Ovid, *Metamorphoses*, 15, 420–25;
translated by Arthur Golding

Whither, O city, are your profits and your gilded shrines,
And your barbecues of great oxen,
And the tall women walking your streets, in gilt clothes,
With their perfumes in little alabaster boxes?
Where is the work of your home-born sculptors?

Time's tooth is into the lot, and war's and fate's too.
Envy has taken your all,
Save your douth and your story.

Agathias, in *Anthologia Palatina*, 9, 153;
translated by Ezra Pound

Troy, that art now nought but an idle name,
And in thine ashes buried low dost lie,
Though whilome far much greater then thy fame,
Before that angry Gods and cruell skie
Upon thee heapt a direfull destinie;
What boots it boast thy glorious descent,
And fetch from heven thy great genealogie,

Sith all thy worthie prayses being blent
Their ofspring hath embaste, and later glory shent?

Most famous Worthy of the world, by whome
That warre was kindled which did Troy inflame,
And stately towres of Ilion whilome
Brought unto balefull ruine, was by name
Sir Paris far renowmd through noble fame;
Who, through great prowesse and bold hardinesse,
From Lacedæmon fetcht the fayrest Dame
That ever Greece did boast, or knight possesse,
Whom Venus to him gave for meed of worthinesse;

Fayre Helene, flowre of beautie excellent,
And girlond of the mighty Conquerours,
That madest many Ladies deare lament
The heavie losse of their brave Paramours,
Which they far off beheld from Trojan toures,
And saw the fieldes of faire Scamander strowne
With carcases of noble warrioures
Whose fruitlesse lives were under furrow sowne,
And Xanthus sandy bankes with blood all overflowne.

Edmund Spenser, The Faerie Queene, III, ix, 33–35

The irrepressible Thomas Coryate visited the Troad in 1612,
finding plentiful ancient remains—though unfortunately what he
actually visited was the Hellenistic city of Alexandria Troas—and
enlivening the visit with his pranks.

> From this Towne [Sio] I sailed in an English Ship, to
> the Trojan shoare, where I landed Feb. 22. with foureteene
> English men more and a Jew or Druggerman, all well
> weaponed for feare of any hostile invasion by the Turkes: by
> the way as we were going thither, we found a bare little plot of
> ground, not farre from the Sea, where their Oxen trode out
> wheate, according to the custome of most of these Asiaticke
> Countries; we walked towards the mould or haven of Troy;
> but before we came thither we observed divers antiquities
> worthy the relation . . .

> It grieved me to the heart that I could not learne either by
> inscriptions, or any other meanes, whose Monuments these
> were: for it is vaine to be induced by conjectures, to say they
> were these or these mens; onely I hope no man will taxe me
> of a rash opinion, if I beleeve one of them might be the Mon-

ument of King Ilus, the enlarger of the Citie of Troy; for I remember that Homer saith in his eleventh Aeneid, that Ilus was buried in the open, as this was; and that another of them might be the Monument of King Priamus, it is not altogether unlikely, for Virgil writeth in his second Aeneid that King Priamus, after the late fatall destruction of the Citie, was slaine by Pyrrhus the Sonne of Achilles, neere the Trojan shoare: for thus saith he—jacet ingens littore truncus. Now through mercilesse Achilles persecuted the dead carkase of Hector with that Barbarous crueltie, as to dragge him starke naked at a Carts taile, three times about the wals of the Citie: yet it is likely they would so much honour the old silver haired King Priamus (especially since they had now fully satisfied their furie, both by burning of the Citie and massacring of all the most Noble Citizens, and with the rest their last King) as to cover his body with some royall monument beseeming his regall state; pardon me (gentle reader) for this my conjecture. I affirme nothing certainely, onely I gesse, as another industrious traveller would doe, that hath or shall observe the same things that I have done, that one of those goodly Monuments might be the Sepulcher of King Priamus.

It happened that when wee had thoroughly satiated our eyes, with contemplation of these ancient ruines, the Chiefetaine of the company, a sworne Brother of mine, whom I have often named before in this my Booke, Master Robert Rugge, observing that I had taken paines for some few houres in searching out the most notable Antiquities of this the worthiest part of Troy to yeeld mee some kinde of guerdon or remuneration for my paines, in a merrie humour drew his Sword out of his Scabberd, and ascending to one of these great stones that lye in the open part of this middle Gate Knighted mee, that kneeled upon another stone on my right knee, by the name of the first English Knight of Troy, and at the Knighting of mee, pronounced those wittie Verses ex tempore.

> Coryate no more, but now a Knight of Troy,
>   Odcombe no more, but henceforth Englands Joy.
> Brave Brute of our best English wits commended;
>   True Trojane from Aeneas race descended.
> Rise top of wit, the honour of our Nation,
>   And to old Ilium make a new Oration.

Two poore Turkes that stood but a little way from us when hee drew his naked Sword, thought verily hee meant to have cut off my head for some notorious villany that I had perpetrated. Those Verses I answered ex tempore, also our Musketeeres discharged two volleys of shot for joy of my Knighthood.

> Loe heere with prostrate knee I doe embrace
> The gallant title of a Trojane Knight.
> In Priams Court which time shall ne're deface;
> A grace unknowne to any Brittish Wight.
> This noble Knighthood shall Fames Trumpe resound,
> To Odcombes honour maugre Envie fell,
> O're famous Albion throughout that Iland round,
> Till that my mournfull friends shall ring my knell.

Thomas Coryate,
in *Purchas his Pilgrimes* (1625); Hakluyt Society edition
(London, 1905), vol. 10, 389ff.

William Lithgow enjoyed this part at least of his Greek travels:

When we landed, we saw here and there many relicts of old walles, as we travelled through these famous bounds. And as we were advanced toward the east part of Troy, our Greeke brought us to many tombes, which were mighty ruinous, and pointed us particularly to the tombes of Hector, Ajax, Achilles, Troylus, and many other valiant champions, with the tombes also of Hecuba, Cresseid, and other Trojane dames: Well I wot, I saw infinite old sepulchers, but for their particular names, and nomination of them, I suspend, neither could I beleeve my interpreter, sith it is more then three thousand and odde yeares agoe, that Troy was destroyed.

> Here tombes I viewd, old monuments of times,
> And fiery trophees, fixd for bloody crimes:
> For which Achilles ghost did sigh and say,
> Curst be the hands, that sakelesse Trojanes slay;
> But more fierce Ajax, more Ulysses Horse,
> That wrought griefes ruine; Priams last divorce:
> And here inclosd, within these clods of dust,
> All Asiaes honour, and cros'd Paris lust.

And loe here is mine effigie affixed with my Turkish habit, my walking staffe, and my turban upon my head, even as I travelled in the bounds of Troy, and so through all Turkey: before my face on my right hand standeth the easterne and sole gate of that sometimes noble city, with a piece of a high wall, as yet undecayed: and without this port runneth the river Simois (inclosing the old Grecian campe) downe to the marine, where it embraceth the sea Propontis: a little below, are bunches of grapes, denoting the vineyards of this fructiferous place; adjoyning neare to the fragments and ruynes of Priams pallace, surnamed Ilium: and next to it a ravenous eagle, for so this part of Phrygia is full of them: so beneath my feet ly the two tombes of Priamus and Hecuba his Queene: and under them the incircling hills of Ida, at the west south west end of this once regall towne; and at my left hand, the delicious and pleasant fields of olives and figge-trees, wherewith the bowells of this famous soyle are interlarded: and here this piece or portracture decyphered; the continuing discourse, enlarging both meane and manner.

William Lithgow, *Totall Discourse of the Rare Adventures and Painefull Peregrinations* (London, 1632)

Like these others, Lady Mary Wortley Montagu was filled with archaeological enthusiasm by the Troad.

> Not many leagues sail from hence I saw the point of land where poor old Hecuba was bury'd, and about a league from that place is Cape Janizary, the famous promontory of Sigaeum, where we anchor'd; and my Curiosity supply'd me with strength to climb to the top of it to see the place where Achilles was bury'd and where Alexander ran naked round his Tomb in his honnour, which, no doubt, was a great comfort to his Ghost. I saw there the ruins of a very large City, and found a Stone on which Mr W[ortley] plainly distinguish'd the words of Sigaeon polin. We order'd this on board the Ship but were show'd others much more curious by a Greek Priest, thô a very ignorant Fellow that could give no tolerable Account of any thing. On each side the door of his little Church lies a large stone about ten foot long each, 5 in breadth, and 3 in Thickness. That on the right is very fine white marble, the side of it beautifully carv'd in bas Releif. It represents a woman who seems to be design'd for some Deity sitting on a Chair with a footstool, and before her another woman weeping and presenting to her a Young Child that she has in her Arms, follow'd by a procession of women with Children in the same manner. This is certainly part of a very ancient Tomb, but I dare not pretend to give the true Explanation of it. On the

Stone on the left side is a very fair Inscription, which I am sure I took off very exactly, but the Greek is too Ancient for Mr W[ortley]'s interpretation. This is the exact Copy. [*Here follow eleven double lines of Greek, apparently copied in another hand.*] I am very sorry not to have the Original in my possession, which might have been purchas'd of the poor Inhabitants for a small sumn of Money, but our Captain assur'd us that without having Machines made on purpose, twas impossible to bear it to the Sea Side, and when it was there his long Boat would not be large enough to hold it.

Lady Mary Wortley Montagu, Letters, 31 July 1718

Most visitors until this date had assumed that in visiting the ruins of Alexandria Troas they were walking where King Priam had trod, and where Helen had pointed out from the ramparts the leaders of the Greeks. Not only Coryate and Lithgow, but Pierre Belon, Pietro della Valle, and Thomas Dallam included this false Troy in their accounts. George Sandys and George Wheler both identified Alexandria Troas correctly, but it was not until 1785 that Jean-Baptiste Lechevalier, a member of the diplomatic staff at Constantinople, proposed an alternative site for Troy, at Bunarbashi (Pinarbasi). Here in 1801 came Lord Elgin, accompanied by Professor J. D. Carlyle; they encountered E. D. Clarke, the Cambridge mineralogist, on the plain, and the two dons quarreled violently over the site. In 1840 Gustav von Eckenbrecher identified Hisarlik as the site, while Charles McLaren, founder editor of the *Scotsman*, published a book championing the claims of this hill in 1863. After Schliemann began his excavations in 1870, Eckenbrecher published his account, modified to harmonize with Schliemann's finds, which conclusively established the site of Troy.

In conclusion, I flatter myself with the hope that, as a reward for my enormous expenses and all my privations, annoyances, and sufferings in this wilderness, but above all for my important discoveries, the civilised world will acknowledge my right to re-christen this sacred locality; and in the name of the divine Homer I baptize it with that name of immortal renown, which fills the heart of everyone with joy and enthusiasm: I give it the name of TROY and ILIUM, and I call the acropolis, where I am writing these lines, by the name of *Pergamus of Troy.*

Heinrich Schliemann, 4 August 1872
from Troy and Its Remains;
translated by L. Dora Schmitz (1875)

Izmir (Smyrna)

Smyrna is one of the oldest Greek cities, one of the claimants to be the birthplace of Homer. In the nineteenth century, it was a mercantile city as prosperous as Alexandria. After the First World War the Greek inhabitants were removed in the exchange of populations between Turkey and Greece. Here is a short selection of visitors' accounts.

Alexander Drummond (d. 1769), the consul at Aleppo from 1754 to 1756, reached Smyrna in 1744. He published his *Travels* in 1754. (Dr. Johnson so far betrayed his principles, when on his tour of the Western Isles, as to read the book on a Sunday—until he discovered a volume of sermons hidden in a corner of his host's house.)

As I have mentioned the lodge of free masons, I cannot help congratulating myself upon the opportunity I had of making so many worthy brethren in this place, and of forming the only lodge that is in the Levant; but my joy is still the greater, when I reflect that all the members are gentlemen of amiable characters, and must reciprocally reflect and receive honour in their association with the society of free and accepted masons. The lodge of Drummond Kilwining, from Greenock, has reason to be proud of this her first daughter; and, I assure you, I am not a little vain of being the father of such a flock.

> For ages past, a savage race
> O'erspread these Asian plains,
> All nature wore a gloomy face,
> And pensive mov'd the swains.
>
> But now Britannia's gen'rous sons
> A glorious lodge have rais'd,
> Near the fam'd banks where Meles runs,
> And Homer's cattle graz'd;
> The bri'ry wilds to groves are chang'd,
> With orange trees around,
> And fragrant lemons fairly rang'd,
> O'ershade the blissful ground.
>
> Approving Phoebus shines more bright,
> The flow'rs appear more gay,
> New objects rise to please the sight
> With each revolving day.
>
> While safe within the sacred walls,
> Where heav'nly friendship reigns,

The jovial masons hear the calls
Of all the needy swains.
Their gen'rous aid, with chearful soul,
They grant to those who sue;
And while the sparkling glasses roll,
Their smiling joys renew.

Forgive this crude performance, with which I close my
account of Smyrna . . .

Alexander Drummond, Travels (London, 1754)

Mark Twain was ready as usual to make sport of whatever he found.

The ascent of the hill of the citadel is very steep, and we
proceeded rather slowly. But there were matters of interest
about us. In one place, five hundred feet above the sea, the per-
pendicular bank on the upper side of the road was ten or fifteen feet high, and the cut exposed three veins of oyster shells,
just as we have seen quartz veins exposed in the cutting of a
road in Nevada or Montana. The veins were about eighteen
inches thick and two or three feet apart, and they slanted along
downward for a distance of thirty feet or more and then disappeared where the cut joined the road. Heaven only knows
how far a man might trace them by 'stipping'. They were
clean, nice oyster shells, large, and just like any other oyster
shells. They were thickly massed together, and none were scattered above or below the veins. Each one was a welldefined
lead by itself, and without a spur. My first instinct was to set up
the usual

NOTICE:

*We, the undersigned, claim five claims of two hundred feet each (and
one for discovery) on this ledge or lode of oyster shells, with all its
dips, spurs, angles, variations, and sinuosities, and fifty feet on each
side of the same, to work it, etc., etc., according to the mining laws
of Smyrna.*

They were such perfectly natural-looking leads that I
could hardly keep from 'taking them up'. Among the oyster
shells were mixed many fragments of ancient, broken crock-
eryware. Now how did those masses of oyster shells get there?
Broken crockery and oyster shells are suggestive of restaurants—but then they could have had no such places away up
there on that mountainside in our time, because nobody has
lived up there. A restaurant would not pay in such a stony,

forbidding, desolate place. And besides, there were no champagne corks among the shells. If there ever was a restaurant there, it must have been in Smyrna's palmy days, when the hills were covered with palaces. I could believe in one restaurant on those terms, but then how about the three? Did they have restaurants there at three different periods of the world? Because there are two or three feet of solid earth between the oyster leads. Evidently the restaurant solution will not answer.

The hill might have been the bottom of the sea once, and been lifted up, with its oyster beds, by an earthquake—but, then, how about the crockery? And moreover, how about *three* oyster beds, one above another, and thick strata of good honest earth between.

That theory will not do. It is just possible that this hill is Mount Ararat, and that Noah's Ark rested here, and he ate oysters and threw the shells overboard. But that will not do, either. There are the three layers again and the solid earth between—and besides, there were only eight in Noah's family, and they could not have eaten all these oysters in the two or three months they stayed on top of that mountain. The beasts—however, it is simply absurd to suppose he did not know any more than to feed the beasts on oyster suppers.

It is painful—it is even humiliating—but I am reduced at last to one slender theory: that the oysters climbed up there of their own accord. But what object could they have had in view? What did they want up there? What could any oyster want to climb a hill for? To climb a hill must necessarily be fatiguing and annoying exercise for an oyster. The most natural conclusion would be that the oysters climbed up there to look at the scenery. Yet when one comes to reflect upon the nature of an oyster, it seems plain that he does not care for scenery. An oyster has no taste for such things; he cares nothing for the beautiful. An oyster is of a retiring disposition and not lively—not even cheerful above the average and never enterprising. But above all, an oyster does not take any interest in scenery—, he scorns it. What have I arrived at now? Simply at the point I started from, namely, *those oyster shells are there*, in regular layers, five hundred feet above the sea, and no man knows how they got there. I have hunted up the guidebooks, and the gist of what they say is this: 'They are there, but how they got there is a mystery.'

Mark Twain, *The Innocents Abroad*,
(Hartford, Connecticut, 1869), chapter 39

The American poet Samuel Green Wheeler Benjamin, who was born at Argos in 1837 and lived in Greece until the age of eighteen, before returning to Boston to pursue a career as a marine painter, has an eloquent sonnet on the lovely city, which can serve as an elegy for the Greek past of Ionia's coast:

> The sunset gun has died along the sea;
> It is the evening of Bairami's fete;
> The torches on each tapering minaret
> Flash in the rippling waters of the bay,
> And languid vapor dims the droning town:
> From Smyrna's dewy gardens floats the scent
> Of myrtle, rose, and citron, softly blent,
> Like votive incense by each zephyr blown
> Round the blind minstrel's cave. Since he began
> His deathless song, weird city of the dead,
> Aged Smyrna! thou hast heard the busy tread
> Of buried millions where the caravan
> Now wends its tinkling way by Meles' stream,
> Where ramparts moulder in the moonlight beam.
>
> S. G. W. Benjamin

14

Envoi

A Spring Wind

Spring shakes the windows; doors whang to,
the sky moves half in dark and half
shining like knives: upon this table
Elytis' poems lie
uttering the tangle of sea, the 'breathing caves'
and the fling of Aegean waves.

I am caught here in this scattering, vagrant season
where telephones ring;
and all Greece goes through me
as the wind goes searching through the city streets.
Greece, I have so much loved you
out of all reason;
that this unquiet time
its budding and its pride
the news and the nostalgia of Spring
swing towards you their tide:

Towards the windmills on the islands;
Alefkandra loved by winds,
luminous with foam and morning, Athens,
her blinded marble heads,
her pepper-trees, the bare heels of her girls,
old songs that bubble up from where thought starts,
Greek music treading like the beat of hearts;
haunted Seferis, smiling, playing with beads.

And since especially at this time
statues and blossoms, birth and death require
we give account of manhood and of youth,
the wind that whirls through London also rings
with the bang and echo of the Easter gun,
as in days gone,

from where the pilgrims' torches climb
over a darkening town
to set that bony peak Lykahvetoss,
Athens, and all the opening year on fire.
Bernard Spencer, in *Aegean Islands*
(London, 1946)

Bibliography

Abbott, G. F., *Songs of Modern Greece*, Cambridge, 1900

Adams, P. G., *Travellers and Travel Liars 1600–1800*, Berkeley, California, 1962

Aicard, J., *La Vénus de Milo. Recherches sur l'histoire de la découverte*, Paris, 1874

Alliterative Romance of Alexander, ed. Rev. Joseph Stevenson, London, 1849 (Roxburghe Club)

Anderson, Patrick, *The Smile of Apollo*, London, 1964

Andrews, Kevin, *Athens Alive*, Athens, 1980

Angelomatis-Tsougarakis, Helen, *The Eve of the Greek Revival*, London, 1990

Anon, *A Sheaf of Greek Folksongs gleaned by an old Philhellene* (with an introduction by Countess Evelyn Martinengo Cesaresco), Oxford, 1922

Ashmole, Bernard, "Cyriac of Ancona," in *Proceedings of the British Academy*, 45 (1959), 25–41

Asse, Eugene, *Les Petits Romantiques*, Paris, 1900

Aubin, Robert A., *Topographical Poetry in Eighteenth Century England*, New York, 1936

Baggally, John W., *The Klephtic Ballads in Relation to Greek History (1715–1821)*, Oxford, 1936

Barba-Pantzelios, *To Tragoudi tou Daskalogianni*, ed. Basil Laourdas, Herakleion, Crete, 1947

Beaton, Roderick, *Folk Poetry of Modern Greece*, Cambridge, 1980

Beckmann, J., *Literatur der älteren Reisebeschreibungen*, Göttingen 1807–09; repr. Geneva, 1971

Bevis, Richard, *Bibliotheca Cisorientalis: An annotated checklist of early English travel books on the Near and Middle East*, Boston, 1973 (I have not seen this work)

Bodnar, Edward W., SJ, *Cyriacus of Ancona and Athens* (Coll. Latomus 43), Brussels, 1960

Bordeaux, Henri, *Voyageurs d'Orient*, I–II, Paris, 1926

Bracken, C. P., *Antiquities Acquired*, Newton Abbot, 1975

Brown, Wallace Cable, "English Travel Books and Minor Poetry about the Near East, 1775–1825," in *Philological Quarterly*, XVI, 8 (1937), 249–71

— "The Popularity of English Travel Books about the Middle East," in *Philological Quarterly*, 15 (1936), 70–80

— "Byron and English Interest in the Near East," in *Studies in Philology*, 34 (1937), 55–64

Caminade, Gaston, *Les chants des Grecs et le philhellenisme de Wilhelm Müller*, Paris, 1913

Cary, George, *The Medieval Alexander*, Cambridge, 1956

Casson, Stanley, *Greece and Britain*, n.d.

Cheetham, Nicholas, *Medieval Greece*, New Haven and London, 1981

Chew, Samuel C., *The Crescent and the Rose*, New York, 1937

Chronicle of the Morea, translated by H. E. Lurier as *Crusaders and Conquerors*, New York and London, 1964

Constantine, D. J., "Poets and Travellers and the Ideal of Greece," in *Journal of European Studies*, 7 (1977), 253–65

Cook, J. M., *The Troad*, Oxford, 1973

Covel, Dr. John, *Diary*, ed. J. T. Bent, London, 1893 (Hakluyt Society, vol. 87)

Cox, E. G., *Reference Guide to the Literature of Travel*, Washington D.C., 1935–38

Crook, J. Mordaunt, *The Greek Revival*, London, 1972

Cyriac of Ancona, *Journeys in the Propontis and the Northern Aegean, 1444–1445*, ed. Edward W. Bodnar, SJ, and Charles Mitchell, Philadelphia, 1976

—, in R. Sabbadini, "Ciriaco d'Ancona e il Peloponneso," *Fontes Ambrosiani*, II 1–53

—, *Epigrammata reperta per Illyricum a Cyriaco*, ed. Carlo Moroni, 1660 (apparently the mutilated volume in the British Library, shelfmark 664.h.5(2))

Dallam, Thomas, *Diary, 1599–1600*, ed. J. T. Bent, London, 1893
(Hakluyt Society, vol. 87)

Dickie, James, "The Grecian Urn: An Archaeological Approach,"
in *Bulletin of the John Rylands Library*, 52 (1969)

Dowling, T. E., and Fletcher, E. W., *Hellenism in England*,
London, 1915

Durrell, Lawrence, *The Greek Islands*, London, 1978

—, *Prospero's Cell*, London, 1945

—, *Reflections on a Marine Venus*, London, 1953

Eliot, C. W. J., "Athens in the Time of Lord Byron," in *Hesperia*,
37, 2 (1968), 134–58

Fauriel, C., *Chants populaires de la Grèce moderne*, Paris, 1824–25

Fermor, Patrick Leigh, *Mani*, London, 1958

—, *Roumeli*, London, 1966

Fourmont, Abbé, "Relation abrégée du voyage littéraire fait dans
le Levant par ordre du Roy dans les années 1729–30 . . ."
(Mémoires de littérature tirez des registres des assemblées de
l'Académie), in *Histoire de l'Académie Royale des Inscriptions et
Belles Lettres*, vol. VII, Paris, 1733, 344–59

Galt, George, *A Journey through the Aegean Islands*, London, 1986

Hasluck, F. W., "The First English Traveller's Account of Athos
(1677)," in *Annual of the British School of Archaeology at Athens*,
17 (1910–11), 103–31

Herakleides, *Reisebilder*, ed. F. Pfister, Vienna, 1951; and in
Müller, *Geographi Graeci*, s.v. Dicaearchus

Hopkins, Adam, *Crete: Its Past, Present and People*, London, 1977

Hosemann, J. J., *Les Étrangers en Grèce*, 1826 (The Bibliothèque
Nationale in Paris, the only library I know of to list this work
in its catalogue, has lost it)

Iorga, N., *Les Voyaguers français dans l'Orient Européen*, Paris, 1928

Jeannaraki (or Giannares), Antonios N., *Kretas Volkslieder*,
Leipzig, 1876

Kalonaros, P. T., *Digenes Akritas*, 1941; 1970

Larrabee, Stephen A., *Hellas Observed: The American Experience of Greece 1775–1865*, New York, 1957

—, *English Bards and Grecian Marbles*, New York, 1943

Lawson, J. C., *Modern Greek Folklore and Ancient Greek Religion*, Cambridge, 1910

Legrand, E., *Recueil de chansons populaires grecques*, Paris, 1884

Levin, Harry, *The Broken Column: a Study in Romantic Hellenism*, Cambridge, Mass., 1931

Llewellyn Smith, Michael, *The Great Island*, London, 1965

Longfellow, H. W., ed., *Poems of Places: Greece, and Turkey in Europe*, Boston, Mass., 1878

Lucas, F. L., "The Literature of Greek Travels," in *Royal Society of Literature of the UK, Transactions*, n.s. 17 (1930), 17–40

Malakis, Emile, *French Travellers in Greece 1770–1820: An Early Phase of French Philhellenism*, Philadelphia, 1925

Matton, R., *La Crète au cours des siècles*, Athens, 1957

Mavrogordato, John, *The Erotokritos*, Oxford, 1929

—, *England in the Balkans: A Hellenic Note on British Policy*, London, 1916 (Anglo-Hellenic League papers, no. 24)

Miller, Helen Hill, *Greece Through the Ages*, New York, 1972

Miller, Henry, *The Colossus of Maroussi*, 1941

Miller, W., *The Latins in the Levant*, London, 1908

—, *The English in Athens before 1821*, London, 1926

Morgan, Gareth, "Cretan Poetry: Sources and Inspiration," *Kritika Chronika*, Herakleion, xiv (1960), 7–68

Notopoulos, J. A., "Homer and Cretan Heroic Poetry: A Study in Comparative Oral Poetry, I. The Song of Daskalogiannis," in *American Journal of Philology*, 73 (1952), 225–50

—, "New Sources on Lord Byron at Missolonghi," in *Keats-Shelley Journal* (Winter 1955), 31–45

Papagregorakis, Idomeneus I., *Kritika Rizitika Tragoudia*, Canea, Crete, 1956–57

Paris, Matthew, in *Purchas his Pilgrimes, vol. II, Book VIII: The Continuation of the Ierusalem Expedition, and other Additions, gathered out of Matthew Paris*, London, 1625

Passow, Arnold T. G., *Popularia Carmina Graeciae Recentioris*, Leipzig 1860; reprinted Athens, 1958

Paton, James Morton, *Medieval and Renaissance Visitors to Greek Lands*, Princeton, NJ, 1951 (Gennadeion Monographs, III)

Paul the Silentiary, in *Corpus Scriptorum Historiae Byzantinae*, ed. I. Bekker, Bonn, 1837

Penrose, B., *Travel and Discovery in the Renaissance*, Cambridge, Mass., 1952

Plomer, William, *The Diamond of Jannina: Ali Pasha 1741–1822*, London, 1970

Plott, J. A., *Greek Love Songs and Epigrams*, London, 1911

Powell, Dilys, *The Villa Ariadne*, London 1974; reprinted Athens, 1982

Raizis, M. B., with A. Papas, *American Poets and the Greek Revolution 1821–8, a Study in Byronic Philhellenism*, Thessaloniki, 1971 (Institute of Balkan Studies, publ. no. 127)

—, *The Greek Revolution and the American Muse: a Collection of American Philhellenic Poetry 1821–8*, Thessaloniki, 1972 (Institute of Balkan Studies, publ. no. 128)

Ramsey, Robert W., "Sir George Wheeler and his travels in Greece, 1650–1724," in *Essays by Divers Hands; Transactions of the Royal Society of Literature*, xix (1942)

Reinach, S., "La découverte de la Vénus de Milo," in *Revue Archéologique*, 7 (1906) 193–202

Reutern, G. von, *Hellas: Ein Führer durch Griechenland aus Antiken Quellenstücken*, Munich, 1958

Rice, W. G., "Early English Travellers in Greece and the Levant," in *Essays and Studies in English and Comparative Literature* (University of Michigan) x (1933)

Rodd, J. Rennell, *The Customs and Lore of Modern Greece*, London, 1892

—, *The Englishman in Greece*, Oxford, 1910

St. Clair, William, *Lord Elgin and the Marbles*, Oxford, 1967

—, *That Greece Might Still Be Free*, Oxford, 1972

Sheridan, Charles Brinsley, *The Songs of Greece*, London, 1825

Sherrard, Philip, *The Pursuit of Greece*, London, 1964

Simopoulos, Kyriakos, *Xenoi Taxidiotes stin Ellada*, I–, Athens, 1970–

Skeat, W. W., *William of Palerne, and a fragment of the Alliterative Romance of Alexander*, 1867, 177–218 (Early English Text Society, Ex. Ser.)

Smith, Harold F., *American Travellers Abroad*, Illinois, 1969

Spencer, T. J. B., *Fair Greece Sad Relic*, London, 1954; reprinted, 1974

Stern, B. H., *The Rise of Romantic Hellenism in English Literature*, Menasha, 1940

Stoneman, Richard, *Land of Lost Gods: the Search for Classical Greece*, London, 1987

Stoye, J. W., English *Travellers Abroad*, London, 1952

Synesius, "Letters," in Migne, *Patrologia Graeca*, vol. 66

Tozer, Henry Fanshawe, *Islands of the Aegean*, London, 1890

Tregaskis, Hugh, *Beyond the Grand Tour*, London, 1980

Trypanis, C. A., *Greek Poetry from Homer to Seferis*, London, 1982

—, *Medieval and Modern Greek Poetry*, Oxford, 1951

Tsigakou, Fani-Maria, *The Rediscovery of Greece*, London, 1982

Vin, J. P. A. van der, *Travellers to Greece and Constantinople*, Istanbul, 1980

Walpole, Robert, *Memoirs relating to European and Asiatic Turkey*, London, 1817

Watkin, David, *The Life and Work of C. R. Cockerell*, London, 1972

Webb, Timothy, *English Romantic Hellenism*, Manchester, 1982

Weber, Shirley H., *Voyages and Travels in Greece, the Near East and Adjacent Regions*, Glückstadt, 1952 and 1953 (Catalogues of the Gennadius Library, I and II)

Wheeler, Sara, *An Island Apart*, London, 1993

Woodhouse, C. M., *The Philhellenes*, London, 1969

Zakythinos, D. A., *The Making of Modern Greece, from Byzantium to Independence*, Oxford, 1976

Literary Sources

Acknowledgment is due to the following for permission to reproduce copyright material:

"On Acrocorinth" and extract from "Hymn to Artemis Orthia" by A. Sikelianos, translated by E. Keeley and P. Sherrard. Reprinted by permission of George Allen and Unwin and Harper Collins Publishers, New York.

"Drinking the Sun of Corinth" and "Ode to Santorini" from *Odysseus Elytis: Selected Poems*, translated by Edmund Keeley and Philip Sherrard. Copyright © 1981 by Anvil Press Poetry. Reprinted by permission of Anvil Press, London.

Extract from "The Gloria" from *Odysseus Elytis: The Axion Esti*, translated by Edmund Keeley and George Savidis, and published by Anvil Press Poetry in 1980. Copyright © 1974 by Edmund Keeley and George Savidis. Reprinted by permission of Anvil Press and the University of Pittsburgh Press.

Extract from "The Archipelago" from *Poems and Fragments* by Friedrich Hölderlin, translated by Michael Hamburger. Reprinted with the permission of Cambridge University Press and Michael Hamburger.

Extract from "The King of Asine" from *Collected Poems* by George Seferis, expanded edition, translated by Edmund Keeley and Philip Sherrard. Copyright © 1967 and preface copyright © 1981 by Princeton University Press. Reprinted by permission of the author's estate, the translators, Princeton University Press, and Jonathan Cape, Publisher.

"Ithaca" from *The Poems of C.P. Cavafy*, translated by John Mavrogordato (1951). Reprinted by permission of Chatto & Windus, Publisher, and Rogers, Coleridge & White, Ltd.

"Patmos" by Friedrich Hölderlin, translated by David Gascoyne. Reprinted by permission of J.M. Dent, Orion House, London.

Index of Places

Place-names are generally given in their modern form, except where an English form is current. Earlier names, where different, are noted as follows: Ancient and classical names are indicated by *A*; medieval and Frankish ones by *M*; Ottoman ones by *O*. Many classical names have been resurrected since 1945, not always attached to the correct sites.

Index of Names

Robson, Rev. Charles, 243–44
Rodd, J. Rennell, 4
Rottmann, Carl, 99, 129, 268

St. Clair, William, 185
Sandys, George, 3, 4, 251,
254–55, 321
Sappho, 254
Savary, Claude-Étienne, 4, 277,
294–95, 302, 303
Scheffer, Ari, 187
Schliemann, Heinrich, 3, 5, 36,
94, 321
Seferis, George, 15, 88–89, 267
Servius Sulpicius, 99–100
Shakespeare, William, 64, 196,
225, 230, 315
Sharp, William, 141
Shelley, Percy Bysshe,
53–54, 125
Sheridan, Charles Brinsley,
10, 189
Sherley, Thomas, 10
Sibthorp, John, 4, 173,
222–23, 241
Sidney, Sir Philip, 48
Sigourney, Lydia H., 12
Sikelianos, Angelos, 15, 39,
72, 104
Simonides, 220
Sitwell, Sacheverell, 94–96
Skeat, W. W., 228
Snell, Bruno, 43
Solomos, Dionysios, 189, 254
Sophocles, 12, 118–19, 257, 302
Soutsos, Panagiotis, 237
Spencer, Bernard, 326–27
Spender, Stephen, 161
Spenser, Edmund, 316–17
Spratt, Thomas Abel Brimage,
283
Stanhope, Lady Hester, 278–79

Stillman, William James,
143, 148
Stoneman, Richard, 96–97
Swan, Rev. Charles, 71, 261–62
Swinburne, Algernon Charles,
297–98
Synesius, 133–34

Teonge, Henry, 29–31
Thackeray, William Makepeace,
3, 12, 151, 280–81
Theocritus, 272–73
Theognis, 105
Thomson, James, 16–17, 61–62
Thucydides, 262
Torr, Cecil, 158
Tournefort, Joseph Pitton de, 4,
241–42, 295–97
Trelawny, Edward J., 6, 35–36,
49, 174–75
Trypanis, C. A., 216–17, 267,
305–6
Twain, Mark, 12, 152–54,
323–24

Urquhart, David, 201–2

Vere, Aubrey de, 3, 180
Vernon, Francis, 3, 66–67
Vigny, Alfred de, 252–53
Virgil, 43–44

Waller, Edmund, 8
Walter of Châtillon, 226
Watteau, Antoine, 82
Welcker, Friedrich Gottlob,
59–60
Wheeler, George, 3, 106–7,
184–85, 321
Wilde, Oscar, 39, 41
Williams, H. W., 6–7, 115

Richard Stoneman was born in Devon in 1951. He was educated in Devon, England, at Rugby School, and at New College, Oxford; he did research in Greek literature at Christ Church, Oxford, and the University of Cologne. He has published several learned articles and reviews for various periodicals. He has traveled widely in Greece and other countries, including Italy, Iran, and Germany. He is the author of *Daphne into Laurel: English Translations of Classical Poetry from Chaucer to the Present* (1982). He lives in South London with his wife and son.